# Just Around the Corner

## Encouragement and Challenge for Christian Dads and Moms

### Volume 2

## by Steven & Teri Maxwell

CCI Communication Concepts, Inc.

Just Around the Corner

Ordering information:
Managers of Their Homes
2416 South 15th Street
Leavenworth, Kansas  66048
Phone: (913) 772-0392

Website: www.Titus2.com

Published by: Communication Concepts, Inc.

Website: www.we-communicate.com

ACKNOWLEDGMENTS

Scripture taken from the HOLY BIBLE, KING JAMES VERSION.

ISBN 978-0-9771420-5-7

Printed in the United States of America.

1

This book was created in Microsoft Word. QuarkXPress 6.5 and Adobe Photoshop were used for layout and design. All computers were Windows-based systems running Windows XP.

Christopher Maxwell designed the cover, and Sarah Maxwell designed the interior of this book.

# This book is:

Dedicated to Nathan and Melanie's precious Susannah Joy, born March 21st, 2007, and slipped into the arms of Jesus March 24th, 2007. She will be a treasure to the lives she has forever touched.

"I thank my God always on your behalf, for the grace of God which is given you by Jesus Christ" (1 Corinthians 1:4).

# Contents — Mom's Corners

Contentment—Part 2

# Contents — Dad's Corners

# Preface

The Lord has finally provided the time to compile *Just Around the Corner,* Volume 2. This project has been on our hearts for a couple of years. Regularly we have been asked when there would be a second volume. At the publishing of this book, we have been writing monthly articles to encourage Christian parents for seventeen years. Some of our children have grown to be adults and begun their own families during these years. Others of our children are still at home.

We are very grateful for the path the Lord Jesus has brought us down in our parenting, and we delight in sharing that with others who seek to have a Christ-led family. The joy of fellowship and purpose in a Christ-led family is beyond measure. It is our desire that every family would have this same experience.

Moms, there is a caution we have for you concerning the Dad's Corners. Steve writes very much to a man's heart. Steve wants to "talk" man to man with your husband without setting any expectations in your heart. We would suggest that you not read the Dad's Corners unless your husband has read them first, and he encourages you to read them as well.

We are thankful to Sarah, our oldest daughter, for her efforts in collecting the Corners, proofing them before they went to the proofreader, generating the index, and formatting the book. She spent many hours on this project. Christopher, our second-oldest son, does the cover design and layout.

Without readers for the monthly Dad's and Mom's Corners there would be no reason to write them. If you'd like to receive the Corners via e-mail each month, you're welcome to sign up on our website, www.Titus2.com. Thank you for your faithfulness and yearning to raise your children in the nurture and admonition of the Lord Jesus. We are always blessed by your words of encouragement.

Occasionally, you will notice a particular month's Corner "missing" from the book. Some months the Lord did not put a Corner topic on Steve's heart. A couple of months we re-used Corners that we had already printed in *Just Around the Corner,* Volume 1.

In Christ Jesus,
*Steve & Teri*

# The Retraining Parade
## *by Teri*

Tonight we had a parade through the Maxwell house! Usually the children delight in parades, but for this one, they were uncharacteristically warm and subdued. One child had on her heavy winter coat, sweatshirt, stocking cap, and an extra pair of shoes over her hands—all in addition to her normal clothing. Another child sported her sweatshirt, bike-riding dress—over her play dress—with shoes dangling on her shoulder. The other three of our younger children had donned varying degrees of similar costumes. They were all busily marching around the house. Soon each one returned to Mom eagerly asking her to come see what they had just accomplished. You might ask, what exactly is going on at the Maxwell house?

We were reaping! Unfortunately, Mom has become slack in giving consequences to the children for leaving their things out. Steve has regularly encouraged me to have the children wear or carry whatever of their personal property is not properly put away. His suggestion originally came because I brought him the ongoing problem we have in our home of sloppiness. My efforts toward positive training of the children in orderliness were not being fruitful.

I have done some mental calculations of what it would be like at the Maxwells' if we didn't stay on top of picking up. There are ten of us living in this home. If we were each to leave out ten items a day, which wouldn't be terribly hard, we would have one hundred things lying around at the end of the day. After a week, a whopping seven hundred pieces of Maxwell personal property would be strewn across the house.

I truly believe in the importance of training our children to put their things away properly. I am certain that their spouses will thank Steve and me if we are successful, and they will be disappointed if we aren't. My children report to us that they really prefer to live in a neat home. This information generally comes after they have visited in a cluttered or messy home. Putting each item where it belongs is a valuable time saver. How many hours have been lost looking for a child's missing shoe? "Go to the ant, thou sluggard; consider her ways, and be wise" (Proverbs 6:6).

Our home is also a testimony—of Christ, homeschooling, and, in our case, large families. We regularly have non-Christians stop by our home unexpectedly. Tonight it was the British Army officer for whom Steve is doing some work. Last week it was our policeman neighbor from across the street. Sometimes it is the retired bank president for whom Sarah gathers the mail and papers when he and his wife are away. I am convinced that if the house looks more than simply "lived in," the testimony of each area it represents, such as homeschooling, is tarnished.

Having the children wear what they have left out has been a most effective way of getting them to pick up their clothing. However, if Mom is not consistent with consequences, the children manage to lose the good habit they have acquired! "Correct thy son, and he shall give thee rest; yea, he shall give delight unto thy soul" (Proverbs 29:17). Tonight we were having a retraining session. The children were wearing clothing items they had left out while they searched the house for other things that belonged to them. They were now eager to put their belongings away. Then they were happy to come ask Mom for an inspection. This was because the removal of each extra piece of clothing was dependent on Mom not finding any more of their things out.

Despite all the benefits I know there are to be gained from teaching my children to put their personal items away when they are done with them, I still struggle with being consistent. When I am consistent, they succeed! When I am inconsistent, they fail!

So, if you pop in at the Maxwell house and observe five children wearing very odd outfits while busily rushing here and there, you will know what is happening. May I encourage you in whatever area you need to be more consistent with your children. It is not too late. It is not too much work, and it is certainly well worth the effort!

# A Daughter's 'Titus Two' Woman

## *by Teri*

As I entered my forties, younger women whom I counseled or encouraged would occasionally refer to me as a "Titus Two" woman to them. This term comes from Titus 2:4-5, which outlines specific areas in which older women are to teach the younger women. "That they may teach the young women to be sober, to love their husbands, to love their children, *To be* discreet, chaste, keepers at home, good, obedient to their own husbands, that the word of God be not blasphemed" (Titus 2:4-5). Having me referred to as a "Titus Two" woman made for a few rounds of laughter at our dinner table when my family teased with, "Mom, you know what that means? You are an OLDER woman!"

One day I was thinking about my own teenage daughter in relation to Titus 2:4-5. I realized as she grew up she was going to be looking for a "Titus Two" woman in her life. I wanted to make sure I had made a concerted effort to be that woman for her even before she felt a need for one.

I knew that being my daughter's "Titus Two" woman would grow naturally out of a healthy mother-daughter relationship. However, as I evaluated my time usage, I noticed that I was encouraging Christian homeschooling moms via e-mail each day. I also would usually meet with a local homeschooling mom on a monthly basis in a mentoring relationship. I desired to invest dedicated time such as this in my own daughter's life.

I began the process by scheduling a monthly outing for just my daughter and me. This is exactly what I did when a friend asked me to mentor her. Why not do the same with my daughter? While my oldest daughter and I had occasional excursions together, it was not on the regular, consistent basis I wanted. I always had good intentions of going out with her. However, in reality, time slipped away with no "feet" being given to the intentions. I found that when evening came, I didn't have the energy left to take my daughter out unless we had planned it ahead of time.

For about four years, Sarah, my nineteen-year-old daughter, and I have gone out to eat together on the first Monday of the month. We both look forward to this special time. Occasionally, Sarah will invite one or both of her younger sisters to join us. Generally, though, this is an evening for just Sarah and me. Sarah often brings up areas she is struggling with in her personal life. We can discuss these issues and find biblical ways to deal with them. She feels the freedom to ask questions and bring up topics she might not be comfortable talking about at home where little ears are always about. During our evening out, we talk with each other, relax, and enjoy the freedom of not making or cleaning up dinner. I plan a simple dinner for the family at home that Daddy and the children can easily make. We are even a bit practical by running errands after we eat. Both of us have fond memories of these past four years' outings and can hardly believe we have been having them for that long!

The second purposeful way I set out four years ago to be my daughter's "Titus Two" woman was by planning weekly time to study together. This wasn't to be study such as we did in school. I wanted it to be much more personal—a sharing of hearts, not simply learning academic information. "To be sober, to love their husbands, to love their children, *To be* discreet, chaste, keepers at home, good, obedient to their own husbands"—these have been my curricula and guidelines as Sarah's "Titus Two" woman.

Sarah and I scheduled our study time. My days were already filled to the brim with homeschooling and caring for a house full of children. Sarah had her own school time, working for her dad, household helping, and much more. I prayed, asking the Lord for creativity in finding the needed minutes for Sarah and me, knowing this would be quite a task. Our study time was planned for a half an hour two nights a week, right after the younger children went to bed. We purposed to be faithful to this appointment. However, we gave ourselves some leeway since if we missed our time together one night, there would still be another night that week to meet.

These study times together are rare opportunities for Sarah to relate to me as another woman, an older sister in Christ, rather than strictly as her mother or her homeschool teacher (when she was still a part of our homeschool). Since this is not part of our school, there are no grades or expectations other than that she want to grow in her relationship with her Lord Jesus Christ. Sometimes our study causes us to be very serious and even grieved as we evaluate our lives in light of Scripture. Other times we laugh and are silly.

I am very grateful as I look back on these past four years for what the Lord has done in developing my "Titus Two" relationship with Sarah. It would have been so easy to stay busy with life and to ignore this vital area. Often, when a friend finds out about my monthly outings with Sarah, she will say, "Oh, that is such a good idea!" I completely agree!

What about you? Are you seeking opportunities to be your daughter's "Titus Two" woman? Even if your girls are young you can focus some of your conversation on "Titus Two" topics. If your daughter is a teen, then it is even more imperative that you are teaching her specifically in the areas Titus 2 lays out for older women to teach younger women. May we give the same time and opportunities to our own daughters to learn from the lessons the Lord has taught us that we give our friends. Mother, may I encourage you to be your daughter's "Titus Two" woman.

# Decisions for the New School Year
## *by Teri*

As another school year winds down, homeschooling moms begin to think ahead to the upcoming academic year. The new homeschool catalogs arrive in the mail, homeschool conventions are available, and decision time is upon us! Perhaps there are some lessons the Lord has taught me through sixteen years of homeschooling that I could share with you to help this time be more peaceful and more fruitful for you.

First, I had to learn the hard way to bathe all of my school plans and curriculum decisions in prayer. I can mull a school purchase over and over in my mind for weeks, not coming to any conclusion and gradually becoming more anxious simply because I cannot make a decision. I will think about the pros for the decision going one way and then the cons. However, it is balanced by the pros and cons associated with making the decision a different way.

I remember needing a different phonics program than I had been using because of the unique needs of a particular child. Each program I looked at had strengths and weaknesses. None seemed to offer exactly what I wanted. Rather than resting in the Lord and praying about the decision, I let it pressure me. I felt I had to make the decision simply to relieve my anxiety over it, while at the same time having no idea what to decide! This was not productive for my spirit toward my homeschooling nor toward my decision.

When prayer over school decisions is the basis of my thoughts, then I can have a peaceful heart as I wait for the Lord's direction rather than forcing myself to make a choice simply to have it done.

"Be careful for nothing; but in every thing by prayer and supplication with thanksgiving let your requests be made known unto God. And the peace of God, which passeth all understanding, shall keep your hearts and minds through Christ Jesus" (Philippians 4:6-7).

If I will follow the truth of Philippians 4:6-7 not to be anxious about anything but to present my requests to God, then I can set my thoughts about it aside. Usually, when I come back to the decision, I don't have the same level of frustration over it. If you begin to feel yourself becoming tense, worried, or fearful about any of the decisions, stop thinking and begin praying.

Next, I have needed to learn to be content. Philippians 4:11 says, "Not that I speak in respect of want: for I have learned, in whatsoever state I am, *therewith* to be content." Here is what would happen to me during a school year. Things would be going well in our school, but I would hear about this new spelling program "everyone" just loved. I would see it advertised in the homeschool magazines and look at the program's website. It sounded so perfect! Very quickly I found myself discontent with our spelling program and thinking about all of its weaknesses. In reality, I had invested time learning the spelling program we were using, and it was working. I had no leading from the Lord to change our spelling. All I had was a desire not to be left behind the rest of the homeschooling crowd.

If you have a curriculum that has been working for your family, don't change it. You have invested time learning the material and are now experienced with it. This is such a time saver for you as a homeschool mom! Even if others are raving about what they are using, be grateful for the experience and success the Lord has given you with your curriculum. Unless the Lord is clearly directing you to something else, stick with what you already know.

I discovered I was a wise woman to seek my husband's input. I try to type out information for Steve so that he can help me make upcoming school decisions. I include what has been problematic for us in the current school year. I write out the pros and cons of a new curriculum I am considering and how I believe it will impact our school. With this background, Steve is often able to help give needed direction on the decisions.

My schedule was another tool that was instrumental in helping me make curriculum decisions. When I had completed a school year where I could have comfortably devoted more time to school, I would expand and add more subjects or extras in. I could also consider a curriculum that was more teacher intensive. However, when I was completing a school year where I felt extremely busy with school and where we were barely accomplishing the essentials, I looked for ways to streamline my curriculum.

You, too, can use your schedule to help you with school choices for next year. If you are pushed for time this year, pray for curricula that will be less time intensive for you or the children. Please consider the importance of your curricula truly reflecting the available time you have. So often I see moms who are struggling with homeschooling because they don't have time for it. They have not been willing to trade off a time-intensive curriculum for one that takes less teacher time in order to maintain their own peace of mind and the overall integrity of their homeschool.

Whatever challenges you are facing as you start your preparations for the next homeschool year, may you be realistic about what you can do and content with what the Lord has already provided. Step out boldly in a new direction the Lord is leading, but only if He is leading! Don't think you have to follow the crowd. Perhaps you will be given the chance to honor your husband by following, without questioning, his suggestions. My prayer for you through the school decisions you are making as a homeschooling mom is that this becomes an enjoyable season for you. I encourage you to use each choice you must make as an opportunity to pray and then rest in the Lord.

# Time for Summer Schedule Planning
## by Teri

One of my children asked me this week if they would be doing math over the summer. That question prompted me that it is time to begin praying about and planning our summer schedule. We have just finished our normal school year and begun our two weeks of "break," then it is summer for us! What about you? Have you considered the use of a daily schedule during the summer? Since I am beginning to think about our summer schedule, I feel that it is time for me to encourage you to begin on yours!

I was amazed by the reports of several of the moms who tested our book on scheduling for homeschool families, *Managers of Their Homes* (see Additional Resources, page 385), before it was printed. After they had been on their schedules for a school year, some decided not to make and use a summer schedule. Their feedback was that they would not make that choice again. Their summer had rushed away without getting to the activities they had wanted to accomplish, and there was a greater level of disharmony among the children.

Summer is perfect for catching up on organizational and cleaning projects for which the school year does not allow time. I schedule one hour a day for these kinds of projects, and I am always surprised and delighted at how much I can do during this hour through the course of the summer.

The temptation is to continue working on the project past the allotted hour. However, this then undermines the rest of my summer schedule, in which I have other priorities planned for the remainder of the day.

I keep a running list of projects I would like to get done during that organizational hour, prioritize it, and jump in when summer begins. I also like to look back over what I have done during previous summers to help me know what to tackle this year.

This is my list right now, but I will come up with other projects as the summer progresses: pack away and label children's winter clothes, box this year's school books, create a school portfolio for each child, clean kitchen cupboards, clean and organize closets, put photos in albums, and plan 2001/2002 school schedule.

I may schedule Joseph, my twelve-year-old son, to spend my organizational hour playing with the younger children outside. This way I would have fewer interruptions for that time, and the children would be getting some exercise. Because we live in Kansas, this hour is scheduled for right after breakfast before it becomes unbearably hot.

Planning for a summer schedule is a great time to pray about whether year-round schooling would benefit your family. Year-round school is one way to eliminate some of the time pressures faced during a normal nine-month school year. When you spend a couple of hours schooling each day throughout the summer, you free up that time during your full-time school year. It also gives your children something constructive to do with their summer days and keeps their skills fresh. We have found that we can skip the first quarter of a math book when we move into it right after finishing the previous one because that first part is all review.

I will also be praying about how much school to continue through the summer. Usually I schedule math, which will necessitate my involvement. I try to make the other school time self-instructional and self-correcting so that as much of my time is freed up in the summer as possible.

I want to spend more time playing with the children during the summer. I put this in my schedule as well because it gives me needed accountability. I am likely to find something I feel I need to do or want to do rather than go outside with the children—especially when it is hot!—if that time isn't scheduled. When the children are looking forward to our outside time, I don't want to disappoint them.

Summer is a perfect opportunity to teach your children new chore skills. You can revise your chore schedule by moving jobs from child to child, training them on new ones, and making sure they can do them well.

Some of you do gardening and canning. Your summer schedule can help assure you that the gardeners in your family are seeing to their tasks in a timely fashion. When canning days come along, you will evaluate your schedule, dropping the least important activities to allow time for the extra hours canning will require.

Having a summer schedule does not prevent you from taking whole days or weeks for activities that don't fit into your normal schedule, such as a trip to the zoo or building a swing set. Your schedule is your tool. Use it when it is helpful. Leave it be when it isn't workable.

We want our summers to involve a change of pace. However, we don't want to lose the direction, productivity, and peace our schedule lends to our home. Therefore, we simply pray about a summer schedule, seeking the Lord for His priorities for our summer days. Then we are ready to put together the summer schedule and look forward to what we can enjoy and accomplish.

Ephesians 5:16 and Colossians 4:5 both mention "redeeming the time." May we see the productive possibilities for a summer schedule to help us in this important directive of "redeeming the time." May I encourage you to consider a summer schedule if you have not used one before. If you already believe in the importance of a summer schedule, may I suggest you begin now to pray about and plan for the details of that schedule.

# A Mother's Influence
## *by Teri*

At the opening of our church's mother/daughter banquet, the mom who was the banquet coordinator shared with us her love for gardening. This enjoyment of gardening began when she was just a little girl and would be included in her grandmother's daily garden time. Her grandmother talked to her and gave her appropriate tasks to do. All of this was the beginning of a lifelong pleasure in many aspects of gardening.

When I was a little girl, we frequently visited my grandparents for periods of time during the summer. Those summer days at their house were filled with pleasant memories. Beside my grandparents' driveway was a bed of flowers they called moss rose. These flowers bloomed with a variety of colors all summer long. Can you guess what my favorite summer flower is? Yes, every year I ask Sarah, our gardener, to please plant me a crop of moss rose.

I don't like to garden. For me, working in a garden is hot, dirty, and backbreaking—totally devoid of any pleasure. Perhaps, though, if my grandmother had been a gardener who loved her gardening, I would have picked up from her that same feeling toward gardening.

While my grandma, with her hay fever and asthma, could not garden, she did love to bake cookies. We never visited her home without finding several containers of freshly baked cookies in the pantry. Meme passed that same enjoyment of baking on to my mother. My mother has passed it on to me, and now it is effortlessly being handed down to my girls. When there is a quiet, rainy day, one of my first thoughts is, "What a great cookie baking day!"

The purpose of these stories is to encourage us to consider how critical it is that we cultivate good memories in our children's minds. Consider my delight in moss rose flowers. My grandparents didn't even know that the flowers they liked so much would become my favorite as well. This simply happened because of the love and sweet memories from those summer visits with my grandparents. I believe these are valuable lessons for us as Christian mothers and home-schooling moms as well. We have the incredible ability to influence some of our children's likes and perhaps their dislikes too.

I remember when my seventh-grade son was beginning kinder-garten. We had a half hour set aside each afternoon to do math together. Almost before we started our first day, he had decided he didn't like math. Each day he would complain that he didn't like school and didn't want to do the work. This was the beginning of my fourth child's homeschool career!

I must admit to feeling rather powerless against this early level of grumbling. We were not doing difficult work. He was using manip-ulatives in addition to do one workbook page each day, plus I was sit-ting right with him. Math just didn't get any better than that!

I knew I could give him consequences for his murmuring that would cause him to stop. However, I also realized his feelings would probably still be there; he just would not be vocalizing them. I saw this as an opportunity to influence his attitudes toward his school time.

When Joseph would start griping as we began our math work, I counterattacked. "Joseph, I want you to know this is one of the best parts of Mommy's day. I love doing school with you. I like to have some time for just you and Mommy to be together. You know math is very important, and you will use the math you are learning in some way or other almost every single day. I am so happy that I can be the one to teach you how to add and subtract. This is a special time each day for Mommy."

It wasn't the first day I looked Joseph in the eye during math and said those words to him, nor was it after a week, but very gradually, I began to see a change in his spirit. He complained less and less about joining me for math. He perked up and put forth more effort into his work. Finally, there was our day of triumph. After once again sharing with Joseph my joy in spending math time with him, he responded with, "Mommy, I really like this time, too!"

Steve shares with our children how his mother taught him to like to work. She would tell her children over and over that they would be working all of their lives so they might as well learn to enjoy it. Those words may not sound terribly profound, but they were said often enough and pleasantly enough that they impacted Steve's life. He is a man who learned to enjoy his work—in all the various forms it takes.

Moms, our attitude toward homeschooling is going to affect our children's attitudes toward their studies now and toward homeschooling their own children. If we grumble and complain about the burden of homeschooling, are short-tempered and irritable with them during school, and look forward to school time being over, what attitudes will they pick up from us?

I believe our children will acquire many attitudes from us toward not only homeschooling but also the daily routines of life. Scripture says, "Pleasant words *are as* an honeycomb, sweet to the soul, and health to the bones" (Proverbs 16:24). When we have a smile on our faces, a happy lilt to our voices, and pleasant words coming from our mouths, our children will automatically be drawn to having good memories of their days in our home. It is likely these memories will actually determine some of their future likes and dislikes.

I know how easy it is for me to fall into the habit of focusing on myself and my workload. Sometimes with being a wife, mother of eight children, homeschooling, homemaking, and other ministering, my tasks can look overwhelming. If I start to complain and murmur about my jobs, my children quickly pick up on my negative attitudes. It is entirely possible that if these attitudes were the habit of my life, my own children could decide not to homeschool their children because of the burden Mom portrayed homeschooling to be in her life.

Are we being hypocrites to act pleasantly and cheerfully toward daily tasks we really don't care to have to do? Philippians 2:14 tells us to "Do all things without murmurings and disputings. . . ." I see making the choice to have a good attitude toward what we don't like as choosing obedience to God's Word. We should certainly pray for the Lord to work in our hearts so that our positive attitude comes from a heart that is truly pleased to do what we are called to do. However, if that heart is still struggling, choose not to let it show on the outside.

Proverbs 25:11 says, "A word fitly spoken *is like* apples of gold in pictures of silver." We moms have such tremendous potential for positive influence on our children's future. I want to challenge us to consider the importance of our words toward each area for which the Lord has given us responsibility. We would do well to see to it that those words are, as Proverbs says, "fitly spoken."

As you think about how your own likes and dislikes have been shaped by your childhood memories, consider the influence you want to have on your children. May we not become so caught up in ourselves that we lose sight of the impact our words will have on our children's attitudes. May we build pleasant memories of every aspect of daily life for our children by guarding our own attitudes and by keeping them pleasant and positive.

# She Prayed — Part 1
## *by Teri*

I expect, as Christian women reading Ephesians 5:22-33, we would agree that the Bible teaches wives to reverence their husbands and to be submissive to them. However, I wonder how we apply the practical, daily aspects of reverencing and submitting. In particular, how do we handle situations where the Lord puts on our hearts a conviction or direction but not on our husbands'?

We may wonder if we should bring the subject up. Should we share our heart concerns unsolicited, or should we wait to see if he asks our input? Do we speak of it once and then drop it? Do we bring it up every few weeks? Do we share others' stories in the area or ask him to read a book on the topic?

In this Corner, I am not giving you specific answers to those questions. What I am going to do is point you to one sure biblical way to deal with the problem. Philippians 4:6-7 says, "Be careful for nothing; but in every thing by prayer and supplication with thanksgiving let your requests be made known unto God. And the peace of God, which passeth all understanding, shall keep your hearts and minds through Christ Jesus."

Several years ago part of our roof began to leak. As the head of the household, Steve was very concerned about the leak's potential damage to the house. He immediately said we needed a new roof. The problem was that we did not have the cash for a new roof and were committed to no more borrowing.

However, Steve decided that we would borrow the necessary money for a new roof. I spoke my heart passionately concerning our agreement not to be in debt and asked if there wasn't some interim solution while we saved money as quickly as we could for the roof. He was determined to have the new roof and save the house.

I knew after that conversation that I had pushed as hard as I could push. I had met with a level of resistance on Steve's part that was very unusual. I was so distraught I cried, when I was alone, over the possibility of borrowing for a roof. I also began to pray. It was the only avenue I felt I had left.

I prayed and waited as Steve had two roofers come out to give estimates. I kept praying. Then Steve started talking about some possibilities for redoing just the flashing area on the valley of the roof to see if that would keep the rain out until we could afford a new roof. That's what he ended up doing! The "stopgap" project worked. We saved money judiciously for most of a year, and we finally had a new roof—debt free!

I once asked for some testimonials in this area of a wife praying when her heart does not agree with her husband's. I received several stories from women who gave me permission to share them with you. These are examples to encourage you to see prayer as an ally in resolving differences between you and your husband. God can use it to change your husband's heart, change your heart, or simply give you peace in the midst of unrest.

*I worked part-time as a secretary before our first daughter was born, but before I ever got married, I knew I wanted to stay home with my children. My husband didn't see this as an option, but almost as soon as I found out I was expecting, I prayed that God would make a way for me to be able to stay home with my child. However, as soon as my daughter turned six weeks old, my husband instructed me to call the company I worked for to let them know I would be back the following week. So I made the call, and to my husband's disappointment, I was told I was no longer needed.*

*I felt relieved at not having to leave my precious infant daughter, but not for long—he told me he wanted me to begin searching for a new job. This was a point of strife between us for a short while, but after receiving some wise counsel from someone I confided in, I told my husband I was willing to submit to his wishes and would begin looking for a new job.*

*It was at that point that God answered my prayers, and my husband told me he did not want me working outside the home, even if it meant putting off the purchase of a new home for a while (which it did). It's interesting that God answered my prayer in this matter when I did what was required of me, which was submitting to my husband instead of arguing with him. Jill*

*My husband had a vasectomy six years ago, after our having three children. Because I was raised to be in submission to my husband, I signed the papers for him to have a vasectomy. He was convinced that this was the right thing for us, and no matter how much I cried and pleaded, he wanted the vasectomy.*

*For the next three years, I was so angry with him! And I was unbelievably hurt, even though he assured me that he did not think I was a bad mother. He honestly thought that my emotional health would be hurt by having more children because I was so often frustrated, short-tempered, and exhausted with the three we had.*

*In the late summer of 1999, I read testimonies of women whose husbands had had vasectomy reversals and were hoping that God would give them more children. I began to mention this to my husband, who simply listened to me, but didn't say anything one way or the other.*

*Then I started praying for his heart to be changed about having more children, and I asked the Lord to show me that his heart had changed before our anniversary, which is in October, without my having to say a word about it.*

*A couple of weeks before our anniversary, out of the blue my husband asked me if I wanted to adopt a baby! I was stunned! I asked him why he was even considering it, because he had always been totally against adoption in the past. He said he didn't really know why, just that God had opened his heart toward more children!!!*

*Over the course of two or three months, he apologized to me for making such a major decision without me and not giving me any choice in the matter, and he talked to our pastor about adoption. Our pastor suggested a reversal.*

*At this point, we haven't taken any steps in either direction, adoption or reversal. I have left that in God's hands, to guide my husband. An unexpected blessing for me was the total peace that God gave me about the whole thing. I used to agonize over not having any more children, and then was up in the clouds at the possibility of having more. But now I can truly say that I am ready for whatever God has planned for us. If I never have another baby, I am at peace about it.*

*So God has blessed my prayer and trust in Him, too! I know that my husband will follow God's leading. He is a very godly, dedicated man whose life's desire is to please God. Susan*

*My husband and I have four children. After number four, we used birth control because I was so afraid of getting pregnant again. I wanted more children, but was afraid of labor and finances. My husband was supportive of this decision. He felt like we were done and readily accepted the birth-control decision.*

*About seven months went by and my guilt increased daily. I felt like we had taken something that was God's and made it ours. I began to pray that God would show us what to do. I talked to my husband, and he said that he didn't think it would be wise for us to have more children. He wanted us to be done.*

*The next few weeks we didn't talk about it much. I continued to pray that God would have His way with our family. One day my husband and I had a conversation. I told him that I really did not feel like it was okay to use birth control. I felt like God should decide how many children we had. He was the giver and taker of life, and I would not get pregnant if it was not His will. He said he agreed with the concept, but didn't know if we could do it financially, etc.*

*The next few weeks passed with more prayer. Then we had a very different conversation. My husband now believes that we shouldn't try to have another baby, but we shouldn't prevent it either. He says that it is totally in God's hands. Jennie*

While these testimonials deal with three of the bigger issues on which a husband and wife may have differing opinions, they illustrate maintaining a quiet, trusting spirit through prayer and then resting. The results may not always be as we have read here, but God is sovereign. We can trust Him no matter what the outcome is or when it comes. I would much rather have the Lord change Steve's heart than for me to talk, cajole, and push him into it. I would also rather not have Steve's heart change if it isn't the Lord's will. If Steve gives into a decision simply to please me, then we run the risk of being out of God's will.

These issues concerning how a husband and wife relate to each other arise daily and are ongoing. May we, as Christian women, bless our husbands by being women who pray about our differences rather than being drippy faucets.

(Update: since this Corner was written, I have begun giving a session called, *Loving Your Husband.* In it, I encourage you to develop and strengthen your relationship with your husband, and I share many personal examples. For more information on the CD, see Additional Resources, page 385, or www.Titus2.com. Also, Dr. S. M. Davis has two excellent resources we highly recommend on reverence and attitudes: *How a Wife Can Use Reverence to Build or Save Her Marriage* and *The Attitude No Lady Should Have,* see www.Titus2.com for more information.)

# She Prayed — Part 2
## *by Teri*

Last month the Mom's Corner focused on praying in situations where there is a difference of opinion between a husband and wife. In this Corner, I want to go further on the issue of a wife's praying.

We can know the importance of praying for our husbands. We can plan to pray for them on a daily basis. However, do we follow through, or do we find our prayer life steps up only when there is a crisis? I would rather be praying positively for my husband daily when all is going well than to wait until the difficulties arise.

When we begin praying for our husbands, particularly concerning areas where we disagree, we must be very careful that our motives are pure. It is easy to get caught up in the "I am right" syndrome and pray pridefully for our husbands to switch to our way of thinking.

Two times in our marriage Steve has been led to change churches when I didn't agree with him. While I conceded there were good reasons to leave the current church, I was afraid of the unknown. I was settled in the present church and comfortable. The children had ministries and friends. I didn't want to "rock the boat." My prayers were not in support of Steve and the decision he was making.

We made each of those church moves despite my reluctance. In retrospect, they were good decisions on Steve's part even though they were not the ones I wanted. The work the Lord did in our lives through each of those new churches was wonderful. Now I would not change those decisions for anything. In these cases, my opinions on leaving a church were not right, but I sure thought they were at the time!

Fear was ultimately at the heart of my desire to stay in churches that weren't right for our family. I was uncertain of what the future would hold with a move. 1 Peter 3:6 says, "Even as Sara obeyed Abraham, calling him lord: whose daughters ye are, as long as ye do well, and are not afraid with any amazement." We are encouraged not to be afraid as we follow Sara's example.

How many times are our prayers about differences with our husbands based on fear? We are afraid that if we follow our husbands in these decisions, it will mean we may face financial difficulties, we could lose our children's hearts, or perhaps we will be embarrassed in some way. Our Lord Jesus does not want our prayers for the situation to be resolved as we think it should simply because we are afraid. Rather, He wants us trusting in Him.

Keep in mind the biblical stories where everything looked terrible, but God had a purpose in it and brought about good: Joseph being sold into slavery, Samuel being raised by Eli the wicked priest, Moses taken from his mother to be raised by Pharaoh's daughter. Our trust must be completely in the Lord and not in what makes sense to us.

Of course there are legitimate issues where it is clear the husband is making poor choices. When we are considering praying for changes in our husbands' hearts, I would caution that we can easily be consumed with this and develop a critical spirit toward them.

It is important to lay a necessary groundwork for a careful guard against a critical or condescending spirit in a wife toward her husband. If we are praying in one area after another for a change in a husband's heart and doing this day after day, it could keep our focus on the perceived failings of our husbands. This would fuel our critical spirits.

To avoid this, I would suggest being careful how we pray. For example, in my situation when I didn't want us to go into debt for a new roof, I think I was asking the Lord to change Steve's heart so that he didn't want to go into debt for the roof. On the other hand, I could have prayed for the Lord to provide the funds for a new roof or another

alternative that would keep us from debt. Do you see the subtle difference in those two prayers and how the latter would keep my thoughts
off of my unhappiness with the direction Steve was headed?

What about the mom who didn't want to have to go back to
work? She can petition the Lord to change her husband's heart, or
she could ask the Lord to provide for the family without her having
to work. Again, a very subtle difference, but one worth noting.

Proverbs 31:11-12 says, "The heart of her husband doth safely
trust in her, so that he shall have no need of spoil. She will do him
good and not evil all the days of her life." Is it possible that by
allowing a critical, prideful spirit to develop in my heart toward my
husband, I am doing him evil rather than good?

My heart's desire is that, as wives, we truly learn the role the
Lord has for us. Since areas of disagreement are bound to arise
between a husband and wife, may we make it a priority to be much
in prayer about each of them. May we rest in the Lord even if we
don't see the changes we would like to have happen.

# Hard Work — Part 1
## TAKING THOUGHTS CAPTIVE
### by Teri

Here is part of a recent question that was asked of Teri:

*My children are 8, 6, 3, and 17 months. I homeschool. I had a mis-carriage 5 months ago. Sometimes I feel like I'm drowning in everything to do. The home stays relatively picked up. It stays cleaned. We don't have fancy meals, but they're always on the table and usually on time. The children are well-behaved most of the time. They have issues that continually crop up because they're human and sometimes these overwhelm me. So what is the problem? I feel like I'm going non-stop. Jennie*

Can you relate to Jennie? Have you felt like this? Maybe you are struggling with some of these same emotions.

Through my twenty-seven years of being a wife and twenty-five years of being a mother, I have come to see that what the Lord has called me to do is just plain "hard work"! There are no guaranteed vacation days, no promised full nights of sleep—not even an uninterrupted trip to the bathroom! However, Scripture tells us in Romans 8:18, "For I reckon that the sufferings of this present time *are* not worthy *to be compared* with the glory which shall be revealed in us." There is nothing of more eternal value that I could invest my life in—if working hard is even truly suffering—than my husband and the children the Lord has given to me.

## Expectations

My first step in how to handle my emotions concerning "hard work" is through my expectations. If I expect to complete my work by dinnertime so I can sit and relax all evening, then I am frustrated and perhaps even angry with circumstances or people whom I see as robbing me of "my" time. On the other hand, if my expectation is that being a mother is a difficult job that goes from the time I get up in the morning until I go to bed at night—plus some nighttime interruptions—then I am only doing what I expect to do!

## Purpose

My next step is to recall why I am doing what I am doing. In Romans 12:1 we find these words, "I beseech you therefore, brethren, by the mercies of God, that ye present your bodies a living sacrifice, holy, acceptable unto God, *which is* your reasonable service." Isn't this what we are doing every day as we serve our families? We are choosing to be living sacrifices that are holy, acceptable to God, and our reasonable service. We could be investing our time in many areas of our own pleasures and interests. Instead we are making the choice to be a living sacrifice and obediently follow what Jesus Christ has called us to do.

Galatians 6:9 says, "And let us not be weary in well doing: for in due season we shall reap, if we faint not." In John 12:24 we find: "Verily, verily, I say unto you, Except a corn of wheat fall into the ground and die, it abideth alone: but if it die, it bringeth forth much fruit."

I have not been called to follow my pursuits. Rather, I have been given a specific calling to "well doing" that says I am to be sober, to love my husband, to love my children, to be discreet, chaste, a keeper at home, good, and obedient to my own husband, that the word of God be not blasphemed (Titus 2:4-5). This is "hard work." It starts the minute I open my eyes in the morning.

## Acceptance

The final suggestion I want to make is to simply accept the "hard work." Now, please don't misunderstand me. I am not saying there will never be any time for rest, relaxation, or pursuing something I am interested in doing. What I am encouraging is that it not be my focus and goal. I don't want a craving for "my" time to cause me not to have the meek and quiet spirit that is of great worth in God's sight (1 Peter 3:4).

It is interesting that the more I submit my heart to the Lord's direction to be content (Philippians 4:11) and to be grateful (1 Thessalonians 5:18), the more my "hard work" is what I like doing. It becomes what I choose to do even if I don't have to do it.

When my mind is set on things above (Colossians 3:1-2), then days filled with work and activity are blessed and a joy. I feel a sense of peace and contentment in the tasks set before me. How easy it is, though, for me to take my eyes off the Lord and His calling to be an obedient, living sacrifice and instead have them on me.

This is most likely to happen when I get tired. Then my thinking becomes particularly skewed. Here are the kind of "poor me" thoughts I will have: "No one picks up anything in this house except me! The children will never do their chores without being reminded or disciplined! I have more to do than is possible!"

These thoughts are not true! At that point, I should battle the thoughts through prayer. So often, though, I am too tired to even do that and tears combined with those false ideas are my companions. However, with a good night's sleep, I find the Lord's mercies are new every morning. I am again ready to face the day, where the truth is that the children do accomplish some of their chores without being reminded, family members do put things away, and I can do what the Lord has called me to do.

## Encouragement

This Mom's Corner is not about schedules, timesaving suggestions, or ways to simplify our lives. These are important, and I will be writing about them in next month's Mom's Corner. However, I think we would do well to also encourage each other in the "hard work" we have set before us. Our labors are our living sacrifices—the sacrifice of ourselves. Through our "hard work" we die to ourselves, but live to the Lord. The rewards we will see in our husbands, children, those around us, and even our own hearts are the rewards that truly matter!

Sisters, may I encourage you that you have chosen a good thing when you obey the Lord's calling on your life to invest it in your family by serving them. May I also suggest that this lifestyle is one that requires constant, vigilant, "hard work" with bountiful rewards now and in eternity. Let "hard work" be our expectation, one which we seek the Lord to help us embrace with joy. May we die to the wants we have for our "free time" and invest all that it takes in the areas in which the Lord has called us to serve. May we simply, contentedly, and happily accept the work that comes with serving our families!

# Hard Work — Part 2
## PRACTICAL HELPS
### *by Teri*

The tasks set before a Christian wife and mother are high callings from the Lord. While they can involve a great deal of hard work, we want to embrace our jobs with joy. In last month's Mom's Corner I discussed this part of the workload of being a mother. Now let's look at some of the practical aspects. Are there ways to manage our workload and perhaps even lighten it?

I simply cannot speak highly enough of the benefits a schedule brings to a mom in her ability to keep up with life. I knew a daily schedule helped me immensely. However, since the publication of our book on scheduling *(Managers of Their Homes)*, I have heard the same thing from many other moms who have begun to schedule their days.

While I am not going to try to recap all that is in *Managers of Their Homes,* let me share with you a few benefits a schedule has that apply to a mother's workload. First, your schedule makes you more productive. You know what to do throughout each scheduled segment of the day, so you are not wasting time trying to decide what to do or simply doing nothing because it all looks too overwhelming.

You can schedule time to accomplish your work tasks, but you can also schedule in time for other priorities. This should most importantly include daily time with the Lord. Other scheduled personal-time activities might be exercising, crafting, reading, or napping. With a schedule making you more productive, you might discover you actually have time for projects you would like to accomplish. Plus, it is put into your schedule to assure it happens!

A schedule causes you to realistically evaluate what you can and can't do. A mom who is away from home a great deal may have trouble keeping up. This could make her believe her workload is too great. If you are trying to do too much within the home, you will have the same struggle. Putting all you would like to accomplish on paper brings a level of realism that isn't found any other way. If the planning stages of a schedule cause you to see that you have more to do than time to do it, taking the problem back to the Lord and to your husband may help you know what you can release.

It is imperative that a mom gets the amount of sleep she needs if she is to have any hope of keeping up with her work and having the right attitude toward it. It is tempting to continue working until way past a reasonable bedtime, night after night, in an effort to accomplish all we "think" needs to be done. On the other hand, we may find ourselves so exhausted we do nothing productive in the evening, but neither do we go to bed to get needed sleep. When we are tired, everything looks overwhelming!

We will do our families and ourselves much good if we take our thoughts captive (2 Corinthians 10:5). All the "I-have-to-do-this-before-I-can-stop" thoughts that cause us not to go to bed at night need to be taken captive to the truth that our sleep is more important. When we are well rested, no matter how much work we have to do or how busy we are, our spirits will deal with it in a much better manner than when we are tired.

Please, please schedule a nap each afternoon if you are not able to get the amount of sleep at night that you need. Perhaps you have a nursing baby with whom you are up one or more times in the night. Maybe you go to bed later than you would choose because that is your husband's preference. Whatever the reason, if those nights are shorter than the sleep your body requires, have a nap scheduled for the afternoon.

Schedule exercise time into your day even if you don't think you can afford the time. You will discover that the minutes spent exercising will multiply themselves many times over in your energy level.

When you are feeling better, you will be able to accomplish more and keep up better with the work of being a wife and mother.

Sometimes I ask Steve for help. I am designed by God to be Steve's helpmeet. There are times, though, when I simply request that Steve help bail me out of what have become overwhelming circumstances to me. This might mean that he says "no" to some tasks I have thought I could keep up with. It could be that he will physically pitch in and help make dinner or clean up. He could even send me to bed for some added sleep!

Be sure to train your children to help. You are not robbing your child of his childhood by doing this. You are preparing him for life. I hear over and over again of moms who say they were not taught as children how to care for household responsibilities. We also are very aware that many men do not know how to help their wives because household chores were never required of them as they were growing up. If you teach your children basic home duties, not only are they lightening your workload, they are also being prepared for life.

Stay home more! It is extremely hard to keep up at home if you are frequently away. Somehow, once we leave home for a meeting, Bible study, activity, trip to the store, or whatever it might be, we don't have the same energy level and momentum for doing our home tasks as we have on the days we stay home. In addition, by being away from home we lose many, many hours that could have been used to accomplish our work. I cannot overstate the importance of limiting outside-the-home activities if one is struggling with a negative attitude toward a day that goes nonstop. If you do choose to be gone from home frequently, then you must accept the trade-off of being extremely busy when you are at home. Your outside-the-home activities are your discretionary time that could be used for rest and relaxing if you were home rather than away.

Finally, look at your schedule and tasks to accomplish and evaluate what you could do less frequently. Are there jobs you currently do every day that could be done every other day or once a week? Take vacuuming, for example. If you vacuum every day, limit yourself to doing it every other day for a month. See if you and your family can live with that level of carpet cleanliness so that you can invest the time elsewhere. What about tasks that you are doing three times a week that you could cut back to once a week? Vacuuming the carpet every day may cause a mom time pressure that leads her to be frazzled. Perhaps it would be better not to vacuum so frequently, choosing instead to put up with a less than ideally clean carpet!

There is absolutely no doubt about it; being a wife and mother means plenty of hard work, but it pays wonderful, eternal dividends. May I encourage you to consider the use of a daily schedule to help you manage your time, including both work and rest. Teach your children how to work and also be willing to ask your husband for help when needed. Remember the importance of staying home and adequate sleep in keeping up with the work of a wife and mother. May we be committed to serving the Lord Jesus by serving our families, even if the cost is hard work!

# Worthwhile Toys, or Should It Be Tools?
## *by Teri*

Regularly I receive e-mails requesting that I write a Mom's Corner on a specific topic. Here is part of one such note:

*There were a couple of areas I would really appreciate Teri tackling in future Corners. One area has to do with toys and suggestions for timeless, durable, worthwhile toys.*

With Christmas quickly approaching, I thought this might be an appropriate subject for the December Mom's Corner. Considering we have eight children in one family, we have had plenty of experience with toys!

Let me begin by sharing some of our goals for our children's playtime that in turn translate into goals for toys. As we began our parenting adventure, Steve and I did not realize that the toys our children played with had an influence on their character development and even their future appetites. If we allowed the children to have a toy with an evil face, they played with it as an evil individual and their play took on an evil bent. If we gave our children an electronic game, they spent hours sitting and playing with it. They lost interest in any type of active or creative play. Your goals, even for how your child spends his playtime, are important.

We choose to shield our children from as much worldliness as possible. 1 John 2:15 tells us: "Love not the world, neither the things *that are* in the world. If any man love the world, the love of the Father is not in him." Therefore, we desire that our children be involved in pure, wholesome types of play. For example, we give the girls baby dolls rather than Barbie dolls. We would like for our daughters to desire to be nurturing mommies rather than possibly giving them a hunger for dating relationships.

We want the children to develop skills while they are playing. That means we will invest in puzzles, games, quality reading books, and even tools. Creativity is on our list of goals for playtime. Therefore, we avoid electronic toys with lots of "bells and whistles"—the kind with a never-ending thirst for batteries. In addition, we choose to avoid toys that are faddish. We didn't have to decide if some of the Star Wars toys were okay or not. They fit into the category of faddish and therefore weren't even considered.

We desire for the children to be developing hearts toward families and service even while they are playing. This, then, needs to be taken into consideration when we are picking out toys. Will this toy help my child toward the goal or hinder him?

## Trikes

Tricycles. We would much rather our children ride trikes for outside playtime than to ride around in a battery-operated sidewalk vehicle. Outside play is the time for exercise to build strong bodies and release energy!

## Educational Games

Playing educational games is an activity I enjoy doing with my children. I feel like my time spent with them is not only quality time, but also time invested in their future. I schedule a half hour each afternoon to spend with just one child. We almost always use this time to play games together. Here are our favorites.

*Takeoff.* Takeoff is a game that teaches the names of countries, their major cities, and flags. Even my six-year-old can play it with a little bit of help. There is some strategy, but not much. My children will often beat me!

*Muggins Math* games. We have Knockout and Muggins. It is a two-sided wooden game board using marbles, numbered dice, and numbered game-board holes. Any child who is able to add and subtract can play these games. All of my children regularly request this game, even the one who can't add or subtract. "You tell me where to put my marbles, Mommy," she says.

*Sum Swamp.* Sum Swamp is a board game for children learning to add and subtract. It has cute little plastic swamp characters such as a frog and snail for game pieces. We have played this game so much that the numbers have worn off the dice.

*Name That State.* Name That State is a board game to teach the names of states and capitals. The younger children simply have to name the state. Older children and Mom have to give the state and its capital. They love it when Mom can't remember the capital of Vermont or South Dakota!

## Puzzles

Each year when I order school curriculum, I also order two to four new puzzles for the preschoolers. I have a wonderful collection of puzzles that my children love to work. Most are floor puzzles. We have puzzles of varying levels of difficulty. Some of the puzzles make for playtime after they are put together. One is a city just the right size for Matchbox cars. Several become props for other play. One is a rainforest. As we put it together, John will say, "Mom, what is this animal?"

"Well, I'm not sure I've ever seen anything like that. Let's look inside the box where it shows all the animals with their names on them."

Our puzzles are kept in a closet, and they are only allowed out by permission. That helps to preserve them and to keep interest in them high each time they come out. I expect to have my puzzles be regularly asked for by my grandchildren in future years when they are at my house!

## Legos and Playmobils

Legos are the timeworn standard in the Maxwell house. Sons and daughters, older and younger play with them day after day after day. We purchase the city, police, fire, rescue, and arctic sets. There are many sets that aren't acceptable to our family's standards. Usually this is because of an evil theme, or because they encourage play that we wouldn't allow in real life. We were even able to purchase a large wooden display table from a store going out of business so the children can keep permanent Lego set-ups.

The children have spent hours and hours of playtime during cold winter and hot summer days with their Legos. They build and build; then they enjoy what they have made. The buildings and vehicles are redesigned and rearranged. A new play theme is begun. While many toys the children have had stay stuffed on a shelf, Legos are forever used in our home.

Playmobils are the second long-standing favorite of our children. While the sets are expensive, they are played with for years and years. We often rotate having Playmobils out or Legos. Every few months when the changeover occurs, the children will have an added excitement in their play.

## Tools

As our boys enter their middle elementary grades, we begin looking for tools we can give them as gifts. Because we are training our children for their lives as adults, we want them to begin to see value in work and find it rewarding, even as a child. Our boys are given age-appropriate work tools such as hammers, screwdrivers, and even cordless drills. Of course, it is important to use discretion as to when a child is mature enough to safely handle the tool he would be given. Also, rules as to the tool's usage and adult supervision while the child is handling it are musts!

One year when John was seven and Joseph was nine, they were each given a cordless drill for Christmas. They were thrilled. Steve had a project planned for after Christmas that he knew they could help him with, using their new drills. Over the past three years they have used them often in other work projects with their dad. They have even been able to loan them to their big brother for work on his house.

By giving your son tools, he will learn valuable home-maintenance skills, develop a willingness to work, build his personal tool supply, and have as much fun as playing. Collecting tools will provide a young man with the supplies he needs to help him maintain his home, yard, and vehicle when he is married with a home of his own.

## Set Your Goals and Make Your Choices

Our children have grown up without television. They have enjoyed parental sheltering even in the toys they are allowed to play with. While some would mock such choices, we are watching pure, wholesome, delightful children grow into the same kinds of adults. Appetites are developed in childhood. Consider well what appetites the toys you are giving to your children fuel within them. May I encourage you to pray and seek the Lord for the biblical goals He would give you for your children's playtimes. Then translate those goals into the toys you allow your children to have.

# From Negativism to Thanksgiving
## *by Teri*

When I picked up the phone, it was my dad. "I am inviting your children to drive to Post with me to see the chapel that burned on Sunday morning. Your mom says there is all kinds of activity there. I am sure your children would be interested in watching what they are doing."

Having no doubt that my crew would enthusiastically say "yes," we made arrangements for the children to walk over to his house since we live next door. Delighted hoops and hollers filled our halls as five children from age twelve down to five heard the plans.

While my children enjoyed an unexpected field trip, I really believe the Lord put together that outing for another reason. I had been struggling emotionally all day. Although I was not falling deeper into the negative spiral, neither did I see victory on the horizon. Suddenly I had a silent house with no responsibilities that had to be fulfilled at that minute.

I headed straight to my rocking chair nook with my Bible and a tissue. I knew I needed time with the Lord. My negative thoughts were so overwhelming that I pulled out a small notebook and began to write down all the areas of my life in which I seemed to be failing. I knew that at least if they were on paper I could realistically evaluate them with the Lord. I quickly filled up a page and a half!

I had decided I would work my way down the list, confessing each area as sin and then reading Scripture that applied to it. As I glanced over the list, however, I saw that my emotions had totally distorted my thinking. While each portion of the list had things I was asking the Lord to grow me in or eliminate from my life, none represented truth. They were all globalized with words like "never," "nothing," "won't," and "can't."

While confessing sin, asking forgiveness, and seeking the Lord for His grace to avoid that sin in the future is part of my normal procedure, that wasn't where the Lord took me that afternoon. He quickly put in my mind another direction for attacking this problem. Thanksgiving!

Two verses immediately came to mind before I even opened my Bible. "And whatsoever ye do in word or deed, *do* all in the name of the Lord Jesus, giving thanks to God and the Father by him" (Colossians 3:17). "In every thing give thanks: for this is the will of God in Christ Jesus concerning you" (1 Thessalonians 5:18).

I was most certainly not giving thanks for everything—or really anything at all. Nor did my day represent doing all in the name of the Lord Jesus, giving thanks to God. It had been a day filled with negative responses to the circumstances around me. Rather than giving thanks and praising the Lord in the midst of feelings and situations, I had turned my focus onto myself and my failures.

Through the early part of the day, I didn't confess each wrong reaction and wrong thought as sin. Those would have been the right steps. Instead, as the day wore on, I allowed my thoughts to follow a path of self pity. I knew I was not being the wife and mother the Lord would have me be that day.

However, I didn't want to choose to apply even a small amount of self-discipline to change the pattern and direction. "Casting down imaginations, and every high thing that exalteth itself against the knowledge of God, and bringing into captivity every thought to the obedience of Christ" (2 Corinthians 10:5). I know some might become tired of how often I quote this verse in a Mom's Corner. It is key, though, in our overcoming the difficulties we struggle with—no matter what they may be!

What I needed to do was to bring "into captivity every thought to the obedience of Christ." This takes place in my mind. The Lord has given us His Word about what we can then expect. "Being confident of this very thing, that he which hath begun a good work in you will perform *it* until the day of Jesus Christ" (Philippians 1:6). "I can do all things through Christ which strengtheneth me" (Philippians 4:13).

It was true that, during the day I am describing, I was allowing unresolved sin to continue in my life that needed to be dealt with biblically. It was not true that I allowed such unresolved sin every day. It was not true that I never responded sweetly to anything. It was not true that I always criticized and never praised. It was not true that I always felt distant from the Lord.

I began to go through each item on my list to find something to be thankful for rather than unhappy about. My negative emotions were almost immediately overcome with that grateful spirit inherent in praise and thanksgiving. Here is a sample of my change of thoughts. "Lord, I feel like I am doing this all in my own strength," was replaced with, "Lord, I am so grateful for my salvation and Your never ending work in my life. You have brought me so far and please continue the good work that You began. When I feel like I am doing this in my own strength, I have lost sight that every single good thing that I do is from You. When those feelings overtake me, it is because I have chosen not to be close to You, not to seek You in prayer before thinking or acting, and to allow self pity to overtake me."

"I never respond to anything sweetly," was replaced by, "Thank You, Lord, for each of these children. They are truly a blessing from You. I am grateful to be given the opportunity to love them and teach them about You."

When my children returned from their outing, they must have thought they had a new mommy. Beginning with a simple choice to seek the Lord for help, the negative thinking was dispelled. Please believe me when I say that no matter what is happening around me, it simply isn't worth a bad attitude toward it. My sinful reactions gain nothing while following the Lord's direction profits everything!

Dear Sisters, I expect you know all too well what it is like to have days when many, if not all, of your thoughts are negative. You may not have a God-directed appointment to quietly take your heart to the Lord as I did, but remember Susannah Wesley, who would throw her apron over her head to pray. In the midst of chaos, strife, and busyness, we can still kneel where we are, bow our heads, and turn our thoughts to thanksgiving. May I encourage you to take your thoughts captive, bringing them from negativism to thanksgiving.

# A Merry Heart and a Joyful Mother
### *by Teri*

We are right smack in the middle of the school year, which could mean we are struggling with negative thoughts about finishing school up. Personally, I have also just had one of the most exciting days of my life. With that combination, I wanted this Mom's Corner to be uplifting. I would like to look at several Scriptures that could encourage and lighten our hearts.

Proverbs 23:7 tells us, "For as he thinketh in his heart, so *is* he . . . ." While this verse, in context, is speaking negatively, I believe we can apply it in the positive as well. What about, "A merry heart doeth good *like* a medicine . . ." (Proverbs 17:22)? Our thoughts, in some measure, determine the emotions that are a part of our heart reactions to things.

On Nathan's wedding day, I had a choice to make. I could dwell on my personal sadness of having a son, whom I have loved dearly for twenty-five years and who has lived with us all that time, marry and leave home. I could also choose to think about the joy and delight he would experience on his wedding day and as he began his new life with his bride.

When I put my thoughts on Nathan and his happiness, it made my heart merry. That was truly good medicine, because I was able to go through the whole wedding ceremony without shedding a tear. I always cry at weddings! I didn't think it was possible to make it through any wedding without tears, and certainly not my own son's!

Proverbs 15:15 says, ". . . he that is of a merry heart *hath* a continual feast." Sometimes a merry heart is simply a by-product of feeling happy. Then it is easy; we just act the way we feel. When I am getting ready for my read-aloud time with the children, my heart is merry. I naturally love these moments each day, looking forward to them with anticipation.

Other times I must choose to have a merry heart. I have discovered, in the midst of discouragement, depression, and negativism, that I can make a choice to have a merry heart. It is never easy, though. As is true with each day, it becomes even more important that I am having daily time with the Lord reading His Word and that I am communing with Him in prayer. While I must make the choice about where my thoughts will be, He is the One Who accomplishes the work. "For it is God which worketh in you both to will and to do of *his* good pleasure" (Philippians 2:13). This grows out of the intimacy of my relationship with Jesus Christ.

There are certain times of the month I wake up feeling entirely different than I do on other days. I don't want to face the day at all, but I must. At that point I have a choice to make. Will I act according to my feelings, or will I put on a merry heart that I don't feel? It begins with a heart that cries out to the Lord for help, acknowledging dependence on Him. The Lord's grace is sufficient: "And he said unto me, My grace is sufficient for thee: for my strength is made perfect in weakness. Most gladly therefore will I rather glory in my infirmities, that the power of Christ may rest upon me" (2 Corinthians 12:9).

When I feel irritable, unhappy, surly, tense, or on edge, I can acknowledge to the Lord the negative emotions I am having. I can pray for His enabling to overcome them. Then I can also choose to walk out of my bedroom greeting my family with a happy voice, while cheerfully loving and hugging my family members—even though I don't feel a bit sweet or loving.

I am not being a hypocrite if I act happy when I am not feeling that way. James 1:2 says, "My brethren, count it all joy when ye fall into divers temptations." Scripture tells me that I am to count my troubles as joy; this is obedience.

I remember once hearing a godly man say, "Obedience isn't hard when we are doing something we like and want to do. However, when to be obedient means going against our feelings, then we see true obedience."

I can't "count it all joy" if I am crying, angry, irritated, frustrated, or feeling sorry for myself. This joy does not come from a heart that thinks about and focuses on its troubles. This joy comes from a merry heart—one that is able to rest in the Lord knowing He is in charge of everything that happens to me.

Our joy develops from what comes out of our mouths. "A man hath joy by the answer of his mouth: and a word *spoken* in due season, how good *is it!*" (Proverbs 15:23). When I have given a sweet, loving response to a question one of my children has asked me, my heart is happy. However, when I am short or irritable with that child, my heart condemns me.

Here again, my joy comes directly from the choices I am making. Will I decide to follow Christ's way, allowing the fruit of the Spirit to guide my lips? Will I give in to my selfishness, finding instead that, "For the wrath of man worketh not the righteousness of God" (James 1:20)?

"He maketh the barren woman to keep house, *and to be* a joyful mother of children. Praise ye the LORD" (Psalms 113:9). I was reminded of this verse while Sarah and I were reading *A Woman After God's Own Heart,* by Elizabeth George.

Elizabeth George shared several ways that she incorporated being a "joyful mother of children" into her home when her children were young. One of these was to use the positive words "I love" for every good aspect of their lives. She told her children that she loved praying for them, praying with them, going for walks with them, family dinners, family devotions, the Lord's Day, and much more.

Don't our happy, positive words demonstrate a joyful spirit? Even if we aren't feeling joyful, won't they move us in the right direction if we speak them anyway? If these kinds of words are a part of our daily habit of conversation, it will be much easier to say them when we are not actually feeling them.

Let me repeat for you one more time these verses that have to do with a merry heart and joy. Please don't skip over them, but read them carefully.

"He maketh the barren woman to keep house, *and to be* a joyful mother of children. Praise ye the LORD" (Psalms 113:9).

". . . he that is of a merry heart *hath* a continual feast" (Proverbs 15:15).

"A man hath joy by the answer of his mouth: and a word *spoken* in due season, how good *is it*" (Proverbs 15:23).

"A merry heart doeth good *like* a medicine . . ." (Proverbs 17:22).

If you don't have a merry heart or joy, please start by talking to the Lord about it and asking Him for His help. May each of us make the choice to have a merry heart and be filled with joy! May we all truly be joyful mothers of children!

# Anger — Part 1
## THE CASE AGAINST ANGER
### *by Teri*

I had sent Joseph (12), John (11), and Jesse (7) downstairs to pick up in their bedroom. They were given a half hour of time we would normally get to spend reading out loud together for this task because they hadn't done it during their assigned time. When I went to check on their progress, I heard one son fussing at another that he hadn't been working at all. The other son made an unkind comment in reply. As I listened to this verbal interaction between my sons, I found the emotion of anger rising up within me.

Tonight we had a busy "breakfast" supper. There was much preparation, and most of it needed to be completed at the last minute. We started with salads, but then moved into bacon, pancakes, eggs, and biscuits. While everyone else was beginning to eat, I was still frying bacon and cooking pancakes. After a little while, Steve kindly offered to take over the kitchen work so I could sit down to have a bite to eat. I poured six more pancakes and said, "Here are the last of the pancakes. Please keep an eye on them."

After eating a pancake, I returned to the kitchen. "Yikes, who's watching the pancakes?"

"What pancakes?" Steve questioned. "All you said to do was finish frying the bacon."

"No. Before I sat down, I told you I was putting in the last of the pancakes," was my response.

"I didn't hear that."

I could tell, again, I was beginning to feel angry. While I have come a long way in dealing with anger—from yelling and door slamming to irritated tones in my voice—I still have much to learn in this area. I also have a tremendous desire to be constantly characterized by a meek and quiet spirit.

I am concerned about truly conquering anger in my life, and I know many other moms are as well. I don't want to simply control it on the outside, although that is a starting place. I pray that there would be no anger at all in my reactions.

Scripture has strong words to say about anger. "For the wrath of man worketh not the righteousness of God" (James 1:20). I believe as Christian homeschooling moms, we are seeking for the righteousness of God to be manifested. God clearly says that our anger does not bring about His righteousness.

It is easy to justify anger, and that is a very dangerous temptation. May we never, never allow ourselves to do this. We must not make excuses for our anger but rather see it as sin. As long as my thoughts say that I have a reason to be angry, I am not going to deal with that anger properly or gain victory over it.

In the situation where my boys were bickering, they were sinning. I had a choice set before me. I could allow myself to let the angry thoughts and feelings progress, telling myself that my anger is righteous anger and that they deserve it. After all, when I am angry, I get their attention.

However, to be totally honest, while I am disappointed that my boys are not being kind to each other, my anger is more related to my inconveniences. I am angry that they aren't getting their work done, that I will have to correct them for their unkindness, that we work on their attitudes toward one another but they still are bickering, etc. My anger is focused on the impact of their behavior on me.

If I were truly concerned about the issue of sin in my boys' lives, I would not be angry. I would be pleased that the Lord has given me another opportunity to share God's truth with my sons. I would once again turn their hearts and thoughts to Jesus Christ, the One Who can give them victory over sin. No, that is not the focus of my heart when I am becoming angry. Rather, my heart is selfish.

What happens in my children's lives when I respond to them angrily? First, they, in turn, learn to react with anger. While anger is certainly a part of our sin nature, how often do we hear our own angry voices and see our hard facial expressions mirrored in our children? Our children have picked up angry responses from watching their mothers!

Scripture says, "A soft answer turneth away wrath: but grievous words stir up anger" (Proverbs 15:1). Therefore, when I respond angrily to my child, I am fueling his anger as well. We then have an angry, sinful confrontation on our hands. This is most certainly a no-win situation.

Now let's consider the anger I felt inside when the pancakes were being overcooked. This is a simple matter. What difference does it make if I said something and no one heard me? What difference does it make if the pancakes were burned? (They weren't.) Yet my pride over wanting to be paid attention to and not have distasteful food allowed angry feelings to fester.

Here again, is there anything beneficial or positive that might come from anger over pancakes? Of course not! However, there is great negative potential if I let that anger progress. What would my children see in my relationship with Steve if I respond angrily—or even at all? Where do they see my priority if a burned pancake is more important than a sweet spirit?

Next month I want to delve further into this area of anger and dealing with it. I have a whole chapter on anger in *Homeschooling with a Meek and Quiet Spirit* (see Additional Resources, page 385). My desire in these Corners is not to repeat what I have written there, but to continue, in different ways, to evaluate anger and keep our focus on the need to refuse it any place in our lives.

Sisters, we have a myriad of daily interactions that can cause us to feel angry. May we see anger as God sees it. May we hate the anger in our lives and the consequences it brings about as well. May we consistently be asking the Lord for a heart that not only doesn't let our anger spill out on our family members, but one that doesn't even have angry feelings.

# Anger — Part 2
## THE CASE AGAINST ANGER
### *by Teri*

"*It is* better to dwell in the wilderness, than with a contentious and an angry woman" (Proverbs 21:19). Ouch! This verse hits home with me when we read it in our family Bible time. I always pick it as the one that God is telling me to beware of. Walking on the road toward a heart that is not easily angered is a good road to be on. I am so grateful the Lord has moved me away from being a mom who yells at her children. As you know, though, my earnest prayer is that I would be so filled with the fruit of the Spirit that even angry thoughts or feelings would seldom, if ever, arise within me.

As I evaluate my angry responses to situations, I believe it does me the most good to see what Scripture has to say about anger. It is when my evaluation of anger lines up with what God says that I will stop justifying and excusing it.

Please keep in mind that I write the Mom's Corner articles based on Titus 2:3-5, "The aged women likewise, that *they be* in behaviour as becometh holiness, not false accusers, not given to much wine, teachers of good things; That they may teach the young women to be sober, to love their husbands, to love their children, *To be* discreet, chaste, keepers at home, good, obedient to their own husbands, that the word of God be not blasphemed." At forty-six, I am older than many who read the Corners. My goal through the Corners is to pass on what God has been teaching me in the subjects listed in Titus 2:4-5.

I would like to recommend a powerful resource on anger by a solid Bible teacher. Dr. S. M. Davis' teaching audio, called *Freedom from the Spirit of Anger,* has had a profound, positive impact on Steve and me in the area of overcoming anger. It gives a detailed look at anger in the Bible, delves into whether anger is ever justified, and concludes with practical steps to conquering anger. I highly recommend that each mom reading this article listen to *Freedom from the Spirit of Anger.* It is available from our website (www.Titus2.com).

When I allow anger in my life, I am hurting my family members who must either face or watch my angry responses—even if it is simply a tone in my voice. How do you feel when your husband speaks to you in anger? If he isn't yelling at you, but you discern anger within him, is your heart open to what he is saying? Do you feel loved and accepted?

Personally, I would much rather my husband speak to me in a normal tone of voice, rather than an angry one, if he has something negative to present. As soon as I sense anger in him, I become defensive. My spirit closes down, and I justify myself to him for whatever the anger is pointed toward. To be honest, even if I thought my husband had angry feelings about me that he wasn't expressing, it would make me sad as I desire his unconditional love. It has to be the same way with my children. My anger toward them is not what they want to face. It puts them on the defensive, closing their hearts and ears to what I am saying. It also must convey to them a lack of love on my part.

Ephesians 4:31: "Let all bitterness, and wrath, and anger, and clamour, and evil speaking, be put away from you, with all malice." To me this says that ALL anger is to be put away from me. This is my heart's desire!

"A wrathful man stirreth up strife: but *he that* is slow to anger appeaseth strife" (Proverbs 15:18). This verse indicates that our anger can actually cause additional problems. Often when I become angry it is because I want to see a change that isn't happening. Rather than my anger facilitating the change—whether it is harmony among siblings or pancakes that aren't burned—it stirs up more strife!

*"He that is* soon angry dealeth foolishly . . ."* (Proverbs 14:17). It was 8:30 p.m., time for the children to do their picking up before bedtime. My two youngest children, and biggest mess makers, Jesse (7) and Mary (5), had been reminded several times through the day to put away their playthings before moving to another activity. When I walked into Jesse's bedroom, where they had played that morning, the floor was literally covered with toys. They had obviously disobeyed my earlier reminders, and there was certainly not sufficient time left before bed to put away that quantity of toys.

I felt the anger within. You probably wouldn't have recognized it in me, but I did, and I expect that Jesse and Mary did, too. I then acted foolishly just as Proverbs says. I lectured them with that "tone" in my voice. Then I filled their arms with toys and marched them to the places those items belonged.

Understand, the children did need to put away their toys. They needed consequences for their disobedience. What they didn't need, and what was "dealing foolishly" on my part, was my angry reaction.

As the Holy Spirit convicted me of my anger, I went to each of them after they were tucked into bed. I asked them to forgive Mommy for not being sweet and gentle at pickup time. Children are so quick to forgive! Even though they weren't together when I asked their forgiveness, they both said almost the same words, "Oh yes, Mommy. I forgive you. Will you please forgive me for not putting my toys away earlier today when you told me to?" There had been no remorse over their disobedience while they were in my angry presence. However, as soon as I humbled myself to each of them, their spirits were also humbled and convicted.

Next month I will conclude this three-part series on anger by looking at practical steps we can take to gain victory over anger. In the meantime, listen to Dr. Davis' audio, and you may have anger under control before the next Corner is out! May we be women who desire not to have angry reactions in our lives—ever!

# Anger — Part 3
## OVERCOMING
### by Teri

After realizing my seventh-grade son was not making good progress through his independent study of Spanish, I began taking some of our daily one-on-one school time to review Spanish with him. One day, as I was repeating a phrase we had already gone over many times in that session, Joseph exclaimed, "Mom, you are just getting upset and angry with me!"

"Why, Joseph," I replied, thinking I was speaking truth, "I am not angry with you at all."

"Well, then it must be the spirit of anger," were his next words. He had listened to Dr. Davis' audio, *Freedom from the Spirit of Anger.*

Oh, how I would have liked to react and defend myself. I wanted to convince him I had not been angry. However, as I sat silently replaying the situation in my mind, I realized that he was right. I wasn't yelling at him, but I was irritated, and he could tell it. Irritation is a nicer word than anger, but it is still anger.

So how do we work toward overcoming our anger? Are there practical ways we can be proactive in seeking victory over any anger we experience, or are we stuck with a lifetime of angry responses?

What should I do when those situations arise that I would respond to angrily? PRAY! Does that sound simplistic? It probably does, but do you know what? It doesn't come naturally for me to pray when I am starting to feel angry. What does come innately is either to allow the anger to fester or to try to stuff it down as if it wasn't there. I must discipline myself to cry out to the Lord Jesus the moment those feelings are starting!

How much do I hate my anger? Do I have worldly sorrow or godly sorrow over it? 2 Corinthians 7:10, "For godly sorrow worketh repentance to salvation not to be repented of: but the sorrow of the world worketh death." This was such a hard lesson for me to learn, and I am still growing in it. I would hate my anger, but only because it represented another of my failures, not because it was sin.

When my sorrow over my anger is godly sorrow, then I will spend daily, earnest prayer time for victory. My ability to have the fruit of the spirit evident in my life is totally dependent on the work of the Lord Jesus. Philippians 2:13, "For it is God which worketh in you both to will and to do of *his* good pleasure." I am foolish or prideful or both to think that I could follow a list of steps to overcoming anger and have victory on my own.

It is easy for me to decidedly state that anger is wrong. Almost in the same breath, I will say I want to have victory over it. However, my prayer effort in that direction won't match my words! I must truly mean that anger is wrong, from my heart, and then invest time in crying out to the Lord for His help. This has to be in both my daily personal prayer time and throughout the day.

Since I began writing these articles, I have been so excited about the new progress the Lord has been giving me in overcoming anger. However, it has not come without cost. The cost to me has been a constant focus on the problem. Dr. Davis, in his audio, *Freedom from the Spirit of Anger,* helped me greatly with this. He reminds his listeners that there are some sins that are just too hideous to allow ourselves to consider, let alone actually do. Would I walk in my favorite department store and steal a beautiful outfit I couldn't afford? Never! What about ramming my car into the vehicle of a person who has treated me wrongly on the highway? Of course not! We simply don't do those things. We know they are wrong. Somehow, though, we have come to view anger as acceptable to certain degrees rather than hating it as we might hate stealing or violence.

Colossians 3:8, "But now ye also put off all these; anger, wrath, malice, blasphemy, filthy communication out of your mouth."

Seeing anger as a sin, which I do not have the luxury of indulging in, began to make it worth my efforts to truly conquer it. Gentle anger—remember the Lord had given me victory over yelling and door slamming about ten years ago—ruled my life. When I started observing my anger, I became aware that many of the interactions with my children had just a slight undertone of anger in them. I don't even think the children recognize it in me most of the time, but that doesn't make it okay.

I began not only crying out to the Lord during my morning prayer time for help with this problem, but I also started praying constantly throughout the day. At first, it was terribly painful, because the Lord showed me I had a much greater problem with anger than I was aware of. I wrote this series because I thought I had something to share with you as far as overcoming anger was concerned. Instead, the Lord showed me that subtle anger was as much a problem as overt anger.

This continual awareness of my thoughts, attitudes, and reactions with an ongoing prayer of having normal, loving responses to what is going on around me has been wonderful. I am greatly enjoying the realization that even though I have truly had a problem, the Lord may give me lasting, sustained, life-changing victory!

In the situation I started this article with, my immediate step after prayer was to ask Joseph's forgiveness for not being patient and gentle. Sometimes I, as a mommy, don't want to ask my children's forgiveness. I think it will make me look bad in their eyes, that it will undermine my authority, or that it will paint an unnecessarily negative picture of me. I believe asking my child's forgiveness when I have wronged him by using positive words to describe what I failed to do relieves all of those concerns. At the same time, I am doing what is Scripturally commanded of me.

By asking my child's forgiveness for my lack of patience, love, or kindness, I may be healing hurts that might never be spoken of by my child. By this I mean that each time I respond to a child in anger, my lack of love for him is showing, allowing hurts to be established and then to grow. These hurts can be concealed within the child's heart and not be expressed. However, when I choose to humble myself by acknowledging that what I did was wrong, then I have the opportunity to reinforce my love for him.

This Mom's Corner became too long so I needed to break it into two parts. Perhaps that will, in the end, be a good thing. You will have a month to meditate on your own view of anger in your life. You can begin observing your daily interactions and evaluate which ones involve anger. You should have time to start a diligent, vigilant prayer effort with a heart's desire of overcoming anger. Lastly, you could try becoming accountable to the Lord and others in your family for your anger by asking forgiveness when you have been angry.

# Anger — Part 4
## OVERCOMING
### by Teri

We have been evaluating the real-life problem of anger in moms. While our hearts' desire is to be "victorious, joyful mothers of children," it is not unusual to find a mom struggling instead with angry feelings—perhaps day after day after day.

Let's return to the situation of Spanish time with my son. Remember that by God's grace in my life, yelling at the children was overcome ten years ago. I didn't raise my voice with my son during Spanish. However, he sensed anger in me. I like to call it frustration because it sounds better. When Joseph kindly confronted me with my attitudes, I tried to deny it. After all, I didn't yell, stomp, or slam a door, so I must not have been angry. He was right, though. I was no longer interacting with him in my normal way.

What about choosing simply to close my mouth and say nothing if I am beginning to feel at all angry, irritated, or frustrated? Proverbs 19:11, "The discretion of a man deferreth his anger; and *it is* his glory to pass over a transgression." Consider my Spanish situation with Joseph. In this case, I am not even sure we are looking at a transgression on Joseph's part. It only would have been a transgression if Joseph wasn't trying to learn the Spanish phrase as we worked on it, but instead purposing to be uncooperative. Whether it was a transgression or not, the verse still applies in this instance. Had I just continued to repeat the phrase for him without the other comments I was making, we would eventually have moved beyond the problem. How much better to spend the rest of my tutoring session on this one area than to be angry with Joseph simply so we could complete the material at a faster pace!

Another step toward overcoming my anger is awareness of all my angry responses—from the first feelings of anger to irritated tones in my voice to an outwardly evident angry response. My struggle is with wanting to justify that anger, especially when it seems under control and unnoticeable to others. I don't want to fight a battle with anger, and if I am not angry, I won't have to do that. It is much like the proverbial ostrich with his head in the sand. However, when I admit that the angry feelings are there, then something can be done about them.

The Lord has also shown me the importance of physical touch and closeness in overcoming anger. When I am feeling angry, I want to distance myself from the other person. I don't feel close; therefore, I don't want to be close. Distance between the child and me then fuels the angry feelings. On the other hand, if I choose to put my arm around the child, pull him into my lap, hold a hand, or pat a back, the anger begins to dissipate almost all by itself. It is very hard to be angry with someone you are loving on!

Ephesians 4:32 says, "And be ye kind one to another, tender-hearted, forgiving one another, even as God for Christ's sake hath forgiven you." When I am faced with a situation concerning my children where I feel like responding angrily, obviously the Lord's way would be to handle it instead with love, kindness, and gentleness. Proverbs 25:15, "By long forbearing is a prince persuaded, and a soft tongue breaketh the bone." Anger seldom knows anything about a "soft tongue." That does not mean there won't be consequences for wrong behavior in the children. However, it does mean that I am not contributing more to the problem by being angry.

Sometimes I have been told, or heard it said, that anger is a human emotion, and we must express it, within limits. Consider with me a comparison of two moms, one who believes anger is an acceptable human emotion and another who sees anger as sin, praying and working to overcome it in her life. In which home would you want to grow up? In which home do you think the children will feel more loved? Which home will produce angry children?

Which one will produce children who are sometimes angry, but know how to deal with it in a godly manner?

Recently I took three of my children to the public library. There we had the opportunity to watch the interactions between an angry grandfather and his angry grandson. My children were mesmerized by the scene unfolding before them. It was a bit frightening for all of us even though the anger did not go beyond words and raised voices. On the drive home, we discussed what we had observed. The children were very aware that if people will act like that in public, they will be considerably worse in private. We had an opportunity to talk about what happens in lives when anger is not dealt with properly.

Again, recall with me the situation (in Mom's Corner-March 2002, page 61) of my boys bickering while cleaning their room. My goal is to encourage them to learn to work diligently and responsibly. I also want them to be young men who will praise each other while seeking to motivate, in a positive manner, the brothers who aren't doing what they are supposed to be doing.

Here were the words I found myself speaking with a tone in my voice that my boys can recognize as irritated—fueled by angry feelings although you might not recognize the tone since you don't know me well. "Here I have given you time to do your pickup that you should have done before school started, and what are you doing? Being unkind to each other! You should each be working hard, thanking each other for the help, and responding positively if your brother tells you that you need to put something else away."

I believe the results I desired would have been more quickly achieved had I been quiet longer, listening to the boys' interactions and really evaluating what was going on. That would have given me time to pray, asking the Lord for the fruit of the Spirit to be evident in my rebuke of the boys and thanking Him for the opportunity to teach them God's ways. Then my tone could have been sweet and gentle. My words would have pointed out their wrong behavior and consequences given if necessary—all without anger!

Truly, as I evaluate the road I have been walking along toward victory over anger, I realize it has not required much of me. Here is what it has entailed:

* An awareness of the problem

* A heart's desire to change

* Humility

* Time (but not all that much compared to the joy to be experienced on all sides)

* Putting self aside

While there were times I wanted to give up and decide I was an angry person and always would be, God never allowed my heart to be satisfied with those thoughts. I yielded; He is doing the work! He has brought me to where I am in this battle—not having yelled or slammed a door for ten years. He continues to work as He molds and refines me to overcome even the tones in my voice and concealed reactions that stem from anger.

"Cease from anger, and forsake wrath . . ." (Psalms 37:8). Dear Sisters, may anger be a feeling that we want replaced in our lives by the fruit of the Spirit. May we be zealous enough in our efforts to give it no place in our hearts that we will spend time in earnest prayer about it and seek forgiveness when we fail. Let's draw our children close to us with hugs, squeezes, and whispered sweet words, fostering an environment where anger cannot thrive. May we truly allow the Lord to give victory over anger in our lives.

# Prayer Notebook
## *by Teri*

Have you ever had a friend ask you to pray for a specific situation? Then the following week she comes to you thanking you profusely for your prayers. How do you feel and what do you say when you completely forgot to pray? Has it happened to you?

Not only have I had "egg on my face" in relation to saying I would pray but then forgetting, I sometimes didn't remember to pray for what was truly important in my own life. While I would stew about a situation in our family, did I consistently pray about it? Often I found I did not! I said I wanted God's solution, but there were no "feet" to my desire.

A prayer notebook became a valuable tool in my life to facilitate my prayer time. It is something to help me do what I want to do. ". . . The effectual fervent prayer of a righteous man availeth much" (James 5:16). It facilitates doing what the Lord has told me to do. "And he spake a parable unto them *to this end*, that men ought always to pray, and not to faint" (Luke 18:1). In addition, it is beneficial to others and to me. "Confess *your* faults one to another, and pray one for another, that ye may be healed . . ." (James 5:16).

It is important to understand that my prayer notebook has been a tool. It did not take the place of being quiet before the Lord and letting the Holy Spirit put on my heart what to pray. Rather, it has been a memory device so that I don't forget to pray about the areas the Holy Spirit has directed.

I have been using prayer notebooks, of one style or another, for about nine years now. I am pleased with the benefits they have afforded to my prayer life. I am happy to encourage each of you to put this prayer tool into use in your life as well. Because I am a practical person who loves great ideas but always asks "how," I would like to give you some simple prayer notebook guidelines based on my personal experience. From these beginning stages of a prayer notebook, you can, with time, fine tune and expand your own prayer notebook.

I want to start out with simple and practical ideas so that you can realistically make use of your prayer notebook and continue to use it. If it is too complicated, you will enjoy the process of setting up your notebook and using it for a week or two. However, as soon as you hit your first major life interruption, your prayer notebook will become too cumbersome to maintain.

You will first need to decide what kind of notebook to use. Then you will have to choose how to set it up. I am sharing information to help you with both of these decisions. Please don't let the decisions hold you back. If you can't decide, simply follow my recommendations and go with them.

This notebook will begin by being a prayer request notebook. In it, list prayer requests, leave blank lines, and then fill in with answers as they come. With time, as the discipline to use the prayer notebook grows, other sections can be added. The starting goal of this notebook is to let it be easy so that consistency in its use is achieved.

Any kind of journal book or notebook should work. I am currently using a pretty, hardback, blank journal. The drawback with it is that the pages are not removable, so I face limitations and frustration as some pages fill up, but others don't. I have overcome this by putting a checkmark at the top of every page that has all the requests answered and writing "Completed" beside the checkmark. Periodically, I move all the prayer entries from pages that only have one or two left unanswered, plus the ongoing prayers, forward in the book. The advantage of these kinds of prayer notebooks is that you can find ones with beautiful covers on them, and they are relatively small. Plus, when it is full, it is all contained together in a bound book for storage.

You could also use a three-ring binder—small or large. This would probably involve little or no cost. Often, in our homes, we have unused binders stashed here and there, or they can be purchased rather inexpensively at a store like Wal-Mart.

Having a three-ring binder for a prayer notebook allows you to redo pages if you aren't pleased with them the first time or even after you start using them. You can also move a filled page to the back of the notebook so you don't have to flip through completed pages when you are praying.

The small three-ring binder size has the benefit of fitting nicely on top of a Bible and in a drawer or basket. Its disadvantage is that paper is less easily available. The 8½-by-11-inch size is bigger and more awkward to store, but paper and tabs can be purchased at places like Wal-Mart. It also provides more room for writing.

If even a notebook is beyond the scope of your finances, you can use sheets of paper stapled together for your prayer notebook. The advantage of this is that you can keep your prayer journal right inside your Bible—very convenient.

Start small and simple. Grow your prayer notebook with time.

## Using Your Prayer Notebook

1. Scripture decoration—In the top margin of each page of your prayer notebook, plan to copy in a Scripture verse on prayer that is particularly meaningful to you. You can write them on pages you haven't begun using yet as well.

2. Prayer requests—In your notebook, you will list things you want to pray about every day plus requests that are temporary. This has to be a reasonable list so that you can work through it during your prayer time. When you enter something in your prayer notebook, I would suggest leaving at least two blank lines between entries and perhaps three. This allows you room to write answers or updates.

3. Always date entries in your prayer notebook. This makes it a prayer journal, in many ways, because you know when you started

praying about a particular thing, when it was answered, and how. In preparing to write up this information, I looked back at my prayer notebooks. I discovered the year Steve was laid off from his job and the year we made a major curriculum change. Those were dates we had tried to remember, but weren't able to with certainty.

4. Obviously you can put as many requests in your notebook as you want. The caution is that you keep it simple and not too long so that you can actually pray through your prayer notebook each day, plus have time for anything else the Holy Spirit puts on your heart.

5. You will probably want a mixture of prayer requests in your notebook. There will be important, ongoing entries for you, your family, and ministry. Then there will be short-term prayer requests that will be prayed for a few days or weeks with an outcome.

6. If you choose a loose-leaf prayer notebook, I would suggest having one page for important, ongoing prayer, such as one page for yourself, your husband, and your children. Then put other prayer needs on the page immediately after those pages.

7. You can consider using two different pen colors, one for the request, and one for the answer. The advantage with this is that it makes seeing requests versus answers easy. The disadvantage is switching between pens when you are filling in your notebook. Also, if you lose one of the pens, and it is a color pen you don't have many of around the house, you will likely stop filling in that part of the notebook—until you get a new pen—and who knows when that will happen.

8. Develop a system to note prayer requests when you think of them but do not have your prayer journal handy. This is probably best done by having notepads near the computer and the phones. If you have a prayer need come in via e-mail, you can jot it down on a sticky note, carry it with you to where you have your time with the Lord, and then enter it at a later time.

9. Faithfully fill in answers to the prayer requests as they come. Again, remember that simplicity is our goal. Give the date and as brief a description as needed to understand it.

Just get started. There are drawbacks with almost any prayer notebook/journal. Some are so complicated the user never has time to do it. The easy ones, like we are doing, don't have as much flexibility as far as categorizing and dividing up prayer time. That's okay—just do it. Develop the habit of entering the prayer requests, praying, and recording answers. Then move to more complicated prayer notebooks once those disciplines are in place.

I have been blessed through using my prayer notebook. It has fueled my dependence on the Lord as I have learned to write the concerns of my heart in the notebook and then pray about them rather than worry. That notebook has enabled me to consistently pray for people and issues that are near and dear to me. I am grateful for my special friend, Janice, who first encouraged me to start a prayer notebook. The prayer of my heart is that you, too, might be challenged to begin a prayer notebook, finding it a useful tool in your spiritual walk.

# Protectionism or Isolationism?
## *by Teri*

Do you ever wonder whether it is right to shelter your children from worldly influences such as the TV or playing unsupervised with neighborhood children? Do you struggle with feeling like you are becoming an isolationist? Recently we had a mom ask us some questions along these lines.

*I wonder sometimes if I am doing the right thing by sheltering my children as much as I am. I have a burning desire also to tell others about Jesus! I want to minister—even if in just some small way. I don't feel like I'm doing that by keeping us at home and sheltered from the rest of the world. I feel that I have really begun to isolate my children from everything and wonder if this is the right thing to do . . . I wonder if there isn't more we could be doing. Lisa*

This mom asks several excellent questions—ones that are important for us to answer. What a condemnation on us as a group of Christian homeschoolers if we are secluded in our homes with no outreach for our Lord Jesus!

I would not term what we do with our children as isolationism but rather protectionism. God requires us to protect our children from ungodly influences. Scripture is overwhelmingly full of directives to us, as parents teaching our children and as Christians in general, to live holy lives.

Matthew 18:6-7: "But whoso shall offend one of these little ones which believe in me, it were better for him that a millstone were hanged about his neck, and *that* he were drowned in the depth of the sea. Woe unto the world because of offences! for it must needs be that offences come; but woe to that man by whom the offence cometh!"

Does this mean we live in isolation? Absolutely not! Instead, we minister as a family. For Steve and I, this means we are around our children constantly, serving the Lord Jesus with them and protecting them at the same time. There are so many ways the Lord has given us to minister, serve, and evangelize as a family through the years. I will share a couple of current ones with you.

Steve and the boys minister monthly at the Kansas City men's homeless shelter. Steve is with his boys (from age 7 to 25) and able to oversee their conversations, discuss the consequences of sin in these men's lives, and develop a love in his boys' hearts for others who are very different from us. Every month, in addition to the personal conversation and evangelism Steve and the boys engage in, one of the oldest will preach. Our sons consider their time at City Union Mission a highlight of their month.

Two Saturdays a month, Steve and the children have a church service at the local county infirmary, a low-income nursing home. They have the opportunity to love the elderly residents, talk to them, sing with them, and share the good news of Jesus Christ with them. Joseph, our thirteen-year-old son, preached at the infirmary the last time they were there. He hasn't had a call from the Lord to be a preacher, but we want all of our children to be able ". . . to *give* an answer to every man that asketh you a reason of the hope that is in you with meekness and fear" (1 Peter 3:15).

I would encourage us that the questions we are considering are best answered by being "in the world" (John 17:11) but "not of the world" (John 17:14). We are not isolating our children. We are protecting them and also ministering with them to the lost world.

Let me share another story with you by way of illustration. The UPS man stops by our house every afternoon. Once when there was a substitute for a couple of days, the children asked where the regular driver was.

"You mean Caveman?" the substitute asked. The children's eyes became really big as they realized that the UPS drivers had nicknamed our driver "Caveman." That became our children's name for him as well until we had a discussion one day.

We talked with the children about whether "Caveman" was a respectful name for our UPS driver even if they didn't actually call him that when they talked to him. They agreed it wasn't and determined to find out his real name.

Not many days after that they came to me and delightedly announced, "His name is Mr. Smith. His name is Mr. Smith."

"Whose name is Mr. Smith?" came from my confused mind, which had already forgotten the earlier day's discussion.

"The UPS man!"

Can you imagine what Mr. Smith thinks when he is greeted by five lively children each afternoon shouting, "Hello, Mr. Smith! Hi, Mr. Smith. How are you, Mr. Smith?" Remember, Mr. Smith's coworkers call him Caveman.

Recently, eleven-year-old John gave Mr. Smith a gospel tract. A couple of days later John asked Mr. Smith if he had read the tract. "Oh, yeah!" he replied. "It was good. I even showed it to the other guys at the terminal when I got back."

"Would you read another one?" John asked.

"Sure," answered Mr. Smith.

This recent example, I believe, will show you that a protectionist lifestyle doesn't preclude our children from sharing Jesus with others. However, they are doing it in an environment where their own hearts are being as carefully guarded as possible.

Scripture tells us, "The heart *is* deceitful above all *things*, and desperately wicked: who can know it?" (Jeremiah 17:9). So we know that protecting our children will not keep them from being sinful. However, we also know that temptations to sin are greater when a child has been exposed to sin.

I would encourage each of us, with our husbands, to begin praying about what ministry the Lord would have us do as a family. Consider a nursing home, the homeless shelter, a neighborhood Bible study, an outreach to a widow in your neighborhood, or having neighbors in for dinner—that's just a start! When you have the Lord's direction, begin to serve. You will have no concern about isolationism, but rather you will experience outreach within the protected environment of family ministry.

# Seventeen Down, Thirteen to Go
## *by Teri*

Seventeen years and three graduated homeschooled students ago, we began homeschooling. Now our youngest (unless the Lord has a big blessing in store for us) is entering kindergarten. Thirteen years and five more graduated homeschooled students from now, with a thirty-year homeschool career, I expect to retire from homeschooling.

Recently my mom was doing some cleaning and organizing. She came across the letter I had written to them about our plan to homeschool. This letter was written by a young thirty-year-old mother of three. As I read that letter, tears of gratitude filled my eyes. There was no one less likely to make it a year as a homeschooling mom, let alone what will be a career of it, than me!

I want to share part of that letter with you. As you read Mom's Corners, you may be tempted to think that homeschooling has been a natural part of my life. I expect as you read this letter, though, you will come to a different conclusion. My prayer is that you may be encouraged that if Teri can do it, I can do it!

*Summer 1985*

*Dear Dad and Mom,*

*I almost called you today to tell you what I am going to write in this letter but decided to give you some time to digest this information before we talk rather than have you try to conceal your shock and figure out what to say. Now I'm sure I have your curiosity aroused.*

*I am going to homeschool the boys this year and maybe a few more if this works out. I can hear the silent pause at your end now—you literally can't believe that last sentence. From anyone but me perhaps, but not Teri—not the Teri who often questions whether she loves her kids, who can't stand to be around her boys' fussing, who has such emotional downs and doesn't think she is mother material.*

*Well, you know, as I know, God's economy isn't always our economy, and Steve and I can't figure this out but can see God's possibilities. I have always had a little desire, since I know some did, to homeschool. I always discounted it because I knew I couldn't do it. I couldn't even get Nathan to do his homework without a shouting match. The last three weeks, that desire has grown and grown among much reasoning on my part that there was no way.*

*Finally I brought it up to Steve, and we began to discuss it and pray about it. Last week for three days we practiced school. That is why you got a letter. Seems much more logical to practice writing by doing a letter than by copying sentences. We made our decision this weekend with the proviso of trying again this week.*

*I found some amazing things as we practiced school. First, I wasn't fighting to get Nathan to accomplish what the teacher had said he had to in the way she said. We just did what I said and worked on it for a set amount of time. Although we did have a confrontation, it was the type of thing we had virtually every day after school last spring, and this was only one incident in three days with several concentrated hours together each day. Also, I began to see good qualities in them as we worked together rather than only seeing the fighting and fussing.*

*A major reason we are doing this is to give them more time to pursue their interests. There won't be time for everything, but now there is time for none. Even if it takes as many teaching hours at home, they will gain the two hours they now spend on the bus to and from school.*

*Amazingly, without trying to bias, just presenting facts, the boys both (that is unbelievable in itself) want to do it. I didn't think Nathan would want to give up peer time. Also, because I so often, as a mother, view myself negatively, I couldn't imagine them wanting to be home with me all day every day. Nathan said he will miss his friends but it will be okay because he won't have to go to the board to work a problem and be embarrassed if he messes up.*

*We plan to do this for at least a year. Only if I am a total basket-case will we quit after Christmas. If it is just not a great situation, then we finish the year, and they go back to Christian school next year. That is for a sense of commitment for me so I don't throw up my hands one day and try to enroll them back in school the next.*

*August 24th is a homeschool conference near here which will be a great learning chance.*

*Four-plus pages is a long letter.*

*Bye and love,*

*Teri*

Our reasons for homeschooling have changed immensely since we started. I would like to reminisce in the next Mom's Corner about the benefits our family has experienced through homeschooling. However, this month my testimony is totally on a loving, faithful God Who could take the woman you see described in this letter and support her, mold her, change her, comfort her, challenge her, and grow her so that she could do what He had called her to do.

I believe this verse is the embodiment of my homeschooling life. "And he said unto me, My grace is sufficient for thee: for my strength is made perfect in weakness. Most gladly therefore will I rather glory in my infirmities, that the power of Christ may rest upon me" (2 Corinthians 12:9).

There was nothing in my life to commend me to home-schooling except a heart to hear the Lord and be obedient to Him. If you are struggling in any way with your homeschooling, may I encourage you to rest in the Lord and continue on in your obedience to Him. Then look back in seventeen years to see God's faithfulness!

# What Has Homeschooling Done for Us?
### by Teri

Last month I shared a letter I wrote to my parents seventeen years ago dropping the bomb on them that we were going to begin homeschooling. The main reason we started homeschooling was to allow our little boys the time to play and be children. We entered this alternative education with the thought of taking it one year at a time. Now, with thirteen years of homeschooling still before us, we can't fathom any other type of schooling for our children. Benefits we never dreamed of have come from homeschooling. I would like for this Mom's Corner to be a testimonial to God's working in a simple family who was set to seek His face.

By beginning to homeschool, we were better able to follow the instruction in Deuteronomy 6:4-7 to speak of the Lord when we rise up, sit down, and walk on the way. Our relationship with Jesus Christ could be a focus of our whole day, not just the early morning and evening.

Homeschooling allowed us to put Jesus Christ in charge of our children's education. We could pray about what the children would study, what materials they would use, when they would do their schoolwork, how to address problem areas, and more. No longer did we have to accept others' direction of how and what our children learned.

We became the controllers of our children's curriculum. We could choose their school materials, avoiding the ones that were objectionable to us. We were able to search for curricula that was Christian in content and avoid worldly thrusts. Bible became a priority for us, not only for our family devotions, but also for school time.

We have had the pleasure of spending countless more hours with our children than we could have if they had been away from home at school. I suppose I could do the math on that number of hours. It would be something like seven hours a day times five days a week times thirty-six weeks a year times seventeen years and counting. The childhood years pass quickly. How often do you hear someone say they wish they had had more time with their children?

As a homeschooling family, we were able to set our own schedule. We didn't have to put the children in bed at 8:00 p.m. in order for them to be up by 7:00 a.m. to prepare to leave for school. For us, this translated into a later bedtime and morning rising time. Since Steve had a forty-five minute commute, he often wasn't home from work until 6:00 p.m. We relished the extra family time we gained by not needing to institute an early bedtime.

We reaped financial benefits. We saved the tuition money we had been spending to have two children attend a private school and ride the bus to get there. What would it have cost to send eight children to private school?!! We no longer have lunches to buy nor school clothes to purchase. While we have curricula to purchase and some school supplies, the cost has been a fraction of what we would have spent with the children in school.

Our first goal with the extra money was to buy a computer. Steve said, "Computers are the tools of the future. Our children need to be computer literate." That simple start opened the floodgates to eventually provide computer-related vocations for all three of our adult children. Homeschooling allowed them to pursue their vocational interests as a part of their education before high school graduation. They were each well equipped to begin their careers upon graduation.

One result of allowing our children to pursue vocational interests was that it enabled one son to purchase his home debt-free prior to marriage. Our second born is able to do so now, as well, if he so chooses.

I was able to teach several of my children to read. I had the joy of listening to them sound out their first word. I was the one who encouraged them when the task seemed too difficult. I was the one smiling from ear to ear as they read their first book to Daddy. When I wasn't teaching phonics, it was an older sibling who had that responsibility and the enjoyment that goes with it—not to mention the experience.

Homeschooling allowed us truly to be aware of how each child was doing. We could make sure they corrected mistakes in their schoolwork. We were able to discern whether the errors were from carelessness or from a lack of comprehension.

Individualizing studies was possible with our homeschooling. One child moved ahead in reading because it was easy for him, while another took his math more slowly. We were able to include typing for each child, piano lessons, Spanish—whatever we prayerfully deemed important.

Our children became each other's best friends. They had playtime together off and on throughout the day. The extra playtime encouraged them to become lifelong friends. Sibling friendships remain close throughout life.

We were able to take vacations when other families could not do so. As soon as we began homeschooling, if we could take a vacation, we did it in May or September. That way we avoided crowds and often received off-season, lower rates.

There is one final benefit that causes Steve and I to believe that we could never educate our children in any other way. It stands as a giant above our other homeschooling reasons. Protection! Our children kept their childish innocence throughout their childhood years. Sheltered in the homeschool environment, they didn't have to face vulgar, profane, ungodly, jeering, mocking, or hateful words and actions from other children. We have been so grateful to the Lord for giving us something in homeschooling that we never dreamed would be so precious.

Peer pressure did not push our children to develop an interest in the opposite gender before God's time. It kept them from being around others who were dating through high school and perhaps before, and they maintained their moral purity. They choose not to give their hearts away to anyone except the one the Lord shows them is to be their spouse.

There are certainly days I would love to be at home alone, cleaning my house, answering e-mails, or doing some sewing. There are days when I feel like seventeen years has been long enough of doing something that doesn't come naturally to me. However, I never think of calling the local Christian school to see if I can enroll the children, something I used to do in our early homeschooling days. Reviewing what I see God has done for our family through home-schooling reminds me that it is worth every sacrifice. May each home-schooling mom reading this recall the benefits of her homeschool and be encouraged in the sacrificial giving of herself to her family.

# What About Young-Adult Children?
### *by Teri*

It is not uncommon for questions to be posed to Steve and me concerning parenting young-adult children. Should they live with their parents? Should the parents have rules in the home and discipline their adult children if they disobey? While this may appear to be a topic relating to only a few, in reality, parents of children of any age will someday be facing these situations. We would love to give parents of young children a vision of what it can be like when their children grow up and still live in their home.

All three of our older children have chosen to live at home until marriage. One is twenty-five and has been married since January of this year. Our other two are twenty-three and twenty, and they both live at home. It is our desire that by sharing our thoughts and experiences with adult children living in our home, you might be challenged and motivated in your own thinking.

We have personally seen the benefit to children remaining at home until marriage. Scripture says that a man leaves his father and mother to be joined to his wife (Genesis 2:24, Matthew 19:5, Mark 10:7, Ephesians 5:31). This is why we believe it is biblical and beneficial for adult children to live in their family's home, under parental counsel, until marriage or until the Lord calls them to something else such as mission work.

Here are some other advantages we have personally seen as our children live at home:

✻ There are fewer temptations with the accountability of living at home in a family. We see this as very positive. For example, many godly men and women who travel to conferences go with their spouse, an adult child, or a friend. Why? Because they know the temptations that even spiritually mature adults face. How much greater would such temptations be for younger, less mature men and women?

✻ The children remain under the spiritual protection and counsel of their parents.

✻ Their living expenses are less so they can save for future family needs, as our boys have saved to purchase homes debt-free.

✻ Family ties and relationships are maintained.

Proverbs speaks over and over about the differences between a wise son and a foolish son. One characteristic of a wise son is that he heeds the counsel and rebuke of his parents. It is likely the problems that generate the questions such as are in the first paragraph of this article wouldn't even be brought up if the adult children in the family were spiritually mature. Spiritually mature adult children respect the counsel and boundaries of their parents. We can testify to this from experience.

We haven't had to require our adult children to obey us. When issues come up, they will ask our counsel. We then discuss the situation, pray about it, discuss it some more, and almost always come to a decision in agreement. If a child has asked to do something we believe to be unwise, through our talking and praying time, they have come to an understanding of why we think that to be so, and also an agreement with it. Occasionally they don't agree, but they have respected our judgments and accepted them simply because they respect their parents—again a sign of spiritual maturity. The children have been receptive to our counsel.

With adult children, our roles as parents have changed from disciplinarians to friends and counselors—roles that were developing and growing throughout their childhood. We are all still learning how our new roles work. For us, as parents, this has meant we have needed to let go of being in authority in our adult children's lives.

We have found these years to involve daily opportunities for us to interact with each other in mutual respect. We realize our adult children are to be treated as the adults they are. We are desirous that our relationships with them be characterized by love and deference. "Iron sharpeneth iron; so a man sharpeneth the countenance of his friend" (Proverbs 27:17).

We do not discipline our adult children. The adult child is responsible to the Lord for his decisions. Having our older children's hearts makes it possible to influence their decisions, but we no longer give consequences for bad choices. Consequences at this point, if there are any, come from the Lord.

The peer activities our adult children choose to participate in would not be an evening of hanging out with friends. Rather, it would be Sarah having a friend over for an afternoon to make cookies and scrapbook. It would be Christopher taking one of his friends out for dinner and fellowship.

Steve and I are far from perfect parents! However, we have had hearts to, as fully as we could, love Jesus and apply His Word in every aspect of our lives, including raising our children. This often led us to make different decisions with the children than other parents were making with their children. Despite those who told us it would never work, we have experienced the joy of watching our three oldest children grow through the teen years and into the young-adult years without rebellion. The Lord has clearly been working in their lives, and He gets all the glory for where they are today.

Steve and I both write extensively on the choices and decisions we have made in child raising. If you have younger children and are interested in the background steps to our young-adult children living at home, then we would suggest you read our book, *Keeping Our Children's Hearts* (see Additional Resources, page 385).

If you have a teen or young adult with whom you are having trouble, we suggest Dr. S. M. Davis' resources (www.solvefamilyproblems.com), particularly his audio *Changing The*

*Heart of a Rebel* (also available on www.Titus2.com). We personally do not have the time or the answers to specific questions concerning individual situations but highly recommend Dr. Davis' materials.

We have had such joy in our adult children living in our home. Certainly, there are times of disagreement, but with the Lord's help, we work through them. We have seen the benefits of the added accountability and protection of living in the family home for the purity of our adult children. We have personally observed the help parental counsel has been in these children's lives.

We have loved moving from the role of disciplinarian to the role of counselor. We enjoy conversations and time with our older children. We see them growing in spiritual maturity and often seek input from them on our personal and family decisions. We desire that they feel loved, sheltered, valued, and wanted in our home until the Lord calls them to be married. We would be delighted to see your homes blessed, as ours has been, if your children are living at home as young adults.

# Christmas
## *by Teri*

With the Christmas season upon us, the "have-to's" of traditions can become consuming. Then we find ourselves stressed out rather than enjoying the celebration of the birth of our Savior. Personally, we have several goals for our family through our Christmas activities. In an effort to keep the season pleasant and worshipful, we try to keep our traditions simple, fitted to our spiritual goals.

### Changes

After Steve and I were saved, the Lord directed us to some changes in what we did at Christmas. We first eliminated Santa Claus from our home. For a while we continued hanging up stockings for the children and telling them that Dad and Mom filled them during the night. The children's Christmas stockings were too cute to throw away and too much a part of our family tradition. After a few years, though, we felt that we were compromising as the Israelites sometimes did. We decided to stop any vestige of Santa Claus.

We no longer put up a Christmas tree. The first year without this traditional Christmas trimming was because we didn't want the frustration of trying to keep a toddler safely away from the tree. However, before the next year rolled around, we read Jeremiah 10:3-5 and realized how much the cut tree in the passage sounded like a Christmas tree. Because we wanted to make sure there was no possibility of the tree taking an out-of-proportion role in our Christmas, we chose no longer to have a Christmas tree.

When we made that change, we also decided to make all of our Christmas decorating distinctively Christ focused. That meant quite a purging of the Christmas decorations.

## Simple Yet Meaningful Christmas Traditions

Without purposing to do so, we have created some family Christmas traditions that have become very meaningful to us, kept us Christ focused, and built family memories. We have found that it is important to keep these traditions simple and easy to carry on each year. There have been years when we added Christmas traditions that were a burden rather than a joy. It doesn't take very many of these "good" ideas to make Christmas a dreaded time rather than one to expect with excitement.

We want our children to learn the importance of giving to those who have need. We participate in the Samaritan's Purse Christmas shoebox outreach. On an evening in November, we will take the children to Wal-Mart where they all excitedly give suggestions on what to purchase for the boxes. On another night the children open the items that are to go in the boxes and fill each box up.

This year, one item for the girl's box was a cute little doll. Our six-year-old, Mary, carried that doll throughout Wal-Mart with her. When we came home, she stood by the kitchen counter, where the boxes were temporarily set, holding the doll. We were so pleased, though, that she never once asked to keep the doll. She understood its purpose.

One goal for our family's Christmas is that our children learn, ". . . It is more blessed to give than to receive" (Acts 20:35). The tradition in our home that reinforces this goal revolves around the children planning and buying gifts for family members. This has become very special to each of them. We will frequently hear them discussing how much they love to choose, buy, and give gifts to their parents, brothers, and sisters. Often they will make great financial sacrifices to do this.

We take the month of December to focus our family Bible time on Christ's birth. We will spend some time in the Old Testament looking at the prophecies of Christ's birth. Then we go to the New Testament and read the Gospel accounts of Jesus' birth. We learn about, discuss, and ponder the miracle of Jesus Christ and His birth.

Another desire of our hearts is that our children would learn to serve and minister with no expectations. On an evening near Christmas, we go caroling to the nursing home and also to our neighbors. Last year the highlight was a dear old man confined to his bed in the nursing home and appearing to be almost unconscious. His eyes were closed and his blanket pulled up under his chin. When we started singing "Silent Night," he couldn't open his eyes, but almost immediately he began an agitated moving of one of his hands. As we continued singing, he struggled with his arm and the blanket. Finally, he pulled his hand out, eyes still closed, and lifted his arm in praise to the Lord. I don't think there was a dry adult eye as we left that room.

We want our children to be drawn into worshipful thoughts of Jesus Christ. On Christmas Eve, we look forward to a family ride in the van to look at Christmas lights. While we drive, we listen to the *Twelve Voices of Christmas* (www.backtothebible.org), a dramatic presentation of the key players in the Christmas story. It is moving and awe inspiring, raising all of our hearts in praise for the sacrifice Jesus Christ made for us.

Christmas evening is set aside for reading Luke's account of the birth of Christ. Many years ago, Grandma made up a program for this that we have used ever since. Each person who can read is given, on a slip of paper, a reference for a prophetic or Gospel verse relating to the birth of Christ. Grandad is the narrator, with people reading their particular verses at the designated time. We also have appropriate Christmas carols interspersed. This simple Christmas program is available on www.Titus2.com/christmas-program.htm for anyone whom it might bless.

To increase the excitement and interest level for the children, Grandma has an empty Nativity sitting out on a shelf. All the figures that go into the Nativity have been wrapped in tissue paper and are waiting in a bag by her side. Throughout our Christmas program, one by one, the children will come and take a figure from the bag and set it in the Nativity scene.

Sharing the gospel of Jesus Christ is high on our list of priorities. Christmas affords us an excellent witnessing outreach time for Jesus. Each year, Steve, Nathan, and Christopher choose Christmas cards that are overtly Christian and glorify Jesus Christ to send to their clients. We have the opportunity of giving homemade goodies, which include notes with truths from God's Word, to our neighbors.

We want what we do on Christmas and the days before it to have purpose and meaning. It is a special day and season—one of joy for the Maxwell house. We pray that as your family evaluates its Christmas traditions and activities, you, too, will make it as free of stress as possible with a continual focus on Jesus Christ.

# Contentment — Part 1
## WHAT IS IT?
### by Teri

Recently I had a question posed to me about living a life of contentment. I expect this is something with which we can all easily struggle to one degree or another. Sometimes our lack of contentment is in material things, but often it revolves around spiritual desires—areas we know would be God-honoring if they were changed.

Here is what this mom writes:

*It seems I am NEVER content with anything. So I decided to write a gratitude list, and it was huge. Then I tried to write a contentment list and there was NOTHING. So I wrote a discontentment list. They were things that I don't think the Lord would be content with either.*

*I am grateful that my children's behavior is improving, but I am not content with their behavior. I am not content. I don't have a church. I am not content. I don't have a godly husband. I am not content watching TV every night with my husband. I am not content. We live in such a remote place. I am not content that I'm not more self-disciplined.*

*For each of those things, there are areas I'm thankful about, but I am never content. I always want more. Just because they're godly things I want more of, does that make it all right to live so discontented? The Bible tells us to be content. It also tells us to run the race. I don't think I'm getting it! A mom*

Paul tells us in Philippians 4:11-12 what his experience with contentment has been. "Not that I speak in respect of want: for I have learned, in whatsoever state I am, *therewith* to be content. I know both how to be abased, and I know how to abound: every where and in all things I am instructed both to be full and to be hungry, both to

abound and to suffer need." Paul could relate to our struggles with
contentment, and then some! Let's look at the circumstances Paul
faced that were a part of his road to learning contentment.

". . . in labours more abundant, in stripes above measure, in
prisons more frequent, in deaths oft. Of the Jews five times received
I forty *stripes* save one. Thrice was I beaten with rods, once was I
stoned, thrice I suffered shipwreck, a night and a day I have been in
the deep; *In* journeyings often, *in* perils of waters, *in* perils of robbers, *in* perils by *mine own* countrymen, *in* perils by the heathen, *in*
perils in the city, *in* perils in the wilderness, *in* perils in the sea, *in*
perils among false brethren; In weariness and painfulness, in watch-
ings often, in hunger and thirst, in fastings often, in cold and naked-
ness. Beside those things that are without, that which cometh upon
me daily, the care of all the churches" (2 Corinthians 11:23-28).

How could a man walking in obedience to Jesus Christ, who
experienced these trials because of that obedience, say he had learned
to be content "in whatsoever state I am"? What can we glean from
him about contentment? What is Paul's secret? What is it that helped
him to accept the negative circumstances God allowed in his life?

Paul tells us in his own words, "For to me to live *is* Christ, and
to die *is* gain" (Philippians 1:21). "I can do all things through Christ
which strengtheneth me" (Philippians 4:13). It was Paul's relationship with Jesus Christ that made him content. Our contentment
does not come in our circumstances or lack of them, but rather in
our relationship with Jesus Christ. "Set your affection on things
above, not on things on the earth" (Colossians 3:2).

In Paul's life, it appears that his contentment was rooted in his
total dependence on Jesus Christ and obedience to His will. Living
in prison, being beaten and shipwrecked certainly could not have
been pleasant experiences. However, Paul knew he was doing exactly
what the Lord had told him to do. Therefore, he was content no
matter what happened.

Dr. Adrian Rogers clarifies this further for us in his book *The
Lord Is My Shepherd.* "Perfect contentment, the kind David discovered, only comes when a person puts his or her complete trust in the

Shepherd. You will never have true satisfaction until you can say, 'The Lord is my Shepherd' and mean it. Then, and only then, can you confidently say, 'I shall not want.'"

*Vine's Expository Dictionary* defines the word "content," used by Paul in Philippians 4, as "to be sufficient, to be possessed of sufficient strength, to be strong, to be enough for a thing." Contentment as defined here is the ability to accept and withstand the circumstances, even negative ones.

One thing we may be dealing with is a difference between what biblical contentment truly is and what we, in our culture, think of it as being. We tend to define contentment as being happy with the way things are and having no desire for change. I don't think that is the kind of contentment Paul means. Paul's contentment was rooted in trusting his sovereign God in the situations he was experiencing. However, I expect Paul was happy to be out of prison when he was released.

How does all this relate to contentment in our lives as Christian wives and mothers? For a practical example, let's take one area from the discontent mom, who shared her heart with us. Since we can probably all relate, we will consider our children's behavior and find an analogous situation that Paul faced. "Beside those things that are without, that which cometh upon me daily, the care of all the churches" (2 Corinthians 11:28). We see regularly through Paul's writings that the churches had problems and struggles. They needed to learn and grow. This is true of our children as well.

Did Paul's contentment mean he did nothing concerning the churches, that he had no desire to see them change? No! Paul prayed for the churches, he taught them, he lived in their communities, and he admonished them. Paul did what the Lord directed him to do in relation to his work with the churches. However, his contentment did not mean he didn't want to see these churches change. Rather, his contentment was an ability to trust the Lord to work.

Our goals for our children would be similar to Paul's goals for the churches—that they would walk worthy of the Lord (Colossians 1:10). We obediently do what we are called to do by bringing our children up in the nurture and admonition of the Lord (Ephesians

6:4). We pray for our children just as Paul prayed for the churches. Daily, always, in every prayer, without ceasing: these were some of the words he used to describe his prayers for the churches. Through Christ's strength, we resolutely disciple and teach our children.

We don't become weary when the task of raising our children is long and difficult. Our contentment is in our relationship with Jesus Christ and joy in Him rather than in what is or isn't happening in our children's lives. Contentment, then, means we rest in the Lord's working in our children's lives. "Being confident of this very thing, that he which hath begun a good work in you will perform *it* until the day of Jesus Christ" (Philippians 1:6). We keep our eyes on Jesus and trust Him.

In conclusion, I would like to share a story about a group of people who have had to flee their homes because of government military persecution. They have been forced to leave their lands, homes, and jobs. Many have lost lives as well. These people are living impoverished lives in refugee camps, in a country not their own, with only the barest necessities provided. They have been given no hope of a change in the future. However, here is the report of a visitor concerning some of the Christians in this refugee camp.

*During this time in the camps, he heard singing constantly. Any time day or night, the Christians were singing or studying the Scriptures. They would study into the night and fall asleep at their table, then wake to study some more. At 11:00 at night people were singing. At 3 a.m. he awoke to hear people still singing. Before dawn and throughout the day, everywhere he went, people sang praise to God.*

There is nothing in their circumstances to make these people content, yet the sound of their singing expresses contentment. They have nothing, and yet, because of Jesus Christ, they have everything!

As we desire to be the wives and mothers Jesus Christ would have us be, may we daily be content exactly where He has us. May we serve, love, and minister with hearts learning, as Paul did, ". . . in whatsoever state I am, *therewith* to be content" (Philippians 4:11).

# Contentment — Part 2
## Where to Begin?
### by Teri

In last month's Mom's Corner we delved into the difficult topic of contentment. We saw that Paul had learned to be content in whatever circumstances he found himself. However, we also discovered the root of this contentment was not in the situation, but rather in his relationship with Jesus Christ and his trust in His will. We also realized that Paul's contentment did not mean he didn't desire change or pray for it in a particular situation. Instead, he was able to fully rest in his Lord Jesus and wait for His timing to work.

This leads us to other important questions for Christian wives and mothers to consider in relation to contentment. We may agree that we want to be content and would like to learn this contentment. However, we don't really know where to begin. We are too steeped in our natural inclinations and wrong thoughts. Paul is a wonderful teacher of contentment, so let's again turn to what he has to say. Was there an area of Paul's life that was difficult for him? What did he do about it? What was God's response, and how did that affect Paul?

"And lest I should be exalted above measure through the abundance of the revelations, there was given to me a thorn in the flesh, the messenger of Satan to buffet me, lest I should be exalted above measure. For this thing I besought the Lord thrice, that it might depart from me. And he said unto me, My grace is sufficient for thee: for my strength is made perfect in weakness. Most gladly therefore will I rather glory in my infirmities, that the power of Christ may rest upon me. Therefore I take pleasure in infirmities, in reproaches, in necessities, in persecutions, in distresses for Christ's sake: for when I am weak, then am I strong" (2 Corinthians 12:7-10).

Paul had what he called a "thorn in the flesh." He asked the Lord three times to be relieved from his "thorn in the flesh." However, the Lord's answer was "no." God had a purpose in Paul's difficulty and was going to use it as a demonstration of His grace and strength in Paul's life. What was Paul's response and ultimately his secret to contentment? He chose to "take pleasure in infirmities, in reproaches, in necessities, in persecutions, in distresses for Christ's sake: for when I am weak, then am I strong."

For me, personally, this goes totally against my natural, fleshly reactions to hard circumstances. What I feel like doing is to grumble, complain, be irritated and unhappy, feel sorry for myself, and try to figure out a solution. I am still at the stage in my Christian walk where I must choose to ". . . [bring] into captivity every thought to the obedience of Christ" (2 Corinthians 10:5) because it isn't my first, automatic reaction to take pleasure in what I don't like.

James learned the same lessons as Paul did about contentment and facing the areas of our lives that would rob us of contentment. "My brethren, count it all joy when ye fall into divers temptations; Knowing *this*, that the trying of your faith worketh patience. But let patience have *her* perfect work, that ye may be perfect and entire, wanting nothing" (James 1:2-4). The word "count" means "to consider, deem, account, think" (*Strong's Greek and Hebrew Dictionary*). This is an act of my will. It is a decision I make as to how I will think about my trials. James didn't tell me to simply accept my trouble, to endure my difficulties, or to grit my teeth until it was past. No, he said to "count it all joy." JOY! Doesn't that sound like an impossible reaction to hardship? It is, when I am relying on myself. I have the choice to make regarding my thoughts. God does the work in my life.

There are two sections of Scripture I would like to look at regarding our view of difficulties. These passages show me that God has purposes far beyond just getting through a struggle. What these verses teach me is that my focus is everything. My natural reactions put myself in the limelight. How does this affect my comfort level? Is this to my liking? Can I see anything positive in it? Scripture tells me that Jesus Christ is to be the center and object of my thoughts and therefore, as always, the focus. When this is true, then I can rest. Resting is the place of faith and trust in my sovereign God. It is acceptance that He knows what is best for my life. I am to count it as joy. When I receive trials with this attitude, then I am content. My joy is not in what is happening but rather in my relationship with Jesus Christ.

"Therefore being justified by faith, we have peace with God through our Lord Jesus Christ: By whom also we have access by faith into this grace wherein we stand, and rejoice in hope of the glory of God. And not only *so*, but we glory in tribulations also: knowing that tribulation worketh patience; And patience, experience; and experience, hope: And hope maketh not ashamed; because the love of God is shed abroad in our hearts by the Holy Ghost which is given unto us" (Romans 5:1-5).

"*We are* troubled on every side, yet not distressed; *we are* perplexed, but not in despair; Persecuted, but not forsaken; cast down, but not destroyed; Always bearing about in the body the dying of the Lord Jesus, that the life also of Jesus might be made manifest in our body. For we which live are alway delivered unto death for Jesus' sake, that the life also of Jesus might be made manifest in our mortal flesh . . . For which cause we faint not; but though our outward man perish, yet the inward *man* is renewed day by day. For our light affliction, which is but for a moment, worketh for us a far more exceeding *and* eternal weight of glory; While we look not at the things which are seen, but at the things which are not seen: for the things which are seen *are* temporal; but the things which are not seen *are* eternal" (2 Corinthians 4:8-11, 16-18).

We know that our attitudes are, in large measure, the attitudes of the home as a whole. Seeing that Scripture teaches us contentment is important and knowing this from personal experience as well, may we seek contentment. May we begin to make the choice to "count it all joy" and to take "pleasures in infirmities, in reproaches, in necessities, in persecutions, in distresses for Christ's sake: for when I am weak, then am I strong."

# A Few Helpful Tools for the Homemaker
### by Teri

Several years ago I was given a cute gift basket filled with various "goodies." One of the items in that basket has been such a helpful tool in our home that it is something I want to share with you. I know how busy homeschooling moms are. We want to maximize every moment of our days. I thought it might be helpful to dedicate this Mom's Corner to describing several items in our home that are invaluable tools and time savers for me.

The pretty little "goody" in that basket wasn't edible. It was a skinny pad of paper with flowery decorations and lines on it. It looked like you might use it for lists or for writing notes. In addition, it had a magnet on the back. I put that pad on my refrigerator because it had complementary colors to my kitchen.

One day someone said they needed another bag of socks from Wal-Mart. I suggested they write "socks" on the pad on the refrigerator and title that page Wal-Mart. The next time I thought of an item we were running low on that we purchased from Wal-Mart, I added it to that list. When we went to Wal-Mart several days later, I just pulled the page off the pad and was ready to shop. Immediately, I wrote Wal-Mart on the next page of the pad attached to the refrigerator. I asked my family members to write anything they needed from Wal-Mart on the list, and our shopping list habit was begun.

Within a short time, I purchased another magnetic notepad and put it on the fridge. Now I had a Wal-Mart pad and a Sam's Club pad. Those are the two major places we shop for basic necessities. Anytime we are short of an item or out of it, we put it on that list.

Now whenever someone is going to one of those stores and asks if I need something, I can tear the list off the pad and send it with them.

I can't begin to tell you how simple this plan is and how much time it has saved us in not having to make trips back to the store for forgotten items. In addition, it has freed me from the mental burden of trying to remember what we need the next time we go to the store. I am secure knowing my list is on the fridge and ready to go.

My next time-saving help also is related to a magnet and my refrigerator. In this case, it is a clip with a magnet on the back of it. It also hangs on the fridge and holds the list of evening meals for the week. When I make up the weekly grocery list, it includes a section where the evening meals for the week are listed. I cut or tear that portion of the list off after grocery shopping and hang it in that clip on the fridge.

This list has also saved me much mental time and energy by allowing me to lay out my evening meals and then quickly see what each meal will be. I used to think and wonder and consider through the day what to make for dinner. If I was too busy to think about it, I entered the kitchen in the evening in a state of dismay at having to make a decision on what to prepare. Now it is all set out for me. The decisions are made once a week. All I have to do is to look at my meal list and go to work.

Would you believe one of my favorite household tools is a feather duster? For twenty-seven of my twenty-eight years of being married, I used a dust rag or lambs-wool duster for dusting tasks. I also avoided dusting some things, such as picture frames, door frames, silk flowers, and mini blinds, because they were difficult to do with those dusting methods. Last summer when we purchased blinds for the living room, a feather duster was recommended for cleaning them. I tried my new feather duster for other dusting besides the living room blinds, and I loved it. I even bought one for my mother and daughter-in-law for Christmas.

So what makes a feather duster so great? It gets into nooks and crannies that other dusters don't easily reach. It gives me several extra inches of height so I can reach areas normally out of reach. My feather duster gives me a good angle for dusting, while the lambs-wool duster had to be held in a certain way. When dusting lightweight articles, it doesn't move them around or knock them over. I have to admit I almost think dusting is fun now that I am using a feather duster.

While vacuuming is at the top of my list for household tasks I like to do, ironing ranks near the bottom. However, two ironing tools have made the job quicker, easier, and more pleasant. These items may be ones you will choose to save up for if you decide to try them since they are much more costly than magnetized shopping lists and feather dusters.

When the iron I was given as a wedding gift "died" after twenty years of use, Steve bought me a Rowenta professional style iron. I was absolutely amazed at the difference in ironing. The Rowenta is larger and heavier than normal irons. That means it irons more quickly and efficiently. Now I feel blessed, rather than resentful, every time I need to iron.

One day about two years ago one of my children decided to sit on my twenty-five-year-old ironing board. While Steve is great at fixing many broken things in our home, the ironing board was beyond help. I went out and purchased the most expensive ironing board I could find at Wal-Mart. When I set it up at home, I was appalled at how unsteady it was. With young children, I was concerned about their safety when they were around if I was ironing. We took that ironing board back.

Then we purchased a very nice ironing board at Bed, Bath, and Beyond. I think this ironing board was around ninety dollars, and we had a coupon for 20 percent off. The ironing board from Wal-Mart was less then twenty dollars. I could hardly conceive of spending so much money on an ironing board. However, we decided, based on the board's stability and added safety, to purchase it. I think every penny we spent was worth it. It should last the rest of my ironing life!

Not only did we gain the safety benefit we wanted, but we noticed several other benefits. This ironing board has a much larger ironing surface. That means I can iron more quickly and spend the saved time in another way. The board itself is taller so that I can stand more erect while ironing and not hurt my back. It is much heavier and sturdier so that it doesn't rock when bumped. The ironing board has a place on the side to set the iron in so that it isn't sitting upright on the board itself when someone isn't holding it. Therefore, the iron is less susceptible to being knocked off the board. Each time I iron, I think about how grateful for something as simple as a high-quality ironing board.

The Lord has given homemakers the responsibility of being a keeper of the home. For me, having good tools to save me time and to help me in this process is extremely beneficial. I am happy to be as efficient in my homemaking as possible so that I have more time for mothering and schooling.

# Sleep
## *by Teri*

The topic of sleep is one that is very real to every mother. Pregnancies, babies, busy schedules, homeschooling, outside activities, ministry, relationships—almost every area of life has the potential of robbing us of sleep. If I feel tired throughout the day, is it because I am not getting enough sleep? Does it seem that I don't have the available time to sleep the hours my body requires? Do I envy others who seem to have much more time in their day because they function nicely on fewer hours of sleep than I do?

Recently, a mom asked me:

*I used to sleep up to twelve hours a night and still could sleep ten if I had the time. I find that as I have more tasks to care for, I am cutting down on my sleep. I know the rule that we need eight hours of sleep, but I have seen some women live on seven hours consistently. I also know back in previous days most women (families actually) went to bed at 9 and rose at 3:30 or 4 a.m. I would like to hear from you since you had seven hours sleep time scheduled but still nursed during the night, even if for only the first few weeks. That is the toughest time to get through! Any advice?*

Scripture warns several times about the dangers of loving sleep, "How long wilt thou sleep, O sluggard? when wilt thou arise out of thy sleep? *Yet* a little sleep, a little slumber, a little folding of the hands to sleep: So shall thy poverty come as one that travelleth, and thy want as an armed man" (Proverbs 6:9-11). "Love not sleep, lest thou come to poverty; open thine eyes, *and* thou shalt be satisfied with bread" (Proverbs 20:13).

These verses show us that in general we have to guard against wanting to have too much sleep. We should exercise caution as we evaluate how much time to allocate for sleep. Our tendency is to choose the easy path, the one that includes more sleep. Because of this warning, I believe we have to carefully observe our "need" for sleep and make sure we are meeting true needs and not fulfilling wants in this area. With this warning against too much sleep, I believe we can move on to evaluate how busy moms can get an adequate amount of sleep to function normally.

I don't know about you, but when I don't get enough sleep my whole personality changes. I am more easily discouraged. I become angry at small things. I can't think well. I cry, and nothing seems right. This doesn't appear to be uncommon among women. I have also seen in Scripture several extremely godly men who, at one point in each of their lives, ask God to let them die. To me it seems to be related to them becoming very weary. These men are Jonah (Jonah 4:7-8), Elijah (1 Kings 19:4), and Moses (Numbers 11:15).

I would encourage us to make sure our schedules are such that they allow us to sleep the amount of time we need to each night so that we can function well each day. Our family's schedule helps Steve and me in this area. We have a set time to go to bed each night, Sunday through Thursday, and a set time to get up. There is very little that we allow to interfere with these bed times and wake up times. The consistency of our sleep schedule has enabled us to determine sleep amounts that allow us the greatest amount of productive daytime while still adequately meeting our sleep needs.

It may take some trial and error to determine whether one should have seven, eight, or nine hours of sleep each night. Obviously the number of hours of sleep we need may not be the same as the number we could sleep. In the case of the mom who wrote the note, she said she could sleep ten hours each night, but she may only need eight hours of sleep. That means she must determine how little sleep she can get by with so that she isn't experiencing the sleep-deprived symptoms I listed earlier.

For most of my adult life, I thought I needed eight hours of sleep each night. However, I often couldn't get to sleep when I went to bed. At some point in our married life, Steve and I decided to see if we could get more time in our day by sleeping fewer hours at night. We dropped down to seven hours a night. It was amazing for me. I functioned well on seven hours per night and no longer struggled with having trouble falling asleep. My body didn't need eight hours of sleep.

If you have planned a schedule that allows for eight hours of sleep each night, or whatever your personal amount happens to be, but there isn't time in the day to accomplish what should be done, then what? There are several possibilities. As you evaluate them, it may be that one will be helpful, or you may need to use all of them.

First, make sure you are using a daily schedule for your time and your children's time. This will make you as productive as possible throughout the day. It will help you to discern your priorities and put your time where it is most needed and beneficial. The *Managers of Their Homes* book addresses this topic in detail.

Next, I would encourage the elimination of activities, based on their priority and urgency. Mom's sleep must come before any outside-the-home activity, no matter how important that activity may seem. When we deprive ourselves of sleep for an outside activity, we aren't trading off our personal preferences for our child's best interest. Rather, we are giving away the possibility for our child to have a sweet, godly, loving mother, which has eternal value in that child's life. Generally, we are making this exchange for an activity of temporal value.

Another suggestion may be a difficult one for some—a home business. If Mom isn't able to get enough sleep and she has a home business, then I believe her priorities again are wrong. Anyone who has a home business will have a justification for having it. However, if the home business robs her of necessary sleep (or the ability to homeschool, train the children, be a keeper at home—any of her biblical roles), then the reasons for it have to be reevaluated.

The next area to look at would be time trade-offs. For example, it may be that your preference is to make your own bread and sew your own clothing. At some seasons of life, these may be reasonable tasks. Again, though, if Mom can't find time for the sleep she needs, then these time-consuming choices may have to be eliminated. The priorities should be kept in line, and sleep is higher than homemade bread or home-sewn clothes.

Scheduling an afternoon nap can be another way to allow one to get by with less nighttime sleep. For the years I was pregnant or nursing, I always had a half-hour nap scheduled sometime during the afternoon when the children were taking their naps. This short rest gave me the added boost necessary to keep me going during those months that were taking a higher toll on my body.

Finally, as we look for ways to free up time for needed sleep, consider the type of homeschool curriculum you are using. Here again, we may decide to make different curriculum choices so that school and school planning aren't requiring so much time. Hours that are deterred from a time-intensive curriculum can be given to sleep. Again, this change will likely only be for a season. Then, with another set of circumstances and available sleep time coming from another area, a return to the preferred curriculum can be made.

The Bible warns us first not to love sleep. We must be cautious to discern if our desire for sleep is a want or a need. Throughout our lives, there will be periods of time when we will be living sleep-deprived lives for one reason or another. However, because of what a lack of sleep does to us spiritually, emotionally, and physically, I don't believe it is wise to continue to try, on an ongoing basis, to get by without adequate rest. We shouldn't feel guilty for getting the sleep we need. We aren't being selfish to do so. Rather, we are loving our husbands and loving our children as Titus 2:4 tells us because we are giving them a mom who is sweet, loving, and kind rather than angry, depressed, and sluggish. May we be women who value our families enough to make the necessary choices to allow us each the right amount of sleep.

# Traditional Christian Textbook Curricula
## by Teri

We love traditional Christian textbook curricula for our homeschooling family. Through my eighteen years of homeschooling, however, I have regularly read homeschool literature where this choice of homeschooling materials is criticized. Very seldom, if ever, have I been encouraged by a homeschooling book or article in the direction of using textbooks for education. Many authors have indicated that my children will not love to learn if I use textbooks. Others tell me that my children will not grow up to be godly adults with strong character exhibited in their lives if I use textbooks for their education. At first, reading these books and articles distressed me and caused me to go back regularly to Steve about our curricula choices.

Now, however, we have been using traditional Christian textbooks for our homeschool long enough that I am secure in our decisions. In addition, we have personal experience and visible results in our children to refute those authors who say the negative things about using textbooks. I want to share our reasons for our traditional Christian textbook curricula decision. This may encourage others who have made the same choice but are usually discouraged by the homeschooling articles they read about curricula. It may also help some who haven't considered traditional Christian textbooks as a viable homeschool curricula option.

I might also add that if you have chosen other methods of teaching, I am not trying to dissuade you in any way. Follow the path that God leads you down. In fact, I would suggest you not read this article any further as I don't want to discourage you in your choice. This article is strictly to share the benefits we have experienced and encourage moms who might be struggling with doubts after reading or hearing negative words about traditional textbooks.

For nine years in our early homeschooling, we used unit studies. Then, when Sarah was entering high school, we switched to traditional Christian textbooks. Both Nathan and Christopher, our oldest children, have told us that they would have liked to have had textbooks for their high school education. Why? They observed Sarah's study and learning from her textbooks. The textbooks were comprehensive and methodical. They liked history being completely and chronologically presented. They saw the thoroughness of the science textbooks. The boys believe Sarah received a better high school education than they did.

A traditional Christian curriculum helps us in our goals for our children. We see childhood as a training ground for adulthood. While our children have time to play and enjoy being children, we think their school and chore time should challenge them to learn to work. We want these hours of their day to be very beneficial in helping them grow into responsible, productive, mature adults—ones who don't need to have something be fun in order to choose to do it.

We find the traditional Christian curriculum to be thorough and complete, allowing us to give our children the type of education we want them to have. Studying the same material repetitively on a higher level as the successive years progress helps to cement in our children's minds what they are learning. Rather than squelching their love for learning, textbooks have given our children the tools they need to pursue their personal interests. As a matter of fact, our younger children always ask for school books at age three or four when we don't want them to start school until they are five.

I am able to homeschool my large family to achieve a maximum of learning for a minimum investment of my time. Traditional Christian curriculum helps me budget my school time plus my children's time. I can work with an individual child for a scheduled amount of time. What doesn't fit into that time frame, he can accomplish on his own without direction from me. I can schedule each child the amount of time he needs for each of his subjects, knowing approximately how long that subject will take him each day.

If there is a year when a baby is added into our lives and I don't have as much time for school, I can cut back on my one-on-one school time and let my children do more of their school work on their own. When this is the case, we will spend our individual school time on the subjects with which they struggle, while they will work independently on the other subjects. School doesn't have to be put on hold for several weeks while I am recovering from childbirth.

I love to read history and science with my children, but if there are days, or seasons, my one-on-one school time doesn't allow for this, the children can read the lessons and answer questions on their own. We like to do science experiments during our individual half hour of fun together time. That way it doesn't impact our school time, plus I find it easier to work with only one child when it comes to a science experiment.

With traditional Christian textbooks, I generally don't have to weed out information I don't want my children to be exposed to such as evolution, false religions and gods, mythology and fables. Romans 16:19 says, "For your obedience is come abroad unto all *men*. I am glad therefore on your behalf: but yet I would have you wise unto that which is good, and simple concerning evil." Deuteronomy 12:30 tells us to, "Take heed to thyself that thou be not snared by following them, after that they be destroyed from before thee; and that thou inquire not after their gods, saying, How did these nations serve their gods? even so will I do likewise."

A traditional Christian curriculum requires little teacher prep time for me. Each week, I put the next week's assignments on our assignment sheets or simply write the day of the week on the page in the child's workbook if it is consumable. I don't have to hunt up materials related to our studies, and we never miss school because I didn't get around to doing what I needed to do in preparation.

School does not dissolve into "nothingness" if I don't have school planning time. My children are not completely dependent on my time and availability in order for them to do school. On those occasions when I am sick or away, they can continue with their normal school day. We aren't down with school because I am not available. This also helps to occupy their time when I am unavailable, and it makes those days function much more smoothly.

If I don't have time to check the children's schoolwork, they could actually check it themselves. I have a scheduled time in my afternoon for this, but if I were to be sick or gone for several days, I would allow them to do the checking themselves or check each other's work.

There are other homeschooling families who are making the traditional Christian textbook choice. Here is what one says: *"My children also love their textbooks, and I have met several children going to college now who have expressed that they wished that their parents had stuck with a curriculum that would have provided greater consistency, especially in math."*

Here are the reasons another mom shares for liking traditional Christian textbooks:

* *My husband wants me to!*
* *It offers structure.*
* *It requires less time by Mom for planning.*
* *It follows a logical sequence.*
* *Transcripts and records are easier.*
* *I have looked at other methods, and they do not fit our family type or temperament.*
* *Easier to teach large numbers of children.*
* *Earlier student independence.*
* *More support for questions from publisher.*

Finally, one more mom shares:

* *They have the materials presented clearly and in an efficient way for learning—broken into reasonable "chunks."*
* *They save me a lot of preparation time, making it possible for me to teach children at different levels easily.*

✴ *They provide an orderly way to move through materials year to year.*
✴ *They provide the tools of learning and a core of knowledge my children use to build onto with their own interests and strengths.*
✴ *They help my children learn that learning requires discipline and is not always entertaining.*
✴ *They make it possible for me to teach things in which I have little or no background.*

One area of disappointment for us in some of the traditional Christian textbooks has come in their reading and literature courses. We have found only one acceptable publisher for this. Rod and Staff have the only textbooks we have come across that don't have mythology, fables, violence, or extreme silliness in their elementary reading program. Rod and Staff uses strictly stories taken directly from Scripture until the end of fourth grade. We have chosen to have reading a separate subject from first through fourth grade.

As we choose our textbooks, we are careful to look at the books at a homeschool convention so that we can see if there are any objectionable themes in them. For example, our children have chosen not to date. One high school English textbook had a story running through it that involved a boy-girl dating relationship. Another English textbook had a sports theme in it, and our family has decided not to participate in sports. We want our textbooks to support our choices not undermine them.

These are many of the reasons we have decided to use a traditional Christian textbook curriculum. However, this does not mean that we don't respect and support homeschoolers' decisions to use other types of curricula and methods. We encourage each family to seek the Lord, review what is available, and make informed curriculum decisions for their children—based on discernment of the Lord's goals for those children. What does bother us is when we read books and articles making it sound like no one could effectively homeschool their children using traditional Christian textbooks. We are here to say we are using Christian textbooks, we like them, and they are working!

# A Summer Schedule
### *by Teri*

For many of us, our normal school year is ending with summer bringing a change of pace. Some will take a complete break from any kind of structured learning. Then there may be moms who will have a light school load during the summer weeks. Others may be planning to continue school through the summer. During our eighteen years of homeschooling experience, I have discovered the direction, productivity, and peace a summer schedule brings to our home.

One of the top priorities for my summer schedule will be to help my children manage their time usage. We have found that children left day after day having "nothing" to do generates a multitude of problems. Not the least of these problems is the proverbial, "Mom, I am bored. There's nothing to do." I will plan our summer schedule to prevent this. Our children bicker more when left to their own devices all day. They also are more prone to get into things they aren't supposed to do. Again, our summer schedule will alleviate these difficulties before they arise.

I will include each child in our summer schedule. Steve and I evaluate how much free time we think the children can handle well. We want summer to be a break from their normal school schedule and workload. At the same time, we want to fill some of their summer hours productively.

The children's schedules will include personal Bible time for those old enough to read their Bibles and have a prayer time. Music practice is scheduled. We like for them to keep up their math skills, so most summers they continue doing a math lesson each day. They may also have other academic work scheduled that doesn't involve my time such as typing and handwriting. Daily chores are scheduled. If there are any major projects to be accomplished, they will have some time dedicated to those.

Summer is the perfect time to schedule in those activities you always want to do with the children but never have the available time. I make it a priority to put in the children's schedule and in my schedule time to read out loud. I also want to have individual time with each child at least weekly. Simply include a block of time in the summer schedule and make a list of what you want to do with the children. When we have a schedule in place, this assures that I don't allow myself to be consumed with my personal projects, putting off time I want to spend with the children.

If your child has an area of academic need, scheduling a block of time to work on it during the summer is perfect. Generally, summer days afford the extra hours required to give individual attention in a specific school area. A child who doesn't yet know his basic math facts could spend a few minutes every day doing drills on the computer, on paper, and orally. Writing projects could be tackled knowing there is time to write, revise, and polish them.

As you can see, the children's scheduled activities nicely fill several hours each day. This still allows them to have a great deal of time to play, help others, or pursue their own interests. However, we have easily avoided the pitfalls that come from a summer overloaded with free days.

A priority for my summer schedule will be cleaning and organizing time. There is a host of cleaning projects for which there is simply not time during the school year. I look forward to knocking these out during the summer. My procrastinating nature can easily put these off, though, if I don't have a place in my schedule for them. I love to have two hours a day for these projects but most years I can only squeeze out an hour.

Here is a list of what I will do each summer:

* ✽ Pack away school books and school work
* ✽ Clean kitchen cupboards
* ✽ Clean refrigerator
* ✽ Organize and work in storage room
* ✽ Clean and organize every closet
* ✽ Put photos in albums
* ✽ Plan and prepare for upcoming school year
* ✽ Clean windows

A number-one priority for my summer schedule is preparations for the next school year. This will take up a big chunk of my scheduled cleaning and organizing time. My excitement for a new school year is partially dependent on how prepared I am for it. Using summer for this planning allows me get my school schedule worked out. I can have all the children's books and materials prepared and ready. I am able to order anything I realize we need but haven't purchased yet. I can clean out and reorganize areas of the house dedicated to school materials. This time allows me to be physically, emotionally, and mentally prepared for the new school year.

You wouldn't believe what can be accomplished through the course of the summer by simply tackling cleaning and organizing for an hour a day. I can never remember not getting through my "to do" list by the end of the summer. Often, I have to come up with additional jobs that weren't on my original list because I have more time than projects. Beware, though. The key for me has been to stop my cleaning or organizing when the scheduled time is completed. That way I don't impact other scheduled activities. I also don't burn out by getting too tired. Hour by hour, your projects will be accomplished.

Some may have a garden that needs extra attention through the summer. Remember to put time in your and your children's schedule for these gardening jobs. Schedule in time for any large projects that you would like to accomplish during the summer.

In setting up my summer schedule, the most important part is prayer. I want to make sure the activities put in the schedule for me and for each of the children are what the Lord wants us to do. I also desire to put the amounts of time into each task that would be honoring to the Lord. The Lord has called each member of our family to follow and serve Him. Our schedule is to be a tool to help in this.

There will be days you don't use your schedule for one reason or another. Perhaps you decide to have a spur-of-the moment trip to the park for a picnic and playtime. Then you will probably use your schedule until time to prepare for the outing and decide what the priorities are for the remaining day when you return home. Other days you will be away from home all day. Your schedule should make these days more enjoyable because your daily tasks will be current. Catching up for the day or days away won't be stressful. Let your schedule help you enjoy that trip to the park, visit to the zoo, or cookie baking day.

I want to encourage you to consider making and using a schedule to help you meet your goals and desires for the summer. Some structure to summer days ensures that they will be peaceful and productive. You won't enter your new school year disappointed that the summer weeks slipped by without you or your children accomplishing what you had hoped to do. A daily schedule is a productive instrument we can benefit from making and then using.

# Priorities
## *by Teri*

It isn't uncommon for us to hear a homeschooling mom vent a little frustration about how much trouble she has accomplishing school, keeping her house clean, and preparing meals. In the next sentence, she will, without even realizing it, give us a clue as to why she is struggling. She herself won't be aware of the cause and effect of her two statements because she is so close to the situation. However, as an outside observer only knowing what she tells us, we can quickly discern the problem.

Priorities are very difficult first to define in our lives and then to live by. It seems fitting that a starting place for our priorities would be God's Word. For example, there are two verses particularly aimed at Christian women to which we could look for direction in setting godly priorities for our heart focus and time usage. In Titus 2:4-5 the older women are admonished to ". . . teach the young women to be sober, to love their husbands, to love their children, *To be* discreet, chaste, keepers at home, good, obedient to their own husbands, that the word of God be not blasphemed."

In 1 Timothy 5:10, we see what Paul gives Timothy as criteria to look at in a Christian woman's life that will determine whether she qualifies for church support if she becomes a widow at some point with no other source of care. She is to have been "well reported of for good works; if she have brought up children, if she have lodged strangers, if she have washed the saints' feet, if she have relieved the afflicted, if she have diligently followed every good work."

We can easily see in these verses a blueprint of a woman's priorities. Everything in these verses grows from our relationship with the Lord, so that is a first priority. Then we are to love our husbands and children, be keepers at home, and finally, minister to others. This is a simple list, and yet it appears to be quite powerful. Consider what would happen if we took everything in which we invest time and evaluated each in light of these priorities.

Let's start with setting aside time each day to spend reading the Bible and in prayer. That one is easy since it fulfills priority number one plus is instrumental in helping us with every other priority we have. Not only do Bible reading and prayer take precedence on my "to do" list, they also receive the first part of my day.

What about exercise time? That doesn't seem to fit clearly into one of the priorities—or does it? What is the result of not exercising? Poor health and lack of energy. That means if I don't have exercising as a priority, I may not be able to fulfill my other responsibilities as a Christian woman. Therefore, for me, exercise time stays on my list of profitable time usage.

Does housekeeping make it in my list of priorities? Absolutely. The verses in Titus tell me to be a keeper at home. A part of that would be staying current with the cleaning tasks in my home. This makes a pleasant environment for my husband and children and is a demonstrative way of showing my love for them. What about the directions in 1 Timothy to wash the saints' feet or lodge strangers? I can tell you from personal experience and talking with other moms, we don't want anyone outside our family in our home when it is dirty, messy, or cluttered. That means we aren't willing to have our homes used for ministry and outreach to others when they are in this condition. However, if my home is continually maintained, then preparations for dinner guests are an afternoon affair rather than something entirely avoided or requiring a week-long cleaning marathon.

Many Christian women have chosen not to work outside the home. They often feel they should, in some way, be contributing to producing income for the family. As I evaluate these verses, I don't see this as a priority at all. It isn't even implied in either of these verses. On the other hand, consider what a home business often does for a homeschooling mom. It causes her to live under constant stress and time pressure. It limits and sometimes completely robs her of time for the higher priority of homeschooling her children in order to keep up with business demands. It consumes her thoughts and emotional energy. It can even cost her health.

Where do outside activities for the children fit into a list of priorities? Once again, I don't see them in these verses. For our family, a part of loving our children is teaching them at home. Taking them out for music lessons, sports practice, and co-op classes simply means we wouldn't have the needed time for our schooling. This then would cause me stress, time pressure, angry responses, impatience, discouragement, and sometimes depression. This is the exact opposite of the directive to love my children.

It isn't uncommon to hear a mom say that she needs time for herself. One vehicle she may choose for this is computer time in message boards, blogs, or personal e-mails. She plans to take five or ten minutes but commonly ends up taking a half hour to an hour. In the meantime, the housekeeping, homeschooling, or meal preparation she could have used that time for is left undone. Now she feels rushed and frustrated, which leaves her more susceptible to angry outbursts. If my personal socializing can't be confined to an allotted time and not disturb other priorities, then it needs to be curtailed.

Our priorities are vitally important in determining how we spend every minute of our day, particularly when we are in our child-raising years. Personally, I would vote for children who "miss out" on soccer, homeschool co-op classes, and piano lessons but have a joyful, sweet-spirited mom because her priorities are in line with Scripture. The alternative is too often children who are involved in every possible church, homeschool, and other activity but are growing up in a home filled with anger, stress, frustration, and impatience while not even having time to accomplish homeschool.

I would be thrilled if this Mom's Corner challenged many who are reading it to sit down and determine your priorities. They may not be just like mine, but I encourage you to take them from Scripture and know what they are. Then hold up how you spend your time against those priorities. Evaluate what the outcomes of your time usage are on your family and on you—spiritually, emotionally, and physically. May we be women with godly priorities—ones who wisely choose how to spend their time based on those priorities.

# I Just Want to Be a Mommy
## *by Teri*

Our first year of homeschooling, I had a seven-year-old, a five-year-old, and a three-year-old, plus a constant struggle with depression partly rooted in a lack of spiritual growth. At this time, I found another Christian mom, with children my children's ages, in whom I saw wonderful spiritual maturity. This other mom agreed to spiritually mentor me. For a year, we met together, did a Bible study, memorized Scripture, and discussed the practical aspects of our spiritual walk as Christian women. I was so grateful for the investment this woman made in my life. That year my friend's children were in a Christian school, but the following year she decided to homeschool them.

Although our mentoring time lasted only one year, we continued to maintain a friendship. After a year of homeschooling, my friend chose to put her boys back in a Christian school. I can still remember her words to me that afternoon as I sat in her home, and she justified her actions, "Oh, Teri. I just want to be a mommy. I want to welcome my boys home in the afternoon as their mommy. I don't want to have to be their teacher too. I just want to be their mommy."

I recall driving home that afternoon in tears. "Lord, I just want to be a mommy too. I want all the happy, fun things about being a mommy with none of the difficulties."

In my mind, I pictured my friend's children coming home from school in the afternoon. She would have spent the day in personal Bible study, prayer, exercise, housecleaning, reading, ministry, sewing, and cookie baking. As the children bounced in the door, they would be met by a beautiful, smiling mommy. I was sure she would have taken a long shower and blown her hair dry too. The children would smell the freshly baked cookies and scramble for a seat at the table. There they would happily discuss the excitement of their day in school. Finally, they would head outside to play while my friend started supper in peace and quiet. I just want to be a mommy too!

As I prayed about my heart-wrenching discussion with my friend and my personal feelings about wanting to "just be a mommy" too, the Lord soon began to show me some things. He made me realize that my homeschooling lifestyle was "just being a mommy" in its fullest sense. As we begin a new school year, perhaps you are struggling with feelings of not wanting to tackle another homeschool year. Maybe you have even thought the thoughts of my friend when she told me she "just wanted to be a mommy." It could be that this is your first year of homeschooling, and you are concerned about being both a teacher and a mommy. Perhaps your role as a homeschool mom has lost the joy it once had. Together let's encourage one another in the direction the Lord has led each of us in homeschooling. After all, I just want to be a mommy!

What does being a mommy really mean? Titus 2:4 tells the older women to ". . . teach the young women to be sober, to love their husbands, to love their children." Easily seen then, my role as a mommy is to love my children. Practically speaking, how is this done? Do I have more chance to love my children when they are away from home at school for seven or eight hours or when I have them home with me all day? The answer to this one is obvious: when they are home with me. By loving my children, I just want to be a mommy!

During those extra hours I have to "just be a mommy," I can tell my children over and over again how special they are to me, how much I love them, how wonderful they are, and how blessed I am to "just be their mommy." I have seven more hours a day to give them hugs, pat them, put my arm around them, smile at them, kiss them, laugh with them—opportunities to "just be a mommy." The bottom line is, "I just want to be a mommy!"

What about the time we spend in homeschooling? Have I taken off my "mommy" hat and replaced it with a "teacher" one? I am taking the place of a teacher in a classroom in my children's lives, but I am still "Mommy" in the fullest sense of the word. My mommy role as a teacher began from the first words I quietly whispered in each newborn baby's tiny ear. Almost everything my children have learned in their young lives, this mommy has had a part in teaching them. Being an official teacher in our homeschool is simply an extension of this natural teaching relationship that exists between a mother and her child. Really and truly, I just want to be a mommy!

I thought about what it meant to be a mommy teacher beyond simply teaching my children facts and figures. What teacher in a school loves their students like I love mine? What teacher's main goal in life is to see their students grow up to love the Lord Jesus Christ with all their heart, soul, mind, and strength? What teacher is going to cuddle a sick student on the couch, tucking that student in with extra pillows and blankets, while loving and consoling him through his misery? Hey, I just want to be a mommy!

Perhaps I should consider the time spent in disciplining or correcting my children during school hours. Maybe I am not being a "mommy" then. Once again Scripture assures me that this is part of my mommy role. "My son, keep thy father's commandment, and forsake not the law of thy mother" (Proverbs 6:20). My friend didn't like to have to make her children do their schoolwork. Sometimes they cried about what they were to do for school and this was part of why she abandoned homeschooling in favor of "just being a mommy." One of my most important "mommy" responsibilities is to prepare my children for life. If they face a difficult task in their school and choose to cry about it, this is my chance, as their mommy, to encourage them to pray about it, to put forth some effort, to try again, and to rest in the Lord. What opportunity these hours my children are home with me during school time afford. Wow, I just want to be a mommy!

Every day I have a choice set before me. I can look at my home-schooling with resentment and think, "Lord, I just want to be a mommy," while sending my children away to school and doing what I want to do all day. I might think these same thoughts without acting on them but all the while wishing I could put them in school. It will still affect my attitude toward my children and my home-schooling. Alternatively, I can view homeschooling with rejoicing in my heart and say, "Lord, I am so grateful to just be a mommy. Thank you that homeschooling is part of the mothering I can give to my children. I know there are moms who want to homeschool their children but can't. I know there will be difficult days for us as I home-school my children. Yet, it remains with me as to what I will allow in my thoughts." May we be mothers who relish our roles as home-schooling mommies. Let's never forget, I just want to be a mommy!

# First Day of School
## *by Teri*

August 11th marked the Maxwell family's nineteenth first day of school. We celebrated that night, because it was our very best first day of school ever! Generally the first day of school is one that I look forward to with great excitement. However, the reality of living through it most often has generated discouragement and frustration. It is not unheard of in the Maxwell home for Mom to be crying by dinnertime on those momentous first days of school. I have been known to say to Steve, "It was a zoo here today, dear. I have no idea how we will ever get any real schoolwork done."

Since I have experienced nineteen first days of school, and since I really, really like happy first days of school, and since I truly, truly, truly want to learn from all of our failures, perhaps I can share some of my first day of school experiences with you. It could be that your first days of school have been much like mine, and that you, too, would love to have one you could celebrate.

## First-Day-of-School Traditions

When Nathan started school, he attended a private, Christian school for three years. On the first day of school, I always took a photo of him before he left home in the morning. There he stood with his lunch box in one hand and his pack on his back, sporting his tidy blue-and-white uniform. Each year's photo shows him a bit bigger but just as cute. Therefore, when we began homeschooling, we decided to continue first-day-of-school photos. Without lunch boxes, the children hold their favorite school books in their hands for the picture-taking session.

Another tradition we have for our first day of school is special school supply surprises. While school supplies are on sale at the stores, I will shop for any school supplies the children need. I purchase notebooks, notebook paper, notebook tabs, pencils, pens, colored pencils, pencil pouches, small whiteboards, whiteboard markers, scissors, rulers, glue sticks, crayons, tape—although not each of these every year. Since our materials often last us more than one year, it can be challenging coming up with needed supplies, so sometimes I resort to buying not-so-needed-but-fun supplies. Each child finds a stack of school surprises by his spot on the dining room table on the first day of school.

Because pencils being left out in the house are a problem here, I purchase the children pencils with different outside colors. I discovered that there are pencils with not only yellow on the outside but also green, black, and wood color. There are different colored bands around the yellow pencils in various packs. I give each child a couple of sets of pencils, different from his siblings, and then when a pencil is left out, I know to whom it belongs. Plus, if the child loses all of his pencils before the school year is over, he can buy his own replacements.

Finally, the first day of school will often bring with it a special breakfast. Because of having children living at home who drive, I have the advantage of being able to suggest to Sarah that we could enjoy donuts for the first-day-of-school breakfast if she has time to go to the grocery store that morning. She is very accommodating, and donuts are a great treat in our family.

## The Change

While these first-day-of-school traditions have been in place for quite a while, this is the first year that I realized the biggest failure of my first day of school. We typically do these traditions on the first day of school and also attempt a normal day of academic schoolwork. This year, the week before our first real day of school we had another first day of school. You might call it a pre-first day of school. I scheduled no academic work for that day, only our first-day-of-school traditions. It was a little like registration day used to be when I went to school.

Because each of these practical and memory-making activities we do on the first day of school takes up time, we would be frustrated trying to get normal school completed. We spent several hours doing our pre-first day of school. No wonder I have been frustrated with what I was trying to fit into our previous first days of school.

After the special breakfast and school surprises on our pre-first day of school, I had a one-on-one meeting with each child. We went through his schedule and looked at all his books. For my fourth and fifth graders, I read out loud with them their first spelling lesson because they do that on their own. Often they will struggle with things that are very simple, because they try to fill in blanks without reading the material. This was an opportunity to teach them how to do their spelling lessons effectively.

Each child from fourth grade on up has a school notebook. This year we finally got them organized. We have used notebooks for organizing schoolwork for several years, but I am generally frustrated with them. We hadn't taken the time to plan how many tabs each child needed and what the tabs should be labeled. Then the history tests and quizzes were mixed in with the daily history work and difficult to find come "study-for-nine-week-exam" time. The writing was somewhere in the spelling section because we didn't have enough tabs. You get the picture, I am sure.

This year I made a list of what each child would need as far as number of tabs and what they should be labeled. I bought enough tabs for their notebooks and for my notebook. I included the children's tabs in their school supply surprises. During our one-on-one meeting we labeled the tabs and alphabetized them, too. That was another problem. With three children (four this year) with schoolwork in notebooks, I was always struggling through the tabs to locate the right one. Every child had the tabs set up in a different order. I don't care much for checking schoolwork to begin with, so anything I can do to make it easier is a benefit to me. Even having readable tabs that are in order helps.

After lunch, Sarah, one of our family photographers, did the first-day-of-school photos. Getting five children to choose their photo props, get the camera setting correct, pose each one individually for photos, and then put them together as a group is not a five-minute project. Again, this was time that was pulled from what normally was a full academic school day. None of us likes to finish school at dinnertime.

While what we did on our pre-first day of school are small, little tasks, each one adds up to extra time away from schoolwork. Having these activities planned for a day when we weren't going to do any normal schoolwork was wonderful. I know it was a major factor in our super-duper, best-ever first day of school. May I encourage you to look at your previous first days of school, and if they aren't what you would like them to be, try to determine why they weren't. Then make the necessary changes. You will be glad you did, and perhaps it won't take you nineteen years of trying.

# A Grumbly Spirit
## *by Teri*

For several weeks recently, I had been allowing myself to think negative thoughts. The result was that I hadn't felt happy, had forced myself to do what I needed to do, and had been generally unpleasant. This had been a continual burden on my heart as I prayed each day. One morning I brought up my struggles to Steve while we were talking on our daily walk. He encouraged me. That discussion also began quite a thinking process as I did my cleaning later that morning. The Lord and I have some of our best "discussions" during Friday morning cleaning.

The Lord showed me the root of my problem. I had been complaining in my heart—complaining about my day being full of things I didn't want to do. I didn't want to grade schoolwork. I didn't want to write Mom's Corners or books. I didn't want to write Christmas letters or figure out what to get people for Christmas. I didn't want to pick up after people. I didn't want to be careful of what I ate. There was more, but I think you get the idea.

These were all things I either was doing or was going to have to do soon that I didn't want to do but were my responsibility. Looking at that list, I see that there is nothing at all awful, bad, or even that difficult about those tasks. As a matter of fact, they are activities that I can enjoy if the circumstances are right—although I am not sure I ever enjoy checking schoolwork. It is likely some of you reading this article would think the jobs I was complaining about are wonderful jobs. For me, though, they had become burdensome to the point of a grumbling, negative overall spirit.

The Lord caused me to realize that my problem is not what I have to do but my attitude toward it. What an ungrateful attitude I had! If I were living in prison for my faith in Christ, wouldn't I be delighted to have the opportunity to be free once again and check my children's schoolwork each day? Wouldn't I be rejoicing each time I sat down with those school papers? I thought about the stories I have read of Christians being separated from their families, put into sparse living conditions in a prison, forced to hard labor for endless hours, and even physically abused. What would they think of the most distasteful task I had set before me? Wouldn't they love to be in my circumstances?

My focus on the Lord and serving had been lost in the midst of what I want to do and what I like to do. I had come to think only of myself. The more I thought about not enjoying certain tasks, the more tedious they became. It was draining—not the job, but my emotional response to it—causing me to feel tired. My thoughts discouraged me. Eleven more years of checking schoolwork! Those kinds of feelings caused me to procrastinate and let things slide to which I should have attended. This was not the kind of wife, mother, and homeschool teacher I wanted to be.

"Casting down imaginations, and every high thing that exalteth itself against the knowledge of God, and bringing into captivity every thought to the obedience of Christ" (2 Corinthians 10:5). My thoughts were not being brought into the obedience of Christ. As a matter of fact, the exact opposite was happening. Those thoughts were self-centered rather than God-centered and other-centered. On top of that, my selfish direction didn't make me happy. I kept feeling more unhappy as I dwelt on what I didn't want to do.

Here is the starting place for change. I have to confess my wrong thoughts, discontentment, grumbling, and unhappiness to the Lord as sin. "If we confess our sins, he is faithful and just to forgive us *our* sins, and to cleanse us from all unrighteousness" (1 John 1:9). This is such a simple step to take. It is very painless except for hurting my pride—which is a good thing to be hurt.

Next comes the truth of Jesus Christ to which my thoughts need to be obedient. "Rejoice in the Lord alway: *and* again I say, Rejoice" (Philippians 4:4). Rejoicing—not grumbling, not complaining, not disliking, but rejoicing. The starting place for moving away from my rut of negativism was to take those thoughts captive. Instead I needed to think truth—rejoicing.

"In every thing give thanks: for this is the will of God in Christ Jesus concerning you" (1 Thessalonians 5:18). When I am murmuring about what I don't want to have to do, I am not giving thanks. This verse tells me clearly that I am no longer in God's will when I choose to be discontent rather than to give thanks. That is a heavy statement worthy of consideration. Sometimes we allow and excuse our bad attitudes when instead we should see them as sin and deal with them as such.

As I pray each day asking the Lord to strengthen me to keep my mind on His truth and not allow me to complain or focus on self, I know that is the Lord's will for me. "I can do all things through Christ which strengtheneth me" (Philippians 4:13). Steve often encourages me that I can make the choice to be obedient. Then, the Lord is the One Who does the work. "And he said unto me, My grace is sufficient for thee: for my strength is made perfect in weakness. Most gladly therefore will I rather glory in my infirmities, that the power of Christ may rest upon me. Therefore I take pleasure in infirmities, in reproaches, in necessities, in persecutions, in distresses for Christ's sake: for when I am weak, then am I strong" (2 Corinthians 12:9-10). It all starts with that choice I make.

If you have been struggling with a negative attitude, a complaining spirit, or a self focus, may I encourage you to begin by recognizing that is not God's will for you. See it as sin and ask forgiveness. Make the choice to be obedient by rejoicing, being thankful, and taking your thoughts captive. Go to the Lord, asking Him to help because His grace is sufficient, and we can do all things through Him.

# Christmas Decorating
## *by Teri*

"If someone walked into your home this Christmas season, would they know by your decorations that you were celebrating the birth of your Savior, Jesus Christ?" Many years ago, this was a question asked of the congregation by our then pastor during his Sunday sermon. Upon hearing this statement, our whole perspective on Christmas decorating changed. "And whatsoever ye do in word or deed, *do* all in the name of the Lord Jesus, giving thanks to God and the Father by him" (Colossians 3:17).

Prior to this, our Christmas decorating reflected what we thought looked nice and Christmassy. No thought was given to the importance of visibly making Christ's birth the central theme of our decorations. The nativity was a part of our Christmas decorating. However, it was also made up of a menagerie of items that had been given to us through the years. Santa Clauses, reindeer, and stockings were sometimes themes of these decorations. "Finally, brethren, whatsoever things are true, whatsoever things *are* honest, whatsoever things *are* just, whatsoever things *are* pure, whatsoever things *are* lovely, whatsoever things *are* of good report; if *there be* any virtue, and if *there be* any praise, think on these things" (Philippians 4:8). This verse was good encouragement for us in leaving behind the worldly trappings of Christmas decorating.

That question challenged my family to reevaluate the Christmas decorations we put up. Was the birth of Jesus evident, even at a casual glance? Would someone else, who didn't know us, be able to see that we worship Jesus Christ? Would they know He was preeminent in our hearts and home? We realized a guest would observe some evidence of Christ since we had a very nice nativity set. However, the whole feeling of our Christmas decorating was closer to what the world thinks of when they think of Christmas than it was a celebration of the birth of Christ. We began a purging of our decorations to eliminate the ones we did not feel fit with the emphasis we wanted to have—celebrating the birth of Jesus.

The weeding-out part was easy except when there was sentimental attachment to an item. At that point, I would think about what I wanted my children's hearts endeared to through the years of putting up the Christmas decorations. Did I want them excited about pulling out the reindeer from the Christmas box or delighted about opening the little glass nativity that sits on a mirror? Where would their joy be—in the cute little Santa or the wall plaque that says, "Jesus is the Reason for the Season"? The items that had heart attachment but no longer fit with our new decorating scheme were easier to let go of as I focused my mind on those thoughts.

I have to admit that, even with thinking right thoughts about eliminating decorations we no longer wanted to use, there were a few things that stayed in the boxes rather than coming out for the first couple of years. I simply couldn't get rid of them. Finally a year came when I was ready. The heart attachments were truly broken. They were pitched in the trash. "If ye then be risen with Christ, seek those things which are above, where Christ sitteth on the right hand of God. Set your affection on things above, not on things on the earth" (Colossians 3:1-2).

We also began to pray for the Lord to show us where to find decorations that would have Him be the focus. What exactly would those decorations look like? The acquiring of replacement decorations was hard since so many Christmas decorations have nothing to do with the story of the birth of Christ.

It was just a year or so later that I saw an ad in a Christian catalog for a fireplace mantle garland with a large ornament hanging from the middle of it that said, "Name Above All Names." There were smaller, scroll-shaped ornaments hanging on the sides with words on them such as, "Truth," "Bread of Life," "Emmanuel." It was perfect for our new Christmas decorating theme. This became the focal point of our Christmas decorating, with our nativity set sitting on the mantle right above the "Name Above All Names." One "name" a year was added to the collection until the mantle displayed as many names as it could hold.

The girls and I try to go to a Christmas craft bazaar each November with Grandma. As that date approaches I begin asking the Lord to give me two or three new decorations to add to the collection. We visit booth after booth, searching for any decoration that refers to Christ or the Christmas story. Sometimes we find this very discouraging because so little of what we see glorifies Christ and much more of what is available is focused on the world's idea of Christmas. However, every year the Lord has provided those two or three special decorations. I rejoice in God's goodness to give us decorations that keep our mind on His birth during the Christmas season.

One year I found a large ceramic ornament with the nativity scene painted on it that can be hung on the wall. I also found a wooden plaque with an image of Mary, Joseph, and baby Jesus painted on it, and the words, "Remember the reason for the season." The third item was another wooden plaque with an angel on one end and "Joy to the World" written on the other.

Each year I come home from the bazaar with our purchases, hang them in my bedroom until the time comes to decorate the house, and delight in looking at them. They truly put my focus on Jesus Christ during His special season.

This change in our Christmas decorating has filled my heart with joy. I love the excitement in our children's eyes as they pull out their favorite decorations from the Christmas storage boxes. Each item puts our thoughts on Jesus Christ in some way. There are no more mixed messages being sent to our children. When a guest enters our home at Christmas, he will no longer wonder what Christmas means to the Maxwell family. He will see Jesus Christ everywhere he looks.

In the years since making our Christmas decorating change, we have been excited to see how God has answered the prayer of our hearts and provided decorations that glorify Christ. Because we have only added one to three new Christmas decorations per year, the expense has been minimal. If we hadn't had the finances for this or simply wanted craft projects, we could have made our own decorations. With Christmas fast approaching, may Jesus be known to our children even by our decorations. May we use them to draw our children's hearts into a deeper love for Jesus as they experience the excitement year after year of getting out those Christmas decorations that remind them of His birth. May our decorations also bring joy to our hearts because they encourage us and our families to reflect on the magnificent miracle of the birth of our Savior.

# Quietness, Confidence, and Strength
## by Teri

Homeschooling moms can find themselves feeling discouraged by the constancy of their job in the midst of what they want to be the most joyful years of their lives. Here are a couple of moms with whom we might relate:

*I am failing miserably and feel awful. I am irritable, cranky, and anxious. Please pray for me that I can get thru this, that God will give me strength, and that I will not be crabby to my children. A homeschooling mom*

*I am feeling overwhelmed and depressed. I have 3 kiddos. First of all, my 5 and 2 year olds constantly run and make noise, noise, noise. I am always tripping over train tracks, etc., because they drag all of it out into the living room. I have tried to carve out times where they play in their room or take quiet time, but they are constantly running out. I feel like I am interrupted so many times that I can't keep a thought in my head, or get any time alone to sort out my thoughts. It is very discouraging to me. Another mom*

" . . . In quietness and in confidence shall be your strength . . ." (Isaiah 30:15). Here we read three words that can be very meaningful to a discouraged homeschooling mother: quietness, confidence, strength. We know that we want quietness of heart and confidence in the Lord; that will be our strength. However, sometimes it appears that the circumstances of noise, disorder, and pressure rob us of any quietness or confidence.

Quietness, confidence, and strength—it all comes back to our focus. Jesus said, "Take my yoke upon you, and learn of me; for I am meek and lowly in heart: and ye shall find rest unto your souls. For my yoke *is* easy, and my burden is light" (Matthew 11:29-30). God's Word tells me that Jesus' yoke is easy, and His burden is light. That is truth. When I feel a heavy burden or difficult yoke, then something has happened that isn't right. I can know for sure the problem lies with me and not with the Lord!

Perhaps the starting point for moving back to quietness, confidence, and strength is, "Be careful for nothing; but in every thing by prayer and supplication with thanksgiving let your requests be made known unto God. And the peace of God, which passeth all understanding, shall keep your hearts and minds through Christ Jesus" (Philippians 4:6-7). For my heart to remain quiet, I can't be anxious about anything. Therefore, Philippians 4:6-7 tells me that I am to lift up my concerns in prayer. Sometimes we may feel like we are doing this, but are we really? It could be that we think about our problems, we worry about our circumstances, and we try to figure out solutions. However, do we truly and simply pray about them? When we pray, they are no longer our problems, difficult circumstances, or solutions. They belong to the Lord. He can deal with them infinitely better than we can.

Paul knew what it was to have difficulties, ones beyond what most of us have experienced. "*We are* troubled on every side, yet not distressed; *we are* perplexed, but not in despair; Persecuted, but not forsaken; cast down, but not destroyed . . . For which cause we faint not; but though our outward man perish, yet the inward *man* is renewed day by day. For our light affliction, which is but for a moment, worketh for us a far more exceeding *and* eternal weight of glory; While we look not at the things which are seen, but at the things which are not seen: for the things which are seen *are* temporal; but the things which are not seen *are* eternal" (2 Corinthians 4:8-9, 16-18).

While the tasks of a homeschooling mom may at times seem mundane, wearisome, and constant, our eyes must be focused not on the temporal but on the eternal. What we are doing in our homes with our children has value that goes far beyond feeding and caring for children. We are impacting their souls for eternity. The opportunity is given to us to mold the hearts of these children for Jesus Christ. The noise, discouragement, and fatigue that may accompany this high calling of mothering are nothing in comparison with the eternal benefits we can reap. Just like Paul, if we are troubled on every side, we are not to be distressed. When we are perplexed, we don't want to be in despair. At times of feeling cast down, we know we aren't destroyed. Paul's secret in this was his total, wholehearted, complete commitment to the calling Jesus had given to him—his mission. That will be our secret at well—commitment to our mission as Christian mothers.

We are being renewed day by day, 2 Corinthians tells us. This doesn't happen apart from where our thoughts are. "If ye then be risen with Christ, seek those things which are above, where Christ sitteth on the right hand of God. Set your affection on things above, not on things on the earth" (Colossians 3:1-2). As we are seeking those things which are above and setting our affections on them, our thoughts will automatically be on Jesus. If we think about ourselves, we set ourselves up for feelings of pity, selfishness, and hopelessness. However, when our minds move to Jesus Christ, then there is joy. "As the Father hath loved me, so have I loved you: continue ye in my love. If ye keep my commandments, ye shall abide in my love; even as I have kept my Father's commandments, and abide in his love. These things have I spoken unto you, that my joy might remain in you, and *that* your joy might be full" (John 15:9-11).

If we are to let quietness and confidence be our strength, then we will choose to give our anxieties to the Lord Jesus in prayer. We will set our minds on what is eternal rather than what is temporal. May we be homeschooling moms who have a greater focus on the calling we have to impact our children for eternity than on our own difficulties or discomforts.

# Our Desire for a Meek and Quiet Spirit
## by Teri

Recently, I received this note and question from a home-schooling mom. I asked her if it would be okay for me to answer it with this month's Mom's Corner, and she agreed.

*I started to read the book* Homeschooling with a Meek and Quiet Spirit *by Teri, and I was wondering this. How do I have a quiet spirit when it seems that my blood is boiling from every little thing? I cry out to God. But I still feel that anxiety. I am really confused about this. Should I just force myself to be soft spoken and cry on the inside? How do I keep from exploding? I just feel like the warden. I was wondering if anyone else might suffer from this. It seems God just did not bless me with these qualities. I have always been loud and outspoken. A homeschooling mom*

I expect almost every one of us can relate to what this mom is saying, and perhaps each of us has also experienced her feelings. I remember hearing the Christian writer and speaker Elisabeth Elliot say something to the effect that she regularly asked the women in her audience if anyone was born with a meek and quiet spirit. She never had a hand go up. That tells me that God has not created women to be naturally meek and quiet. However, He does tell us in His Word that wives are to have a "meek and quiet spirit, which is in the sight of God of great price" (1 Peter 3:4).

Even though many of us, if not all, struggle because we aren't gifted with meek and quiet spirits, this doesn't mean this lack is something we accept and feel doomed to live with throughout our lives. God knew exactly what He was doing when He made each one of us, and yet He also gave us direction in His Word about how to deal with this. I would encourage this mom in several things, while reminding myself of them as well.

Make the desire for a meek and quiet spirit the focus of your time with the Lord each day and of your prayer for yourself. Search the Word, as you read it each day, for verses that help you toward a meek and quiet spirit. Look for ones that give you direction on what you should be doing and what you should not be doing. Here is an example.

"Rejoice in the Lord alway: *and* again I say, Rejoice" (Philippians 4:4). If I were to read this verse in my daily time with the Lord while my life was desperately lacking in being meek and quiet, I would copy this verse out and memorize it. It gives me information on how to have a meek and quiet spirit. I am always to rejoice in the Lord. It is extremely difficult to be angry with the children while rejoicing in the Lord. When I found myself in a stressful situation, I would repeat this verse to myself.

I wrote a four-part Mom's Corner series on anger (see March-June 2002). You might find some helpful information in them. There is much in this series that relates to anger and how to overcome it. I would also suggest that you finish reading *Homeschooling with a Meek and Quiet Spirit,* which you said you had begun.

Be sure to check your heart and relationship with your children. Scripture says, "He maketh the barren woman to keep house, *and to be* a joyful mother of children . . ." (Psalms 113:9). "That they may teach the young women to be sober, to love their husbands, to love their children" (Titus 2:4). That is our hearts' desire—to be joyful, loving mothers of children. However, if we feel like a warden with our children, then something is wrong. It is likely our focus has become ourselves and the personal difficulties and inconveniences of raising children, including disciplining them. This is true if we are continually experiencing anger toward our children.

To be joyful, loving mothers of children, our focus should be on the good of our children—their spiritual and personal growth. If we must stop what we are doing to correct a child, we will feel angry when we are thinking about ourselves and our need to accomplish a particular task. On the other hand, if the interruption causes me to thank God for the opportunity He has given me to bring this child up in the nurture and admonition of the Lord (Ephesians 6:4), then I can receive that interruption joyfully and lovingly.

Can you see how the way I think about a situation determines my response to it? When I am thinking of my time investment with my children as a part of bringing them up in the nurture and admonition of the Lord (Ephesians 6:4), then I see my role in a joyful, loving, positive light. I can accept the difficulties because my eyes are on the future outcome for my child's spiritual benefit rather than the immediate difficulty for me. When my thoughts are on my hardships and myself, then every struggle is cast in a negative light and becomes a burden driving me to anger.

The word "quiet" in meek and quiet doesn't refer to volume, as in loud versus soft. Rather, it is a heart attitude of quietness. It is a picture of resting in the Lord, not being anxious. Even though the word doesn't have to do with the volume of our voices, in a home, loudness associated with anger isn't healthy. So I would encourage you that, yes, it would be good to make yourself respond to the children in a very quiet voice. Scripture attests to this: "A soft answer turneth away wrath: but grievous words stir up anger" (Proverbs 15:1). This doesn't imply to me a loud voice. In dealing with the anger, I also strongly recommend Dr. S. M. Davis' teaching audio, *Freedom from the Spirit of Anger.*

I don't think the Lord wants us crying on the inside except to be calling out to Him. He is the One Who comforts us. "Blessed *be* God, even the Father of our Lord Jesus Christ, the Father of mercies, and the God of all comfort; Who comforteth us in all our tribulation, that we may be able to comfort them which are in any trouble, by the comfort wherewith we ourselves are comforted of God" (2

Corinthians 1:3-4). He is the One Who answers our prayers. "Be careful for nothing; but in every thing by prayer and supplication with thanksgiving let your requests be made known unto God. And the peace of God, which passeth all understanding, shall keep your hearts and minds through Christ Jesus" (Philippians 4:6-7). He is the One Who pours out grace into our lives and the lives of our families. ". . . My grace is sufficient for thee: for my strength is made perfect in weakness. Most gladly therefore will I rather glory in my infirmities, that the power of Christ may rest upon me. Therefore I take pleasure in infirmities, in reproaches, in necessities, in persecutions, in distresses for Christ's sake: for when I am weak, then am I strong" (2 Corinthians 12:9-10).

In our roles as mothers, we want to love, bless, and encourage our children. We would like them to live with mommies who are joyful and loving. A meek and quiet spirit leads us toward these goals, while anger destroys the relationships that are so dear to our hearts. Even though meek and quiet spirits don't come naturally to women, the Lord has shown us that this type of heart and thinking leads to peace, contentment, and blessing. No matter how lacking we have been in our lives regarding a meek and quiet spirit, I think Paul sums up our hope and our direction. "Brethren, I count not myself to have apprehended: but *this* one thing *I do*, forgetting those things which are behind, and reaching forth unto those things which are before, I press toward the mark for the prize of the high calling of God in Christ Jesus" (Philippians 3:13-14).

# Turn Your Heart
## *by Teri*

Malachi 4:6 says, "And he shall turn the heart of the fathers to the children, and the heart of the children to their fathers, lest I come and smite the earth with a curse." From this verse it is obvious that parents' hearts turned toward their children are important to the Lord Jesus. As Christian homeschooling moms, I expect each of us would say that we have our hearts turned toward our children because the Lord has called us to this job. If our children weren't our highest priority after our relationships with the Lord and then our relationships with our husbands, we wouldn't be homeschooling. It seems that homeschooling is a proof to us that our focus is on our children. But I wonder if this is always the case.

I have discovered that having my heart turned to my children involves a choice on my part. Homeschooling certainly plays a role in that. However, I can mechanically homeschool without my heart truly being turned to my children. For me the fruit of a focus on the children is observed through my attitude toward school. Do I look forward to school time as a joy, or do I dread it as an unpleasant task? Do I smile at my children, or is my forehead knit together in frustration with them? Do I speak encouraging words to my students, or do I criticize their attempts to accomplish their schoolwork?

No matter what my feelings are toward school, Scripture tells me that I have a responsibility in what I think about and how I act. The Lord wants me to have my heart turned to my children. 2 Corinthians 10:5 says, "Casting down imaginations, and every high thing that exalteth itself against the knowledge of God, and bringing into captivity every thought to the obedience of Christ." This tells me that if I am struggling with negative feelings about school, then I can take those thoughts captive and bring them into the obedience of Christ by thinking the truth of God's Word. "I can do all things through Christ which strengtheneth me" (Philippians 4:13).

If I feel down and discouraged, I can choose to replace those thoughts with the truth of the Word. "And he said unto me, My grace is sufficient for thee: for my strength is made perfect in weakness. Most gladly therefore will I rather glory in my infirmities, that the power of Christ may rest upon me. Therefore I take pleasure in infirmities, in reproaches, in necessities, in persecutions, in distresses for Christ's sake: for when I am weak, then am I strong" (2 Corinthians 12:9-10). If I feel like lashing out at the children rather than using sweet, encouraging words, I can recall, "The wise in heart shall be called prudent: and the sweetness of the lips increaseth learning" (Proverbs 16:21).

What might be other demonstrations that my heart is turned to my children? I believe one would be what I do with my time. Do I always stay busy with housework so that there is no time for the children? Am I prone to sit at the computer rather than reading a book to the children, playing a game with them, or teaching them a productive skill? What I have found in my life is that it is often easier to vacuum or do something at the computer than it is to spend time with the children. When my heart is turned toward myself, I spend my time doing what I want to do. However, when my heart is turned toward my children, I spend my time doing what they like to do with me or what is productive for them.

I want my children to remember a mommy filled with love for them that was evidenced in part by the time she spent with them. I desire that they grow to be adults recalling special shared memories rather than how clean our home was. Don't misunderstand me. I have time scheduled in my day and week to keep up with housekeeping. That is a part of the responsibility the Lord has given me as a keeper at home. However, I still have discretionary minutes and hours. When my heart is turned toward my children, I will invest that time in them rather than in selfish personal pursuits. "Verily, verily, I say unto you, Except a corn of wheat fall into the ground and die, it abideth alone: but if it die, it bringeth forth much fruit. He that loveth his life shall lose it; and he that hateth his life in this world shall keep it unto life eternal. If any man serve me, let him follow me; and where I am, there shall also my servant be: if any man serve me, him will *my* Father honour" (John 12:24-26).

Dr. S. M. Davis says that keeping our children's hearts is the most difficult task facing Christian parents today and that it should be their highest priority. Keeping our children's hearts begins with a mom turning her heart toward her children and a dad turning his heart toward his children. May we be moms who know the importance of turning our hearts toward our children. May we continually ask the Lord to turn our hearts toward our children. May we be submissive and obedient to the Lord as He prompts us to turn our hearts toward our children.

# Whose Strength?
## *by Teri*

Recently, this question was posed to me:

*I have such an overwhelming desire to be a godly wife and mom. I want to serve my husband and children by providing a clean, cheery home, fresh laundry, and hearty, home-cooked meals. I desire to do this with a pleasant attitude and a meek and quiet spirit. BUT this is soooooo far from reality!! I am consistently behind in all my housework and constantly struggling to stay on my schedule. It seems I either have a good attitude (and the house goes to pot), or I keep my chores done (and get snippy). I am praying for God to work through me and to make me the mom He desires. Yet I find it hard to distinguish between working as hard as I can while trusting God to make the change in me and pushing myself and pushing myself in my own strength. How can you tell the difference? A mom*

I believe this is a common feeling among homeschooling moms. I have thought these thoughts and asked these questions myself. Of course the place we want to go for answers would be God's Word. Does it offer any insights into this?

First, here is what God says about His role in our lives, particularly in our struggles.

"For my yoke *is* easy, and my burden is light" (Matthew 11:30).

"And he said unto me, My grace is sufficient for thee: for my strength is made perfect in weakness. Most gladly therefore will I rather glory in my infirmities, that the power of Christ may rest upon me. Therefore I take pleasure in infirmities, in reproaches, in necessities, in persecutions, in distresses for Christ's sake: for when I am weak, then am I strong" (2 Corinthians 12:9-10).

"For it is God which worketh in you both to will and to do of *his* good pleasure" (Philippians 2:13).

"I can do all things through Christ which strengtheneth me" (Philippians 4:13).

Our desires to be godly wives and mothers, to make our homes a haven for our families, and to have meek and quiet spirits are God-given desires. Scripture tells us that His grace is sufficient for us and that we can do all things through Christ Who strengthens us.

Our schedules are tools we can use to enable us to accomplish what the Lord Jesus has called us to do. That means we are to use them with a good attitude. A clean house and a sweet disposition are not mutually exclusive. When we are short-tempered as we go through our day, we can be assured we are doing it in our own strength. We know this because we are told in Galatians 5:22-23, "But the fruit of the Spirit is love, joy, peace, longsuffering, gentleness, goodness, faith, Meekness, temperance: against such there is no law."

When our spirits don't exhibit the fruit of the Spirit, the Lord can use our awareness of this sin as a chastening. He wants us to learn and grow through these situations. "And ye have forgotten the exhortation which speaketh unto you as unto children, My son, despise not thou the chastening of the Lord, nor faint when thou art rebuked of him: For whom the Lord loveth he chasteneth, and scourgeth every son whom he receiveth . . . Now no chastening for the present seemeth to be joyous, but grievous: nevertheless afterward it yieldeth the peaceable fruit of righteousness unto them which are exercised thereby" (Hebrews 12:5-6, 11).

Since God has called us to homeschool and keep up with our daily homemaking chores, our schedules are to be viewed as our helpers. The schedule needs to be prayerfully made up so that it allows time for each of the areas in which God has given us responsibility. If on a daily basis we are not keeping up in one or more areas, then we must go back to the Master and consult with Him. We know He doesn't give us more to do than time to do it.

Perhaps the schedule is flushing out our own sinful tendencies. Maybe we are behind in housework and struggling to stay on a schedule because we stay up late at night and then don't get up and going in the morning. It could be that we choose not to do what is on the schedule because we prefer to do other things. For example, the schedule may say it is time to do laundry, but that is my least favorite job. I decide to put it off, thinking I will make it up later. However, I don't feel any more like doing the laundry at another time, so it ends up going undone. These are simply indications that my focus is on my own wants, desires, likes, and pleasures rather than on obedience to Jesus Christ.

We have to remember we are called to be sober, to love our husbands, to love our children, to be discreet, chaste, keepers at home, good, and obedient to our own husbands (Titus 2:4-5). Therefore, our jobs as homeschooling moms and homemakers are acts of obedience to the Lord. When this is difficult for us, here is what we can read in Scripture that puts our battle with our failings into perspective: "Ye have not yet resisted unto blood, striving against sin" (Hebrews 12:4).

God asks us to work hard. I think we can look at Paul's life as an example of that. These verses show us his attitude toward the tasks that were before him. "Know ye not that they which run in a race run all, but one receiveth the prize? So run, that ye may obtain. And every man that striveth for the mastery is temperate in all things. Now they *do it* to obtain a corruptible crown; but we an incorruptible. I therefore so run, not as uncertainly; so fight I, not as one that beateth the air: But I keep under my body, and bring *it* into subjection: lest that by any means, when I have preached to others, I myself should be a castaway" (1 Corinthians 9:24-27).

Paul shows us that he had learned to run the race and strive for mastery while at the same time resting in the Lord. I believe these verses give us a clue as to how he accomplished this. "*We are* troubled on every side, yet not distressed; *we are* perplexed, but not in despair; Persecuted, but not forsaken; cast down, but not destroyed . . . For which cause we faint not; but though our outward man perish, yet the inward *man* is renewed day by day. For our light affliction, which is but for a moment, worketh for us a far more exceeding *and* eternal weight of glory; While we look not at the things which are seen, but at the things which are not seen: for the things which are seen *are* temporal; but the things which are not seen *are* eternal" (2 Corinthians 4:8-9, 16-18). "Set your affection on things above, not on things on the earth" (Colossians 3:2).

Here is the problem again, *Yet I find it hard to distinguish between working as hard as I can while trusting God to make the change in me and pushing myself and pushing myself in my own strength.* When we are obedient to the Lord with our focus on Him, we are not pushing in our own strength. Everything good we do is through Him. All of our irritation, negative responses, frustration, anger, worry, and strife is the outcome of pushing in our own strength for our own agenda.

Perhaps these two verses sum it up for us. "Brethren, I count not myself to have apprehended: but *this* one thing *I do*, forgetting those things which are behind, and reaching forth unto those things which are before, I press toward the mark for the prize of the high calling of God in Christ Jesus" (Philippians 3:13-14). May we see our service to our families as obedience to our Lord Jesus Christ and choose that obedience with a willing heart.

# Wise or Foolish Wives?
## by Teri

As Christian wives, we will be making decisions each day that affect our relationships with our husbands. Here is an example of the simple interactions that occur and often cause us the most difficulty. Susie (not her real name), a wife and mother, writes:

*What should we as wives expect in the way of being a part of decisions made in the home? I wholeheartedly agree that our husbands have the final say in all matters, and they have the right to consult us or not. My question is mainly: is it unbiblical to request that my husband come to me before he announces to the whole family a decision he has made? This is not necessarily so I have the opportunity to change his mind but because he will often make changes to plans or make decisions, and I feel like an outsider. I don't have a chance to work through any feelings or problems I see with a problem before he has already told the kids and me. It feels insulting to me that he would tell them and me at the same time.*

*Recently my husband made an abrupt change of plans. The children were disappointed, and I was too. I reacted improperly, and the whole night was miserable. My contention was that if he had made me a part of the change from the start, I could have gotten over my problems and been on his side much easier. Seeing their disappointment coupled with my own and the fact that he didn't bring me in on it was totally overwhelming.*

*The next day we had another major situation that he wanted to take care of in a certain way. He brought me in private and told me what he wanted to do "so I wouldn't have a fit in front of the kids." I had some-*

*thing different in mind, and we were able to discuss it. He gave in to me because he saw my point. I don't expect him to give in to me every time nor do I think it is feasible to do this every time. But this is the way I would prefer things to work. Is this biblical or not?*

I think for Christian women, what Susie described here is a very real situation that many, if not most of us, have faced. It presents us a great opportunity to delve into the husband-and-wife issues at hand here. These are not the extremes of abuse but rather the kinds of everyday happenings that occur in Christian marriages. As wives, we must biblically decide how we will respond. I write this Mom's Corner because the area of submission is still a regular battle for me with my flesh. Right now I need the reminders I will write in this article. I think I make two steps forward only to soon find myself at least one step back again.

First, let's look at Susie's situation where her husband sprang a disagreeable change of direction on the children and her without discussing it with her beforehand. Certainly, the key to a loving, growing husband-and-wife relationship is communication. Generally, decisions will be discussed by a husband and wife and agreed upon. However, it certainly isn't beyond reason to expect times to arise where prior discussion hasn't happened. It may be that the time for talking wasn't available. It could be that the husband doesn't think the situation is major enough to warrant taking communication time. He may feel sure his wife will be in sync with him, so he doesn't see the need for prior discussion. But if she is unhappily surprised, then what?

This becomes our opportunity to test our hearts. It is easy to submit when we agree. It is hardly submission at all, is it? The crisis comes when we disagree. What kind of response do we want from our children if they don't care for what we have asked them to do? Of course we prefer a happy smile and cheerful compliance. We have the chance to model this for our children in these everyday situations with our husbands.

I am ashamed to say that my displeasure, which is evident to both my husband and my children, is seldom, if ever, necessary. It generally rises from my personal biases. We aren't talking sin issues here, but rather preferences. My reactions show my pride, not my meek and quiet spirit. They are a reflection of my continued selfishness and need to control to get my own way.

In Susie's story, she tells us of her reaction to her husband's decision: *I reacted improperly, and the whole night was miserable.* As I read her story, though, rather than repenting of her unsubmissive attitude, I see Susie wanting to blame her husband for her sin—trying to make it his fault rather than hers. I struggle with this so much. In my pride, I don't want to be wrong and, worse yet, to be at fault. I want to find a way to pin my failure on something Steve didn't do right. Then I don't feel so bad or view my wrong reaction as sin. I have an excuse for it.

I would encourage us to accept our responsibility for our failures and not put the blame elsewhere. It is nothing more than my pride that won't let me simply say, "My reaction was wrong. Will you please forgive me?" I want God's grace in my life to help me be a wife that honors, respects, and submits to her husband. What does God say about pride? ". . . God resisteth the proud, but giveth grace unto the humble" (James 4:6). I want and need God's grace. This verse tells me that His grace is given to me through my humility—saying I was wrong and asking for forgiveness—and that He resists me when I am proud—making excuses for my sin or blaming it on someone else.

We want our husbands to be strong, godly leaders. However, we often encourage the exact opposite tendency by our own words, attitudes, and actions. Consider the second situation Susie describes. Her husband does what she asks him to do by sharing his plans with her privately before he tells the children. Rather than using this information to help her have a positive attitude in front of the children, she expresses her disagreement with his direction. Wow, could I relate to that scenario. My own words don't match my actions. Instead of putting up a fight, Susie's husband goes with what she wants. I wouldn't be surprised if he felt he was in a situation where no matter what he did, he couldn't please his wife. Steve has told me that when we were in the midst of a similar situation. We wives seem to struggle so much with letting go and truly letting our husbands lead.

Scripture seems to be full of admonition and warnings of what happens to us, who are wives, and those around us if we choose this path of controlling:

"A foolish woman *is* clamorous: *she is* simple, and knoweth nothing" (Proverbs 9:13).

"Every wise woman buildeth her house: but the foolish plucketh it down with her hands" (Proverbs 14:1).

"*It is* better to dwell in a corner of the housetop, than with a brawling woman in a wide house" (Proverbs 21:9). (Proverbs 25:24 says almost the same thing.)

"*It is* better to dwell in the wilderness, than with a contentious and an angry woman" (Proverbs 21:19).

"A continual dropping in a very rainy day and a contentious woman are alike" (Proverbs 27:15).

Then we have these verses, which give a wife a picture of an obedient walk with Jesus Christ:

"Wives, submit yourselves unto your own husbands, as unto the Lord. For the husband is the head of the wife, even as Christ is the head of the church: and he is the saviour of the body. Therefore as the church is subject unto Christ, so *let* the wives *be* to their own husbands in every thing" (Ephesians 5:22-24).

"Wives, submit yourselves unto your own husbands, as it is fit in the Lord" (Colossians 3:18).

"That they may teach the young women to be sober, to love their husbands, to love their children, *To be* discreet, chaste, keepers at home, good, obedient to their own husbands, that the word of God be not blasphemed" (Titus 2:4-5).

"Likewise, ye wives, *be* in subjection to your own husbands; that, if any obey not the word, they also may without the word be won by the conversation of the wives" (1 Peter 3:1).

We have a choice set before us each day. We can be wise women who build our houses, or we can be foolish ones who pluck them down. I pray that we will consider well how we can build our houses to bring joy and peace to those who live there. Who do we want to please? Jesus Christ? Our husbands? Ourselves? It is our decision. May we be women who take joy in obedience to Jesus Christ through submission to our husbands.

# Where Is the Fruit of Child Training?
## by Teri

Let me share with you a story from a mom with a burdened heart.

*I LOVE my son so much. He is the oldest of 4 boys. We constantly get compliments about what a sweet boy he is or what a BIG heart he has. But, as his mother I feel like a failure. He completely lacks self-discipline, diligence, and independence.*

*If I sit and do school WITH him he does a GREAT job and does it fairly quickly. BUT if I send him to his room to work independently he will either 1) take all day because he just sits there and daydreams OR 2) he rushes through it and does a really sloppy job.*

*We have spent YEARS training this child. My husband has literally taken him into the kitchen and cleaned WITH him step by step, showing him how to do it SEVERAL times. He has done a good job when he knows a reward awaits him (not perfect, but good), but for the most part he tries to get by with as little as possible.*

*If I don't sit on him and make him brush his teeth or take a shower, he won't. If I tell him his hair needs to be combed, he will go grab a hat.*

*He started crying tonight when I corrected him for doing a poor job. He said he feels like there is nothing he does well. Truthfully, I can't think of anything he does well or that I am proud of as far as skill goes. He has a GREAT heart, but well meaning intentions will get him NOWHERE!*
*Concerned Mom*

What Concerned Mom is sharing about her son is something we commonly hear from moms. Often the mom is talking about a child that is seven years old or older. Perhaps this becomes an issue at this age because we begin to have some expectations of seeing the results of our child training by this time.

Our first step, when dealing with any difficult situation, and especially those concerning our children, is to pray. "Be careful for nothing; but in every thing by prayer and supplication with thanksgiving let your requests be made known unto God. And the peace of God, which passeth all understanding, shall keep your hearts and minds through Christ Jesus" (Philippians 4:6-7). We pray for the Lord to work in and through the needs in our children's lives. We also ask what God's purposes are in the struggles. How does He want us to address them? What direction and solutions does He have? What Scripture applies?

Children take time to mature. "When I was a child, I spake as a child, I understood as a child, I thought as a child: but when I became a man, I put away childish things" (1 Corinthians 13:11). What if Concerned Mom thinks back to her son at age five? I expect he has made some progress in these difficult areas since then, maybe even significant progress. Now, what if she remembers back to when he was nine? Again, he will have made progress—perhaps not as much as she would like, but progress.

What we want to focus on is the spiritual and character growth that is taking place in our children rather than the distance they have left to go. This perspective will help our hearts be encouraged and grateful to the Lord for what He has been doing in our children's lives rather than discouraged over what still should be accomplished. "In every thing give thanks: for this is the will of God in Christ Jesus concerning you" (1 Thessalonians 5:18). Concerned Mom's son is a "sweet boy with a big heart." A heart for the Lord and others is one of the major goals most Christian parents have for their children. Being thankful for the spiritual qualities she sees in her son will give Concerned Mom a starting point for giving her son positive feedback.

I would encourage Concerned Mom to continue working with her son in the areas where she sees her son should improve. Scripture admonishes us that we are to "bring them up in the nurture and admonition of the Lord" (Ephesians 6:4). This is a long-term project the Lord has given us. Concerned Mom hasn't failed but rather the Lord is making her aware of continued needs in her son's life. This isn't to discourage her but to give her direction in where to concentrate her efforts. Her commitment to helping her son is very important. From what she has shared, Concerned Mom is on the right track in teaching her son by showing him what to do, giving him responsibility, and then having consequences if he doesn't follow through.

I would encourage Concerned Mom to find ways to help her son learn the steps to thoroughness for what he needs to do. She can make up checklists for him since she sees that he requires step-by-step direction to accomplish a task. Giving her son a scheduled time for particular jobs with deadlines and consequences may be useful. In addition, it is important to be consistent on a daily basis for an extended period of time. It is common to give up on what we are trying to do before it has time to work.

Concerned Mom could let her son take all day to do his schoolwork, without emotional anxiety over it. He likely won't continue to take all day, and if he does, then she doesn't need be concerned about it. It was his choice. When he tires of spending all day doing school, he will work harder to stick with it and get it done earlier.

When Concerned Mom's son doesn't do something well, she can simply send him back to do it again. Remember that a mom should do all of this with a meek and quiet spirit rather than with anger or resignation. Eventually, the son will decide to do a better job in the first place. I believe a key is being unemotional in dealing with all of this. Simply be matter of fact.

Another key ingredient in this process is keeping our children's hearts, the subject of our book, *Keeping Our Children's Hearts*. In this case, I would suggest that Concerned Mom make it a priority to work with her son on some of his chores on a regular basis. She and

her husband can spend time with him doing the tasks that are difficult. She can reinforce details of the job. Working together is a part
of building relationships. While they work, Concerned Mom can
talk to her son about his problems—not strictly when the crisis is
flaring but at other times as well.

Concerned Mom will be able to encourage her son that keeping
these issues before him to be worked on is a positive step. What
about using his failures to help him see his dependence on Jesus
Christ and need to rely on Him? "I can do all things through Christ
which strengtheneth me" (Philippians 4:13). These parents can
explain to their son that his reactions to failure and correction show
pride in his life. ". . . God resisteth the proud, but giveth grace unto
the humble" (James 4:6).

Looking at verses in Proverbs that have to do with a son
receiving correction would be a good study to do with a twelve-year-
old boy. "A wise son *heareth* his father's instruction: but a scorner
heareth not rebuke" (Proverbs 13:1). Keeping the relationships
strong, with lots of loving communication, hugs, back patting, and
enjoyable time together, is vitally important.

At age twelve, this boy's family still has several prime years to
work with their son. I think Concerned Mom should be encouraged.
What she is doing will produce results. Her priority is to stay
prayerful, loving, and consistent. She wants to find things for which
she can praise her son. It might not seem like there are any, but if she
thinks about it and looks for them, they will be there—starting with
him being sweet and having a big heart. She wants to make sure that
praise comes out loud and clear.

I believe most homeschooling moms have areas in their children's lives where they know growth is needed. May this be our
theme verse as we face and tackle these necessary issues. "And let us
not be weary in well doing: for in due season we shall reap, if we faint
not" (Galatians 6:9). The fruit comes from years of praying, loving,
teaching, consistency, and investing in the lives of our children.

# Benefiting from Summer Chores
## by Teri

This week seven-year-old Mary, eleven-year-old Anna, and I spent fifteen minutes each day polishing kitchen cabinets. That is a task that looked daunting to me, although I am serious about trying to tackle it at least once a year. My engineer husband has convinced me that if I want my kitchen cabinets to stay nice, I need to take care of them properly. As we evaluated this need and my time, we realized that this was the perfect opportunity to include the girls in a job where they could work with Mom. Each day it seemed that our fifteen minutes was up almost as soon as we started. Our time was filled with happy chatter, typical of mommies and their little girls.

After two days, our nine-year-old son said he would like to join us in our project. At that point, I headed to the store to purchase two more bottles of furniture polish. As we polished and buffed, I asked the children if they could explain the purpose of what we were doing. They did well in knowing that the polish cleaned and protected the wood. Next I questioned them on why we wanted to take care of the cabinets. They decided it was so that they would stay in good condition and look pretty. I presented them with a third question, asking why we wouldn't just let them get messed up and then replace them. That question was a stumper for them. In their minds, it sounded reasonable just to have Daddy buy new cabinets when they no longer looked acceptable. This headed us into a discussion of being good stewards of what Jesus has given to us. That evening in our family Bible time, stewardship came up. Jesse piped in with, "Oh, yes, Mommy talked to us about being good stewards this morning when we were working on the cabinets."

A simple fifteen minutes of time with my children for several days has netted our family many positive benefits. (For further information, see *Managers of Their Homes*.) The girls have learned a skill they may need in their own homes one day. They are being taught in one of the areas that Titus 2:4-5 tells the older women to teach the younger women, and that is in being a keeper at home. My son experienced the pleasure found in volunteering to give of his time to help another—to take joy in serving rather than having to be served. We enjoyed fellowship and spiritual discussions. In addition, the cabinets will all be polished with just a few more days of work.

Summer, if you don't school through it, is the perfect time to dig into household cleaning and organizing tasks that don't fit into normal homeschooling days and weeks. Rather than dreading these jobs, we can enlist the help of the children and discover benefits similar to those our family found in our cabinet-polishing. My girls didn't complain at all when I explained to them what we were going to do—not on the first day or on subsequent days. They now look at the cabinets with a sense of accomplishment in their eyes. I expect they will be even more careful in the future to have dry hands when they open the cabinet doors and to use the handles. They have seen firsthand how much work it takes to keep up the cabinets. They don't want to make more work.

Consider jobs in your home that need to be done and figure out how to work with your children. Our thirteen-year-old and fifteen-year-old sons are taking over the boys' bathroom cleaning from their twenty-five-year-old brother, who will add one more sibling to the two he is already teaching piano to this year in lieu of extra cleaning chores. The boys will trade off weeks to do the bathroom cleaning. This week I cleaned their bathroom, explaining step by step what I was doing. For several weeks, I plan to be an observer of the bathroom cleaning until I feel they are consistently doing a good, thorough job. The boys are motivated to learn to maintain their bathroom well because, if they do, Daddy may consider it for a needed remodeling.

Here are some verses that have helped Steve and me to see that teaching our children to work will be helpful to them as they grow up. "Go to the ant, thou sluggard; consider her ways, and be wise: Which having no guide, overseer, or ruler, Provideth her meat in the summer, *and* gathereth her food in the harvest. How long wilt thou sleep, O sluggard? when wilt thou arise out of thy sleep? *Yet* a little sleep, a little slumber, a little folding of the hands to sleep: So shall thy poverty come as one that travelleth, and thy want as an armed man" (Proverbs 6:6-11). "The soul of the sluggard desireth, and *hath* nothing: but the soul of the diligent shall be made fat" (Proverbs 13:4). "The sluggard will not plow by reason of the cold; *therefore* shall he beg in harvest, and *have* nothing" (Proverbs 20:4).

Steve and I know how much more we enjoy a work project when we can do it together. We have some fond memories of painting rooms in houses we lived in when first married. Steve did the rolling; I did the trim. We worked until we collapsed at night and talked the whole time. The same would be true for our children. Doing a project with Dad or Mom helps the time pass quickly while experiencing the joy of fellowship.

For many homeschoolers, we have several more weeks of summer left before beginning our new school year. I encourage you to target a bit of this time for working on cleaning and organizing tasks with your children. It is also a prime opportunity to teach them how to do new chores. Working together makes the children more willing participants. May we be moms who help our children toward diligence and away from the curse of being a sluggard.

# School Year Preparations
## by Teri

For many homeschooling moms, the beginning of a new school year is just ahead! In this Mom's Corner, I would like to share with you three suggestions for making the coming school year the success that you want it to be.

As I approached the first day of school last year, I was dreading it! I wasn't ready for the changes full-time school would bring. I knew that if my spirit wasn't right, my children's wouldn't be either. I cried out to the Lord concerning the state of my heart, and He answered me.

The Lord encouraged me to set aside the Saturday night before our first day of school as a time to dedicate the school year to Him. I worked on Friday and Saturday to complete all the practical, weekend tasks I had to do so that my Saturday evening would be free. I shared with my family what I was planning and received my husband's blessing. As I waited for my evening with the Lord, I jotted down areas that I wanted to pray about.

After dinner that evening, I gathered up school books, schedules, assignments—anything that had to do with our school. I carried them into my bedroom and stacked them in piles. I pulled out my prayer notes and started praying for our school, for Steve, and for myself.

Then, child by child, I placed their school materials in front of me. I thumbed through them and made notes as to what I thought might be difficult areas for the child. I noted that on my prayer list. Then I prayed for each child and their school year. If the Lord brought ideas to mind during the prayer time, I paused, made a note, and then continued on.

I had such a sweet, sweet time with the Lord that it completely transformed my heart toward beginning school again. I would counsel any homeschooling mom, whether she is excited about her school year or dreading it, to set aside a special time to pray about and dedicate her school to the Lord. This might even be something a husband and wife could do together in addition to Mom praying alone.

Psalms 37:5 says, "Commit thy way unto the LORD; trust also in him; and he shall bring *it* to pass." I certainly saw the fruit of this as I purposed, in a different way than I ever had in the past, to commit my school year to Him. I am planning to do this every year!

The second area I would like to encourage you in is chore assignments. This would include making a list of each child's chores, scheduling a time for them to accomplish the chores, setting aside time for you to check their chores, and agreeing upon consequences when the chores aren't done properly. I have found that one of the most draining aspects of homeschooling is not the schooling itself, but getting children to fulfill their household responsibilities before and after school. For more information about chores, see our book, *Managers of Their Chores: A Practical Guide to Children's Chores* (see Additional Resources, page 385).

What do you do if the child assigned to wash breakfast dishes doesn't do them or takes five times longer than he should? You need to have thought through the possibilities and have consequences in place so that you aren't frustrated when this occurs. We can handle failure in our children calmly when the consequences have been planned out for future use.

When assigning chores and consequences, try to keep personalities in mind. Don't give your dawdler a mission-critical chore that must be accomplished before school can start. If he is the only choice for the job, try giving him a "first school activity" that can easily be made up in his free time later in the day, since some days he might have to spend that slot of school time doing his chore.

The last area I would like address has to do with curriculum. Having prayed about what to use for school this year, be wary of any dissatisfaction you might experience toward your curriculum. The Lord may have a different purpose for those materials that don't seem to be working out as you expected.

When something isn't going well, we are very quick to desire a curriculum change. I know, because I have "been there" many times during the past sixteen years of homeschooling! Perhaps your six-year-old's phonics program isn't working out the way you envisioned. It may be that you should lead your child through at a much, much slower pace while he matures and gradually grasps the material. Could it be your child needs to learn, even at six, to push himself beyond his comfort zone? Maybe you are to learn an extra measure of patience. We can rob our children, and ourselves, of these valuable lessons by "jumping" curriculum too quickly.

I pray that as we enter a new homeschooling year we will seek the Lord on our knees before we ever start the first day of school. May we look for His solutions in helping our children learn responsibility. May we also rest in His purposes for the curriculum choices He has led us to make.

If you would like to view our current school schedule, just go to: www.titus2.com/d-schedule.htm

# The Importance of Daily Time with Jesus
## *by Teri*

It was a normal Friday morning of cleaning and piano practice for the Maxwell family. Just before lunch, I sat down to do some computer work. Sarah called everyone to eat, and I jumped up with gusto. Between me and my meal lay the vacuum cleaner which I abruptly crashed into with my bare foot. Immediately I experienced that excruciating pain one has when they clobber a toe into an immobile object. In this case, though, the pain didn't subside as quickly as normal because my little toe was indeed broken.

This mishap curtailed my ability to walk with Steve in the early mornings after our personal Bible time—a custom we have enjoyed for many years. I sorely missed the exercise my walk afforded me and the talks Steve and I have while walking. However, I gained a wonderful benefit from those extra minutes of being home each morning. I worked at making myself get up with Steve at our normal time, although the temptation was to stay in bed and sleep a bit more. By maintaining my usual schedule, I was able to spend what had been walking time for more Bible reading and prayer. Spending over an hour with the Lord each morning is something I only dream of because generally a half hour a day for my quiet time of Bible reading and prayer has been realistic and workable in my life. That extra time with the Lord each morning for six weeks was just what I needed.

It is not uncommon for a mom to come up to me after a workshop and want to discuss specific difficulties that she is dealing with in her life. After I listen to her problems, I try to make my first question: "Are you having daily, personal time to read your Bible and pray, knowing that is the key and most important starting point?"

More often than not the answer will be that she isn't spending time with the Lord and that she realizes this is what needs to change before anything else will.

I hear over and over again from moms that they struggle with getting up in the morning to spend time with the Lord. Usually there is a reason why she can't awaken early enough to have Bible reading and prayer. It may be not going to bed at a reasonable hour the night before, a sick child up in the night, a nursing baby, or simply the enjoyment of staying in bed. While it is true that most of these reasons cost us sleep, we also have to make decisions about our use of time based upon our priorities. If we had an important doctor appointment after a late night, we would make ourselves get up so we wouldn't miss the appointment.

Before Steve and I became serious about our daily, personal Bible reading and prayer time, we had to come to the point of seeing our need for and the value of this time. We would say we wanted to rise early enough to spend time with the Lord, but we were quick to let our many excuses for not getting up give us the freedom to stay in bed.

When I was in the years of pregnancy and nursing babies, I had scheduled a nap in the afternoon. This gave me the security of knowing that if I was really tired from getting up early in the morning, I had time set aside later to take a nap. With a newborn, I would sometimes change my Bible reading and prayer time to early afternoon, although it was not my preference nor did I want to leave it this way for long. Still, I could sleep in the morning and also rest knowing I would have time with the Lord, because it was scheduled for right after the children laid down for their afternoon naps. I believe it is best to have time with the Lord first thing in the morning, but when that isn't happening, another time that works is better than not having the time at all.

"All scripture *is* given by inspiration of God, and *is* profitable for doctrine, for reproof, for correction, for instruction in righteousness: That the man of God may be perfect, throughly furnished unto all good works" (2 Timothy 3:16-17). Isn't this our heart's desire: that

God would thoroughly equip us for every task He has called us to do? This verse tells us that God's Word is the key to this equipping. It will teach and correct us. Yet, it is easy to say the right thing—that we want God's grace to direct and help us through our days—but fail to do what we need to do to make it possible for Him.

Psalms 119 is a beautiful chapter showing us the value of Scripture to our daily lives. I challenge you to read through it several times. Let's look at some of these verses to see how God's Word meets the needs we are experiencing.

Do we struggle with sin? "Thy word have I hid in mine heart, that I might not sin against thee" (Psalms 119:11).

Do we need counsel on a difficult area of our lives? "Thy testimonies also *are* my delight *and* my counselors" (Psalms 119:24).

Am I afflicted in some way? "This *is* my comfort in my affliction: for thy word hath quickened me" (Psalms 119:50).

Do I want to be wise and make good decisions? "Teach me good judgment and knowledge: for I have believed thy commandments" (Psalms 119:66). "Thou through thy commandments hast made me wiser than mine enemies: for they *are* ever with me. I have more understanding than all my teachers: for thy testimonies *are* my meditation. I understand more than the ancients, because I keep thy precepts" (Psalms 119:98-100).

Do I need comforting? "Let, I pray thee, thy merciful kindness be for my comfort, according to thy word unto thy servant. Let thy tender mercies come unto me, that I may live: for thy law *is* my delight" (Psalms 119:76-77).

Do I need to know how to make it through a trial? "Unless thy law *had been* my delights, I should then have perished in mine affliction" (Psalms 119:92).

Do I need direction? "Thy word *is* a lamp unto my feet, and a light unto my path" (Psalms 119:105).

Do I need rest and protection? "Thou *art* my hiding place and my shield: I hope in thy word. Depart from me, ye evildoers: for I will keep the commandments of my God" (Psalms 119:114-115).

I know what it is to be busy, homeschool, have a large family, be pregnant, be nursing a baby, have sick children, and have more to do than there seems available time. Yet I am convinced that there is nothing I could have done with that time I spent each day with the Lord Jesus in Bible reading and prayer that would have been any more beneficial to my life, my husband's life, my children's lives, or my homeschooling. I have a dear friend who has gotten up for years in the middle of the night to read her Bible and pray. It is the most consistent, uninterrupted time of day for her. Then she goes back to bed and to sleep. If Bible reading and prayer is truly important to us, we will find time for it and then be disciplined to keep it.

I am convinced that it is the heart cry of homeschooling moms to live in such a way that will honor and glorify the Lord Jesus Christ. Plus, we want to guide our children in the paths of righteousness as well. May I challenge each of us that the starting place for this—the place to begin dealing with depression, anger, laziness, impatience, fear, anxiety (I share more about these issues in *Homeschooling with a Meek and Quiet Spirit)*, and every other need we have—is daily spending time with the Lord. It is likely that the busier we are—and the more we struggle with taking time to read our Bibles and pray—the needier we are for this time. May we each determine, with God's help, that we will be committed to making Bible reading and prayer as high a priority as eating our meals.

# Praying for Our Children
## *by Teri*

As Steve and I continue down this parenting path the Lord started us on twenty-eight years ago, we become more and more convinced of the necessity of prayer for our children. Reading through the New Testament recently, I was reminded of the example Paul has set for us in his prayer life. I believe we can learn much from Paul that will apply to us as moms praying for our children.

Paul prayed constantly for the churches and individuals to whom he wrote. Please bear with me in reading through all of the following verses, because I believe they powerfully show us the heart and passion of a man committed to his spiritual children as we want to be committed to our natural children.

"First, I thank my God through Jesus Christ for you all, that your faith is spoken of throughout the whole world. For God is my witness, whom I serve with my spirit in the gospel of his Son, that without ceasing I make mention of you always in my prayers" (Romans 1:8-9).

"Cease not to give thanks for you, making mention of you in my prayers" (Ephesians 1:16).

"We give thanks to God and the Father of our Lord Jesus Christ, praying always for you" (Colossians 1:3).

"We give thanks to God always for you all, making mention of you in our prayers" (1 Thessalonians 1:2).

"Wherefore also we pray always for you, that our God would count you worthy of *this* calling, and fulfil all the good pleasure of *his* goodness, and the work of faith with power: That the name of our Lord Jesus Christ may be glorified in you, and ye in him, according to the grace of our God and the Lord Jesus Christ" (2 Thessalonians 1:11-12).

"I thank God, whom I serve from *my* forefathers with pure conscience, that without ceasing I have remembrance of thee in my prayers night and day" (2 Timothy 1:3).

"I thank my God, making mention of thee always in my prayers" (Philemon 1:4).

"I thank my God upon every remembrance of you, Always in every prayer of mine for you all making request with joy, For your fellowship in the gospel from the first day until now; Being confident of this very thing, that he which hath begun a good work in you will perform *it* until the day of Jesus Christ" (Philippians 1:3-6).

Paul knows that his example is a positive one: "Those things, which ye have both learned, and received, and heard, and seen in me, do: and the God of peace shall be with you" (Philippians 4:9). Yet, look where his dependence remains in his heart's desire for his spiritual children to grow in holiness and godliness. He is continually lifting his churches and converts to Jesus in prayer. He isn't relying on his own wisdom, strength, or example. He knows his total dependence on the Lord and the dependence his "children" will need as well. It would seem to me that of all teachers, Paul would have had the least need of anyone to spend that amount of time and energy in prayer. However, he was completely aware of his weakness and the weakness of those he loved. He was continually crying out to the Lord for those "children." Isn't that true in our lives and our children's lives as well—aren't we all weak and needy?

*Strong's Concordance* tells us that "without ceasing" means exactly that: "without intermission, incessantly, without ceasing." "Always" means "at all times, always, ever." To me these verses and words indicate a mind preoccupied with prayer. Are we praying for our children when we wake up in the morning, when we are working, when we are with them, when we are doing school, when we are in the car, when we go to bed at night, when they are struggling, when they are disobedient, when they are unkind, when they are peaceful, when they are helpful—without ceasing?

My tendency is to make excuses for my lack of prayerfulness. I am too busy. I can't do school and pray for the children at the same time. I have a one-track mind. Am I busier than Paul was? I don't think so. Wasn't he always preaching, ministering, and serving in addition to working as a tentmaker? Paul was a busy man. My excuses are nothing but excuses. We do what is truly important to us.

As I have evaluated in my life how to make continually praying for my children a reality, three things have stood out to me. First, I must make this a prayer of my heart, acknowledging my need for help in this area and asking God to strengthen me for the task and to bring my children constantly to mind for prayer. I want Him to put on my heart what I should pray for my children as well. Second, I want to feel the urgency of the necessity of never-ceasing prayer for my children. Have you ever had a dear friend or loved one diagnosed with cancer? What happens to your prayer life in regard to that person? In the same way, as I truly see the importance of prayer for my children, it comes more naturally to my heart. Third, I should develop the discipline of prayer. I have discovered that my mind easily gravitates to simply thinking rather than to prayer. I have to make a conscious effort and decision to bring my thoughts around to prayer when I realize I am just thinking rather than praying.

After praying always for my children, the next challenge Paul gives me is to fill my prayers with thanksgiving, just as his prayers are filled with thankfulness for his spiritual children. Look back at the verses we read. How many of them have the word "thank" in them? Here are a few more.

"I thank my God always on your behalf, for the grace of God which is given you by Jesus Christ" (1 Corinthians 1:4).

"We are bound to thank God always for you, brethren . . ." (2 Thessalonians 1:3).

Think about what gratitude to the Lord for our children does as we pray for them. Thankfulness springs from a joyful heart. If we are continually thanking God for our children, it is hard to feel unhappy or angry with them. It prompts us to see our children in a positive light. It gives us hope for the areas of their failure and places their needs before the Lord. Spiritually, gratitude puts our thoughts where they ought to be—on the Lord rather than on anything negative about our children or ourselves. Being thankful for our children allows us to be in a place of rest and contentment concerning them rather than dissatisfaction.

Perhaps as we are challenged by Paul's example of praying without ceasing for our children, our praying for them will be the most important step we can take in the turning of our hearts toward those children. It will be a true focus on them, and the best investment we can make in their lives. It may also be the most significant gift of love and sacrifice we could give to them. Will we be mothers who choose to pray without ceasing for our children? Will our prayers be filled with thankfulness for each of them?

# Praying Scripture for Our Children
## *by Teri*

Praying for our children is a high spiritual priority in the life of Christian mothers. We know that the work of spiritual growth in our children's lives is accomplished by the power of the Lord Jesus. "For it is God which worketh in you both to will and to do of *his* good pleasure" (Philippians 2:13). As an example for us in praying for our children, we have many Scriptures that tell us that Paul prayed for his spiritual children without ceasing and with thanksgiving. If we are to invest heavily in prayer for our children, what exactly will we pray?

"For the word of God *is* quick, and powerful, and sharper than any twoedged sword, piercing even to the dividing asunder of soul and spirit, and of the joints and marrow, and *is* a discerner of the thoughts and intents of the heart" (Hebrews 4:12). "All scripture *is* given by inspiration of God, and *is* profitable for doctrine, for reproof, for correction, for instruction in righteousness: That the man of God may be perfect, throughly furnished unto all good works" (2 Timothy 3:16-17). I believe these verses show us that Scripture is an excellent basis for some of our prayers for our children.

My two favorite Scriptures for prayer are ones Paul prayed. "For this cause I bow my knees unto the Father of our Lord Jesus Christ, Of whom the whole family in heaven and earth is named, That he would grant you, according to the riches of his glory, to be strengthened with might by his Spirit in the inner man; That Christ may dwell in your hearts by faith; that ye, being rooted and grounded in love, May be able to comprehend with all saints what *is* the breadth, and length, and depth, and height; And to know the love of Christ, which passeth knowledge, that ye might be filled with all the fulness of God. Now unto him that is able to do exceeding abundantly above all that we ask or think, according to the power that worketh in us, Unto him *be* glory in the church by Christ Jesus throughout all ages, world without end. Amen" (Ephesians 3:14-21).

"For this cause we also, since the day we heard *it*, do not cease to pray for you, and to desire that ye might be filled with the knowledge of his will in all wisdom and spiritual understanding; That ye might walk worthy of the Lord unto all pleasing, being fruitful in every good work, and increasing in the knowledge of God; Strengthened with all might, according to his glorious power, unto all patience and longsuffering with joyfulness; Giving thanks unto the Father, which hath made us meet to be partakers of the inheritance of the saints in light: Who hath delivered us from the power of darkness, and hath translated *us* into the kingdom of his dear Son" (Colossians 1:9-13).

Do we want our children to choose righteousness over sin? Then praying from Romans 6 would be worthwhile. "Let not sin therefore reign in your mortal body, that ye should obey it in the lusts thereof. Neither yield ye your members *as* instruments of unrighteousness unto sin: but yield yourselves unto God, as those that are alive from the dead, and your members *as* instruments of righteousness unto God" (Romans 6:12-13).

Is your child struggling with worry? You can pray Philippians 4:6-7 for him. "Be careful for nothing; but in every thing by prayer and supplication with thanksgiving let your requests be made known unto God. And the peace of God, which passeth all understanding, shall keep your hearts and minds through Christ Jesus."

Does your child lack a thankful heart? Consider praying that your child would begin, "Giving thanks always for all things unto God and the Father in the name of our Lord Jesus Christ" (Ephesians 5:20).

Do you realize how Scripture can be used to pray for our children? No matter what need you see in your child's life, you can find a Scripture to pray that will relate to that need. If you desire growth in your child in a certain spiritual direction, you can look for Scripture to pray that will support and endorse this growth.

I have begun to memorize the verses that I am praying for my children so that I have them available any time I want them. I can pick out portions of the verses to pray, and I can individualize them by putting my child's name into the words from Scripture as I pray. I have found that everything I memorize to pray for my children is applicable to praying for myself and others as well.

There are some things that I pray for my children day after day, prayer after prayer. Should I stop praying them because I have prayed them so many times? "And let us not be weary in well doing: for in due season we shall reap, if we faint not" (Galatians 6:9). My repetitive prayers for my children fall into this category of what I am not to become weary in doing because, in time, there will be a harvest of spiritual fruit.

"And he spake a parable unto them *to this end*, that men ought always to pray, and not to faint; Saying, There was in a city a judge, which feared not God, neither regarded man: And there was a widow in that city; and she came unto him, saying, Avenge me of mine adversary. And he would not for a while: but afterward he said within himself, Though I fear not God, nor regard man; Yet because this widow troubleth me, I will avenge her, lest by her continual coming she weary me. And the Lord said, Hear what the unjust judge saith. And shall not God avenge his own elect, which cry day and night unto him, though he bear long with them? I tell you that he will avenge them speedily. Nevertheless when the Son of man cometh, shall he find faith on the earth?" (Luke 18:1-8). This parable gives the example that we are to continue crying out to our Lord Jesus Christ in prayer for our children, even if we pray the same or similar things for them very often.

When I pray Scripture for my children, I feel assured in my heart that I am praying God's will and desire for them. "And what-soever ye shall ask in my name, that will I do, that the Father may be glorified in the Son. If ye shall ask any thing in my name, I will do *it*" (John 14:13-14). "And this is the confidence that we have in him, that, if we ask any thing according to his will, he heareth us: And if we know that he hear us, whatsoever we ask, we know that we have the petitions that we desired of him" (1 John 5:14-15).

As you commit your heart to pray for your children, I encourage you to use Scripture as part of those prayers. Memorize the passages that the Lord directs you to pray for your children so that you will have them available anywhere and anytime to pray. Then be faithful in spending much time in prayer for your children.

# Job Woes
## *by Steve*

A friend of mine has had a very successful sales position with a company for six or seven years now. He works hard for this company and has brought in a tremendous amount of business as their star producer. So why does he never sound happy in his job?

It seems like every time we speak, he shares a new story about his company. I don't want you to think he is complaining, as he isn't. He is simply seeking encouragement from a brother in the Lord. Listening to this friend, I have found a common thread in his tales. I suspect that you will see it as well.

First, he told me how the executive staff raised prices and didn't tell the sales people until it was announced to the customers. That may not sound like anything out of the ordinary. However, my friend had asked his company if there were any price hikes coming. He was planning to spend a significant amount of money printing some new sales materials and didn't want it to be wasted. He was told there were no changes coming and that he could go ahead with his project.

Another time the company placed a new manager over the salesmen. This manager did not understand the business, and his new policies were wreaking havoc on sales performance. When the salesmen tried to discuss the problems with their new manager and also with the CEO, there was no interest in listening to the issues that were being raised. You can imagine that this caused great frustration and discouragement within the sales force.

Then there was the time that they had a horrible problem with the home office computer system. The customer tracking software was hopelessly snarled up. The sales people were not able to make follow-up calls or document the calls they did make. Unfortunately, their pay is dependent on those calls and their documentation. So the home office computer breakdown was causing the field not to be paid what they needed to support their families. When this was repeatedly brought to the attention of management, there seemed to be little or no concern about helping the sales force meet their financial commitments while the software was being fixed.

It has been sad to see my friend lose his zeal for a job that he once enjoyed so much and from which he derived great satisfaction. Certainly, God is sovereign and gave my friend the grace to deal with each situation.

I expect many of us can easily relate to my friend's experiences. Did you notice the lack of respect and appreciation that management showed for their employees? Could you see how that manifested itself in an unwillingness to communicate? Because I have seen the same problem through the years of my employment and my own mistakes, I coined a phrase and repeat it when appropriate. "We communicate with those we value."

My friend's situation is analogous to what can happen in a home. For the purpose of an example, the dad is similar to company management and the mom to the salesman. I have found it takes a lot of effort to effectively communicate with Teri. If you haven't noticed, men and women think differently. Neither is wrong, just different!

I believe most of us dads have the head knowledge that the road of a homeschooling mother is a difficult one. Unfortunately, sometimes there can be a huge gap between the head and the heart. I know that if I were to ask my friend's company president if he thought good communication with his sales people was critical to the company's success, he would answer with a resounding, "Yes!"

The challenges that a homeschooling mother faces are of eternal consequence and even more difficult (in my opinion) than the challenges of the salesman who must meet quota. Teri's role as my helpmeet is to assist me in attaining the goals God has set before our family. I must have a clear channel of communication open if I'm to help her when she becomes bogged down. When I'm busy, lazy, or just plain selfish, I tend not to listen well to Teri. It is then no different from my friend's situation.

His company's success was entirely dependent on how well the sales people did their jobs, just as the family's success is largely dependent on how well the mother is able to do her job. If Mom is having difficulties and needs help finding solutions, Dad must take it very seriously. He must listen and make whatever effort is necessary to fix the problem. If Dad doesn't wake up and take the responsibility that God has given him, Mom may become discouraged and struggle with her motivation, just as my friend has with his motivation. "For the husband is the head of the wife, even as Christ is the head of the church . . ." (Ephesians 5:23).

At times I think we can be just like the sales manager who didn't understand the business. Have you ever found yourself making rash decisions without really understanding the situation? It takes time and effort to analyze what is happening and make a careful, prayerful decision. I wish I could say I always do that. Sadly, I know there are times when Teri is telling me about a problem and before she finishes, I summarize in my mind what is happening and what needs to be done. Then I either continue to listen while mentally checked out, or cut her short, coming to her rescue with a "brilliant" solution.

Scripture has a verse that speaks to my brilliance: "Seest thou a man *that is* hasty in his words? *there is* more hope of a fool than of him" (Proverbs 29:20). Teri is not impressed with my love for her when I won't listen long enough to understand the situation. My actions are shouting above my speech. If it becomes a pattern, she will soon be discouraged like my friend.

May each of us love and cherish the treasure the Lord Jesus gave us in our wives. May we listen with our ears and our heart. May we own every problem and do whatever it takes to make our wives be successful in their roles as helpmeets. Lord Jesus, thank You for a wife who has willingly chosen a difficult path on earth in exchange for treasures in heaven.

# In His Image
## *by Steve*

Teri and I take great delight in observing families. Most often we see physical characteristics that are common between the children and their parents. It may be hair color or facial features. Usually there is something that causes us to say, "I can tell they came from the same ingredients." It becomes especially obvious the more children there are to compare.

Isn't it a wonderful thing what God did when He designed the procreation process? The image of the parents is impressed on the children. Many of our physical and even behavioral characteristics become a part of our offspring. There is one family in our church where the father is six foot seven. You ought to see his two sons. One of them has just now surpassed his father. I remember when my sons became taller than me several years ago. It felt very strange and was no small event for them.

I wonder how much each of us resembles our Father in heaven. I'm not referring to mankind in general, even though we were made in His image. I mean those who have been born again by the blood of the Lord Jesus. That transaction made God truly our Father, and we became His offspring.

Jesus evaluated men's conduct and associated their conduct with their father in John 8:44: "Ye are of *your* father the devil, and the lusts of your father ye will do. He was a murderer from the beginning, and abode not in the truth, because there is no truth in him. When he speaketh a lie, he speaketh of his own: for he is a liar, and the father of it."

Because the Pharisees would not welcome truth, Jesus stung them with sharp words by calling them the children of Satan. Here were the religious leaders of Israel being called sons of Satan, and Satan was called the father of lies.

We read in Deuteronomy 32:4 about God, *"He is* the Rock, his work *is* perfect: for all his ways *are* judgment: a God of truth and without iniquity, just and right *is* he." Our Father is a God of truth, and Satan is the father of lies. That puts falsehood and truth in a very black and white light. If Jesus made this distinction and likened those who embraced lies to being in the lineage of Satan, it would seem that born-again believers must endeavor to always speak and live truth.

Recently, Teri and I were watching some videotapes by a well-respected Christian teacher. He referred to a statement he spoke to his child. Then he told the audience with a bit of a wink, "I was lying to him." One other time, he acknowledged in a lighthearted fashion lying to someone. I must admit my respect for this person took a hit just then. Here he was expecting us to believe he was telling us truth, and at the same time admitting there were circumstances where he chose to lie.

I have no doubt this man endeavors to live by and preach truth; however, we must shun anything false. I believe it damages the reputation of Christ when we don't. "Remove far from me vanity and lies: give me neither poverty nor riches; feed me with food convenient for me" (Proverbs 30:8). If we want to walk in righteousness we must not lie, as "A righteous *man* hateth lying: but a wicked *man* is loathsome, and cometh to shame" (Proverbs 13:5).

I believe that one of the most pungent Bible verses is, "A lying tongue hateth *those that are* afflicted by it; and a flattering mouth worketh ruin" (Proverbs 26:28). Here we see that from God's perspective, we hate the one we lie to. If we loved him, we would speak truth to him just like our heavenly Father speaks truth always to us.

One of the greatest struggles I have is my desire to be funny. Sometimes the easiest way to get a chuckle is to say something that isn't true. I know it is wrong, and yet it can create this battle in me as to whether I will say it. Usually, I just "swallow the words," but there are times, especially if I'm tired, that they will come out. Then after we have all laughed, my spirit convicts me.

The conviction to speak truth is what initially led us to quit Santa Claus at Christmas. We realized that, according to Scripture, we could not love our children and lie to them. Yes, that also meant that the "tooth fairy" and "Easter bunny" were eradicated—never to darken our door again.

It is so easy to get caught up in all of our warm, fuzzy memories of being a child and in not wanting our children to miss out on anything. However, it is my greatest desire that my children would not miss out on having a God-fearing father who loves the Lord Jesus with all his heart. If God says I must shun falsehood, then I am not going to justify lying to my children for any reason.

I think what happens is that often we dads can be short-sighted and not patriarchal minded. It is so easy to live for all the fun this world has to offer and lose sight of eternal things. This year I will turn fifty and that seems old, but even if I live to be as old as Silas (a delightful young man of ninety-seven years old), what is that in comparison with eternity? Nothing!

I want my children to think of Jesus' resurrection from the dead when they think of Easter. Yes, the Bible doesn't tell us to celebrate "Easter," but we are told to remember. We choose to "remember" in a more focused way on the day that even unbelievers expect Christians to celebrate. In my opinion, it would be far better not to celebrate Easter at all than to have any part of the "Easter bunny." It is not truth, and to let something else detract from the most glorious event ever—the celebration of the death, burial, and resurrection of the Lamb of God, the Lord Jesus Christ—is unthinkable. We do celebrate and remember Christ's resurrection weekly when we worship, but we choose to make Resurrection Sunday a special remembrance.

If we were somehow to find a way to celebrate Easter and spiritualize the "Easter bunny" in some fashion, I believe we would have a situation analogous to Exodus 32. Aaron had just made the golden calf while Moses was on Mount Sinai receiving God's law. After Aaron finished crafting the calf and building an altar for it, he proclaimed, ". . . To morrow *is* a feast to the LORD" (Exodus 32:5). Aaron announced it was to be a feast to Jehovah, the true God of Israel. Only God knows exactly what was going on in Aaron's mind, but from the outside it appeared to be incredible double-mindedness. Let's look at what happened in verse 6 when the things of the world were mixed with the worship of the true God: "And they rose up early on the morrow, and offered burnt offerings, and brought peace offerings; and the people sat down to eat and to drink. . . ."

That does not sound too bad. They had a very spiritual time with their offerings and then a meal. Then we read on that they "rose up to play." This was not righteous play. We learn later that they were naked. Whatever Aaron intended led to something very unholy.

Please understand, I'm not saying that families who choose to celebrate Easter and include the "Easter bunny" are guilty of the idolatry we read about. I am not making that judgment in any way. What I am saying is: we can see from Scripture that if we mix truth with something false, the result is negative. Nothing holy will be inspired in the minds of those we are called to bring up in the "nurture and admonition of the Lord" (Ephesians 6:4).

Dads, please understand, I'm not condemning you if you do make a choice different from mine, that isn't my place. However, it is my prayer that I will challenge you to consider things in a new light and encourage you to love the Lord Jesus more and walk according to His Word. May God be merciful and gracious to you, and may you be the head of many godly generations.

"And the LORD passed by before him, and proclaimed, The LORD, The LORD God, merciful and gracious, longsuffering, and abundant in goodness and truth" (Exodus 34:6).

# Preparing Sons — Real Life Stories
## *by Steve*

I recently spoke with a homeschooled, eighteen-year-old young man of whom I think highly. Let's call him Eric. He is friendly, respectful, and I have not observed him being silly like many others his age. Unfortunately, there is one disappointing aspect of his life— he has not been working toward acquiring the necessary vocational skills needed to earn a living once he graduates from high school.

What makes it worse is the golden opportunity Eric has had. Eric's father is a computer programmer and would love to have his son learn programming. His father has also produced and sold a number of software products that require telephone customer service. In addition to learning programming, Eric could also have learned valuable customer support skills.

As Eric and I talked, I continued pressing to find out why he hadn't been studying and learning programming. Finally, when he ran out of evasive, general answers, he blurted out the real answer—he wanted to continue trying to make a go of his graphic arts business. What this really meant was that he was too focused on the desires of his heart. He did not understand how God uses parents to lead and equip children. His desire to learn graphic design caused him to ignore his parents' counsel. He was unable to look down the road a short distance, past his heart, to see how God might use programming to establish a vocational and financial foundation for him.

Eric is a man and needs to be working hard—especially considering the three or four years of vocational learning opportunities that have been lost. I explained to Eric how programming and graphic arts complement each other very well. At least this is what we have found in our business. Had he listened to his father, he could have learned programming during his final years of high school and been working full time, for a good wage, upon graduation.

The high school years are vitally important to young men as they prepare for their future. Homeschooled children have a wonderful opportunity that others lack: they are able to tailor their curriculum toward God's future vocational leading.

As well as a strong focus on God, character, and academics, we have tried to maintain a concerted vocational emphasis for our children in their junior and high school years. Christopher, our second born, spent extra time learning accounting and computer-based design. Upon graduation he became the Chief Financial Officer of our fledgling company. It was wonderful because he was ready for some real challenge and we had a need for him to fill that role.

Now, four years later, he truly deserves the title. He does a superb job managing the financial side of the company as well as doing all the computer layout and design we need. His earnings are on par with his responsibilities. His goal of buying his first house debt free, like his twenty-four-year-old brother just did, is looking very feasible.

I hesitate in sharing some of these details because I don't want to boast. However, I do want to encourage you. Homeschooling moms and dads are blessed to be able to prepare their children for life in ways that others can only dream of. Homeschoolers should never think of homeschooling just as a way to teach their children, but as a golden opportunity to ready each child for his future. Even though many public high school graduation speeches talk about the graduates being equipped for life, I know from my own experience that was not the case.

Is the ability to purchase a home debt free a good goal for sons? Think about what a burden rent and/or mortgage payments are. They pressure men to choose work in places where Christians should not be employed. I have also known men, under tremendous financial pressure due to their mortgage, who participated in unethical and illegal business dealings. Concern over loss of income should never hold a Christian to a job with which his Lord would not be pleased.

Now can you see why we have presented our children with this goal of a debt-free house? Many parents may see saving for a house as unrealistic because a mortgage payment has hounded them through their marriage. However, I would encourage you to ask the Lord if it might not be a worthy goal for your sons.

Teri and I would have loved to provide our children with homes according to Proverbs 19:14, "House and riches *are* the inheritance of fathers: and a prudent wife *is* from the LORD." Unfortunately, we are nowhere near being able to do that. However, we can provide them with room and board for as long as it takes them to save up for their house. Even then it is our desire that they would continue to live with us until God provides them a spouse.

If a young man has prepared well during high school, he should fairly easily be able to earn thirty-five thousand dollars or more a year when he graduates. Start with a yearly income and then subtract tithes, offerings, and taxes. Then money must be put aside for transportation, insurance (medical and auto), and other incidental expenses. If your son is frugal he should be able to save 50 percent or slightly more of his income while living at home.

Within six years from high school graduation your twenty-four-year-old son will have saved one hundred thousand dollars, not counting any appreciable interest. I find that very exciting. If he earned less than thirty-five thousand a year, it just means he must save a little longer.

Depending upon the location, size, and age of the house your son will purchase, he might not even need one hundred thousand. There are so many possibilities and intriguing options, but nothing happens unless a son has a vision, and you help him prepare.

My sons have found that as they accumulate a significant amount of savings, the interest starts to really add up. This has given them a true appreciation for earning, rather than paying, interest. That is where the battle is won! When you are successful in motivating toward a goal, your sons will own that goal and work toward achieving it.

As Eric and I ended our conversation, I told him I was going to keep asking him, every time I saw him, until he began studying programming in earnest. I admit I was a bit pushy, but I felt God's leading so strongly that I was very forthright when I might otherwise have been subtler.

Since our conversation I'm delighted to say that Eric has really begun applying himself to the study of programming. He is now able to see that his father's leading was correct and how the skill of programming will benefit him.

I am anxious to see the day when Eric is bringing in a reasonable wage for his efforts. He is a serious enough young man that I don't expect him to waste his money on frivolous things but to save toward a house. What an incredible benefit that will be to him as he begins his adult life.

We have known Troy for quite a while. He was homeschooled, and his first job was as a two-week temporary assistant to the most junior employee in the company. Troy was hired to move heavy archive boxes in the basement. Being his first real job, Troy was determined to do his best regardless of how menial the tasks. That doesn't sound like an impressive start to a career, does it? However, it was amazing to see how God was working. While doing his work assignments, he did his best to learn the archiving system of the company. He also tried to perform each task quickly so he would be available to do other "little" things for his boss.

His temporary position was extended, and after a couple of months, he replaced his "boss" as archiving manager for the company. Throughout the next year or so, he completely redesigned the archive system from the bottom up. This included designing a new database and tracking system for more than 4,000 boxes of information.

Computers have always interested Troy, and he found himself helping various people in the company with small projects in his spare time. While not an expert in formulas and the financial aspects of spreadsheets, his desire to learn enabled him to create, fix, and modify spreadsheets. Thus he began to be used in the process of converting the company's spreadsheets from Lotus 1-2-3 to Microsoft Excel. After a while he was doing spreadsheet and database consulting full time. He completely redesigned their largest financial spreadsheet (which was made up of seventeen inter-working spreadsheets) in a three-month-long development project.

Troy began working for minimum wage, and within two years his hourly rate had climbed to twenty-five dollars an hour. He has chosen to go on to college and has found it extremely easy to continue earning that amount doing contract work for another company near his school. Think about how easy it would be to remain debt free through college by working part time and summers for twenty-five dollars an hour.

My encouragement to you is that any homeschooling parent can have confidence that their son can provide a good income for his family with the proper preparation. This requires determination and hard work on your part and your sons', but the results are well worth it, lasting a lifetime.

For more information on raising sons who can provide for a family, please see *Preparing Sons to Provide for a Single-Income Family* (see Additional Resources, page 385).

# Don't Give Up
## *by Steve*

A couple of weeks ago, I was speaking with a dad and mom at a homeschool conference. They were sharing about some difficulties with their son. They admitted making many mistakes. As a result, they had a very rebellious son on their hands. This couple was at the point of wanting to give up on the child, letting him go his own way.

I also met a precious mommy who had a very young child stretched across her lap. I commented about how peaceful the resting child looked. She told me that her baby had a fatal disease that caused him to be so limp. I watched her lovingly use a suction bulb to clear her son's throat and then give him something to eat through a feeding syringe.

My heart broke as I learned they had lost other children to the same disease. There was not a trace of bitterness in her voice, just a tenderness that was the result of a suffering heart submitted to the Potter's knowing touch. Undoubtedly, the family would continue to minister to this child until the Father took him home too.

In Mark 9:14-29, we read an account of a man who brought his son to Jesus to be healed. A mute spirit possessed the son and would attempt to destroy the child by casting him into the fire or water. It would have been a terrible situation for the parents because the son's life depended on their keeping vigilant watch to protect him. There were likely many times that the father or mother had to react quickly to save their son from destruction.

Think about it. What hope did that father have of his son ever being cured and living a normal life? There was no hope! It would have been reasonable for the father to have despaired, forsaking the child. Even if that father had access to today's medical technology, it would have been of no benefit in dealing with a demon-possessed son.

As some read this, a child of yours may be in a grave situation. Others may be like the Maxwells. While we have no rebellious or terminally ill children, at any given time we have issues with some of our children for which we don't have solutions. These issues aren't life threatening, but they would hinder a child from being all that God intends him to be. For example, we have a child who is struggling in a particular area of his schoolwork. We have tried many different remedies, and none have worked. At times it has seemed hopeless. It has been extremely frustrating for the child, for Teri, and for me.

With others of our children there are often areas that weigh on our hearts. Character issues of varying degrees are common for us to wrestle. It would be most pleasant if there weren't ever problems in our home, but that has yet to happen. I suspect that the source of our difficulty is that both parents in the Maxwell home are sinners (saved by grace, but still sinners) who are committed to raising men and women of God. To make things even more challenging, each of our children is a sinner (saved by grace, but still a sinner).

Homeschooling moms should be the most content, joy-filled moms on the face of this earth. Why? Because they are being obedient to their Lord as they invest themselves in the lives of their children. Unfortunately, it can be a very difficult road to walk. Why? Because they are face to face with the rough areas of their children all day long. (Other moms may not see their children in the same light, most likely because someone else is spending most of the day with their children.)

Homeschooling moms see their children when they are being slothful, irresponsible, argumentative, and even deceitful. This is like an arrow to the mom's heart because she is pouring her life into her children. She desires that they become men and women of God. Raising children is a long-term project, and it is often difficult to see the forest through the trees. It is easy for Mom to come to the point where she asks, "Why try? This is the same problem we have been battling forever, and it is no better!"

However, dads don't usually have the same "opportunity" to observe their children's sin all day long. Therefore, we may tend not to view it as seriously as Mom does. We can reassure our wives that it is okay, and after all they are just children, but that is not going to solve anything. In fact, that kind of response could lead to a situation where the parents wake up one day and ask themselves how they raised a rebellious teenager. So what is the answer?

First, I must communicate with my wife. I need to foster a relationship with Teri where she wants to share her struggles with me and can trust me with what she says. I'm ashamed to say that there have been times when I was not attentive to her words, or I did not take them seriously.

When Teri sees that I have taken responsibility for finding a solution, it is like a weight is lifted from her. That is the way it must be, as she is the one yoked to me. I am to bear the weight of her yoke in the same way the Lord bears the weight of my yoke.

In order to take responsibility for finding solutions to difficulties in our children's lives, we can start by praying. As Teri listens to my prayers, she will sense the urgency of my soul communicating the need to my Lord. If I fully own the responsibility, it will be the prayer on my heart during the day. That also means I'm likely to have questions for her about possible solutions or areas in which I need clarification.

When the need is the prayer of my heart, I'm like the father in Mark 9. He could have told his wife that he was busy taking care of the crops and didn't have time to take his son to Jesus. If he did take the child to Jesus, they might not have enough to eat. Back then, just providing for a family was difficult enough. Isn't it easy to rationalize that it is a man's job to provide for the family, and the wife's to take care of the children? That father knew he was ultimately responsible for his child. He was going to do whatever it took to find help for him.

We must be tenacious. The father in Mark 9 wasn't satisfied after the disciples couldn't free the son. He sought to get close to the Lord as soon as Christ came down the mountain. He did not leave with his son when the disciples weren't successful. He probably saw Jesus as his son's only hope. That is true for us as well. Christ is our only hope of true solutions in the home.

When Jesus was now involved, He did a curious thing in verse 21. "And he asked the father, How long is it ago since this came unto him?" Why did the Lord ask him how long the son was like this? The Lord knows everything and didn't need to ask him. He could have quickly cast out the demon and gone on to the next, but He didn't.

The Lord drew the father into a conversation. The Lord had a target that was as important as healing the son. The father replied, ". . . Of a child. And ofttimes it hath cast him into the fire, and into the waters, to destroy him: but if thou canst do any thing, have compassion on us, and help us" (Mark 9:21-22). Christ now had revealed what He wanted exposed—the father's lack of faith.

We would be wise to realize that many of the struggles in our home are for our spiritual benefit. We have as much to gain from the situation as the child with the problem.

"Jesus said unto him, If thou canst believe, all things *are* possible to him that believeth. And straightway the father of the child cried out, and said with tears, Lord, I believe; help thou mine unbelief" (Mark 9:23-24). The father has now responded from his heart with obvious emotion as he proclaimed what faith he had and asked the Lord to help him have greater faith. Dads, are we owning the needs of our family with the willingness for the Lord to work first in our lives? He desires to use every difficulty and trial we encounter as opportunity for building our faith and trust in Him. Will we let Him?

We may be tempted to see these problems as nuisances and hindrances to our getting along with life when, in fact, they are stepping stones to growth in Christ. It is easy to miss the blessings that God intends for us in properly resolving these issues. Paul said in

Philippians 4:12, "I know both how to be abased, and I know how to abound: every where and in all things I am instructed both to be full and to be hungry, both to abound and to suffer need." He said that he knew how to be abased and hungry. I'm sure there are many stories Paul could share with us as to how he suffered. Yet, we read in verse 13, "I can do all things through Christ which strengtheneth me." That is the prize held out to us if we are but willing to receive the process as well.

Dads, it is good to suffer under the weight of family struggles if we will bring them to our Lord. He wants us to own them and bear them to Him. We need to be willing to be abased as we lead our family and be willing to suffer. We must not give up just because we can't handle the difficulties. We can't resolve them ourselves, and it is our lack of faith that causes us to think we can figure it out alone.

Just like that precious mommy with the failing child, we must let Christ work in our lives. Those parents are in God's crucible, and their faith is being refined. If they let Him, He will purify and polish their faith to a luster that will reflect the light of Christ. "And we know that all things work together for good to them that love God, to them who are the called according to his purpose. For whom he did foreknow, he also did predestinate *to be* conformed to the image of his Son, that he might be the firstborn among many brethren" (Romans 8:28-29).

Dads, are we willing to do the same? Are we willing to own the difficulties of raising men and women of God for our Lord? Are we willing to let Him work first in our own lives? My prayer is that we are. God bless, dear brothers. May we be found faithful.

# A Sure Test of Worth
## *by Steve*

There is a skill that every father needs to learn and then be able to teach his children. It is essential for effectively sharing the love of Christ with your family and others.

Without this ability, you and I will leave people with the impression that we think we are more important than they are. The absence of this is particularly evident at social gatherings. The ones with it are a pleasure to be around, while the ones without it are boring.

If you don't develop this skill, your wife may doubt that you really care for her. If you don't practice it with your children, someone else may steal their hearts away from you.

Jesus was a Master of this. In fact, He amazes me every time I read that He did it. Sometimes I cannot understand why He did this, other times it was pretty obvious. What is this skill?

I commented briefly about it in last month's Corner from Mark 9:21, when Jesus asked a boy's father, "How long is it ago since this came unto him?" Jesus is God, and He knows everything. Why did He ask the question? Was He seeking a confession or some information He did not know? I believe Jesus asked the father the question because He wanted to draw the father into a conversation in order to reveal needs in the father's life.

Jesus was accomplished in the art of asking questions. Why is the ability to ask questions so important in life? First and foremost, it communicates worth to the person you are asking because it says that what they are thinking is important to you.

To my shame, there have been times when Teri was describing a situation to me and "in all my great wisdom" I've quickly figured out the solution to her problem. I've interrupted her with answers she was seeking. However, what I really did was to communicate that she wasn't as important as my time. I had given her a swift answer so I could get on with other things. Jesus could have quickly healed the father's son mentioned in Mark 9:21 without any communication, but He didn't. He took what time was necessary to get to the heart of the matter, which included growing the father's faith as well as delivering the son.

That is why questions are so important. What if I were to wait until Teri finished describing to me her problem? Then, what if I asked her a few questions to verify that I understood the situation, gleaning additional clarification as needed? Wouldn't this communicate that I care about what is important to her and am putting her interests first?

Another example might be the times I've been out all day and haven't had a chance to speak to Teri. Finally I come home and ask her about her day, how she is feeling, or if she had any problems. Aren't I telling her that I love her and that she is important to me by asking the questions and being attentive to her answers? Who am I communicating is the most important if I'm only interested in telling her about my day?

The same is true with our children. Communicating heart to heart involves asking our children questions about their struggles, their likes and dislikes. It is an excellent way of showing genuine interest in them and getting to heart issues.

We cannot effectively witness to someone without asking him questions. It is very difficult to communicate the love of Christ while "verbally shoving" something down someone's throat—and that is what a constant stream of words does.

Consider the following examples. "Jim, you need to be saved so you won't go to hell. You need to confess you are a sinner." Or, "Jim, where do you think you will spend eternity? Would you be interested in learning what the Bible has to say about it?"

"Donny, I have seen you being very mean to your sister, and it better stop." Or, "Donny, I've observed you having some conflict with your sister lately. Would you tell me about it? Has she offended you in some way? Shall we talk about it?"

It will help a child throughout his life if he learns how to ask good questions as a means to get to know others. Think how common it is to spend time with someone you don't know very well. What better way to get to know something about that person than by asking questions?

Years ago, our evening family altar time was interrupted by a knock on the door. Nathan, then thirteen years old, jumped up and said he would see who it was. He stepped outside and didn't come back in for quite a few minutes. When he finally returned, I asked who had been at the door. He said it was one of his lawn-mowing customers. I asked if there was a problem, since he was gone for so long. Nathan said, "No Dad, there was no problem, we just got started talking." The gentleman Nathan was talking to was probably fifty years his senior, but because Nathan is skilled at asking questions, he was comfortable talking to just about anyone.

We have found communicating through questions to be essential for our monthly visits to the City Union Mission. The men we "visit" with are often not refined in their social skills. Carrying on a conversation can be quite difficult at times. Questions that require more than a simple "yes" or "no" answer are the primary arsenal for chipping away the hardened outer layers of these men.

Questions are a surgeon's tools for getting to the heart of man. When guided in a gentle but purposeful fashion, they will unlock a great treasure. They can bring to light hidden hurts that have been long buried. They can be the key to discovering deep waters. When I sense a closed spirit in Teri or the children, loving questions will uncover issues that I need to address or offenses I have committed.

How can we teach our children to gracefully employ the art of communication though questioning? Practice with counsel makes one skillful. Fellowshipping after church or with dinner guests provides wonderful opportunities for children to practice their communication skills. Encourage your children beforehand to think of questions they can ask. Then have them practice the questions with you prior to the guest's arrival. That way you can help them learn what is appropriate to ask and how to be gentle with the questions.

I suppose the most difficult aspect of asking questions for a child is learning what is appropriate to ask and what is not. Questions about the guest's physical appearance are always the most risky. One we have learned to shy away from is, "So when is your baby due?"

There are some dangers with questions. As I just mentioned, some questions are inappropriate because the relationship or an assumption can prove false. Questions can be blunt, insensitive, demanding, or too many. Our tone while asking is very important and often will tip the scales toward appearing caring or toward being pushy and demanding.

Teri and I are amazed at how often we encounter people in social settings who will never ask a single question about our family or us. It isn't that we are dying to tell them about ourselves, it just makes the conversation much easier and more pleasant. By their not asking any questions, they appear to be interested only in themselves, and we run the risk of appearing nosy after asking them question after question.

I would encourage each dad to evaluate his communication skills in questioning. A good place to start is by asking your wife if she feels you show interest in her. Do you ask her about her day, her needs, and her cares? If you aren't doing this, repent of your selfish focus. Then begin to ask your wife and children questions to communicate that you are putting them first and caring about them. Make this ability to use questions a priority in your life, and then teach it to your children.

I have found the art of asking questions one of the most important skills I have. I must give credit to two people in particular. One was a man who taught a sales seminar I attended in 1982 on being successful in sales. The other person is Teri's mother. She is gracious and skillful in interacting with others, and I see much of this is due to her ability to ask questions.

Dads, may we be ready instruments in our Lord's hands through our communication skills and equip our children to be the same. These children will then be comfortable in social situations and will bless you.

# Dad, Are You in Danger?
## *by Steve*

"A prudent *man* foreseeth the evil, and hideth himself: but the simple pass on, and are punished" (Proverbs 22:3). I don't believe I have ever met a dad who would consider himself simple. However, there have been times in my life when I acted in a simple fashion, and I expect that might be true of many dads as well.

Over fifteen years ago, I took a test to qualify for a sales position. It was a personality profiler, and if my profile matched the standard, I could transfer to a potentially lucrative sales position in the company. If my personality wasn't similar to the top sales performers they evaluated, then I would stay in my present job. I passed the test—not because I was similar to the other salesmen, but because I knew how they would answer. Did I lie or cheat on the test? Of course not! Well, at least not according to my reasoning.

I moved my family away from friends, a wonderful church, and across the country from Florida to Washington. I soon was a failure in my job! Everything that could go wrong was going wrong. This simply did not make sense since God had always blessed my work in the past.

I could have saved my family and myself a lot of hardship had I discussed the test at length with Teri. She has such a sensitive spirit that she would have immediately seen that I had not responded honestly on the test. She would have cautioned me about heading down a path based on deceit.

I read about a rancher who made a very bad decision. He had greatly benefited by some men's help, but later, when he had the opportunity to help them in return, he was rude and offensive. His words were so inflammatory that these men purposed to kill the rancher and the men in his household.

The rancher was a good example of a poor leader. His foolish behavior led his wife to feel the need to step in and take leadership. Sadly, that is exactly what happens in many "Christian" homes today. Dad will make a poor decision, and his wife will attempt to come to the rescue to protect the family from perceived consequences.

Frequently Teri and I will observe the agonizing dichotomy a wife is faced with because of her husband's decisions. The wife knows the husband is the head and supposed to lead the family, yet she sees the consequences that are looming ahead. She sees herself with two choices. First, she could decide to be submissive and let the consequences, which may ultimately be used by God to teach her husband a lesson, come upon the family. Second, she could decide to usurp her husband's role, jump in, and possibly miss a growth opportunity.

The rancher I mentioned above was Nabal in 1 Samuel 25. He was so simple his name actually meant "fool." Nabal's wife Abigail understood the situation and knew her husband was in grave danger. She decided to take charge and appease David's anger. Was it for the best? Only the Lord knows. In the end, God chose to take Nabal's life even though David decided not to attack.

Many unbelievers purchase radar detectors for the purpose of breaking the law and avoiding the consequences. In some states radar detectors are illegal because they circumvent the authorities' ability to punish wrong choices. The owners rely upon these devices because they don't want to receive the very punishment that may help them make better, law-abiding decisions. Nathan and I went to breakfast years ago with a state senator who had a radar detector in his car. I couldn't believe it. Here was a man who was responsible for making laws with a device built to circumvent the law. The lost may choose a radar detector, but may a man of God never consider it.

I believe God has equipped wives with a special sensitivity to know when God is about to chastise the husband. Think of your wife as a God-given, legal radar detector of sorts. This "consequence avoider" is given for the purpose of learning before the chastisement is sent. If only we would receive this "help" and humble ourselves by listening to our wives' counsel, I believe we would have the God-given opportunity to learn before the trip to the woodshed.

At one time we were renting an enormous, poorly insulated house in Washington. It was the only rental we could find. We were heating it by wood because fuel oil for the furnace would have been very costly. Unfortunately on some days, the county imposed a wood-burning ban on everyone who did not depend on wood for their primary source of heat.

Using my great rationalizing abilities (Teri has another example in her August 2001 Mom's Corner), I decided that since the fuel oil was prohibitively expensive, our wood stove was our primary source of heat. I was completely satisfied with my decision. Every time I heard the ban announced on the radio and the mention of the consequences for those caught, it did not bother me in the slightest. I was at peace.

Oh dear brothers, may I encourage you to never justify a decision solely because you are at peace with it. I can't tell you how many times I have heard people use that as a reason the decision they made was the right one, when even a cursory, objective study of a few appropriate Bible verses would reveal otherwise. "He that trusteth in his own heart is a fool: but whoso walketh wisely, he shall be delivered" (Proverbs 28:26).

We are sinners at heart and must be on guard because the heart is wicked and deceitful. We can selfishly justify anything. Divorce, adultery, pornography, stealing from an employer (time or materially), and breaking the law (my wood-burning example) can all be rationalized. "Only fear the LORD, and serve him in truth with all your heart: for consider how great *things* he hath done for you. But if ye shall still do wickedly, ye shall be consumed, both ye and your king" (1 Samuel 12:24-25).

One day on the way to church the subject of the wood burning came up. Teri, in a very gentle way, shared that she believed I was breaking the law. I expect you can guess how I responded. I did the only natural thing and was offended, becoming angry with her. How could she say that? Didn't she understand how expensive it was to burn that fuel oil for such a large house? What she didn't understand was why I would choose to break the law.

It didn't take long before the truth of her words broke through my hard heart. I humbled myself to her, asked forgiveness for my anger, and made the decision to turn the oil furnace on. What would have been the consequences had I not listened? I believe someone would have turned me in, and I would have been fined. Maybe the greatest negative result would have been that my testimony would have been harmed had I continued burning wood. I think we too often forget about how our neighbors view our wrong decisions.

As members of the body of Christ, when we make choices contrary to God's Word, the world notices and mocks God. When a Christian gets a divorce, generations will suffer. When Christians commit adultery, even if the marriage survives, the scars will never be removed from those involved and probably from the children as well. When a man commits mental adultery using pornography, he will never be the same again, he will torture the heart of his wife, and his prayers will be cut off until he repents (1 Peter 3:7). The list goes on.

There may be some men reading this who are in grave danger. ". . . There is a sin unto death: I do not say that he shall pray for it" (1 John 5:16). 1 Corinthians 11:30 says, "For this cause many *are* weak and sickly among you, and many sleep." There are times when the Lord will send sickness and death to chasten. Paul was referring to men who were taking the Lord's Supper and had not dealt with sin in their lives. It is very likely that there are some men reading this Corner who are at serious risk.

There may be many others who have ignored the cautions of their "consequence detector" and may be facing some difficulties that could have been avoided. Why put yourself and your family through it? Why not ask your wife if there are areas that she has expressed a caution about and that you haven't heard? Then take those before the Lord with a repentant heart, and ask the Lord what you should do.

There are others who may be missing out on blessings that God desires to give you. I have observed that often it is the wife's heart that appears to be sensitive to the Lord's promptings.

Dads, may I encourage you to go to your wife and ask her if there are issues that are on her heart that she either has brought up previously or has been afraid to bring up. I know there can be times when I will not want to listen to what Teri may be sharing. Usually, the subject matter is something that is a little painful, and I would rather not hear her. I'm not implying that just because Teri has a caution I will automatically receive it and respond to it. However, I have learned that I had better be prayed up and have good Scriptural basis for not responding to her counsel.

God has given each of us a marvelous helpmeet and equipped her with great sensitivity. May we each listen to our wives' counsel in order to grow and avoid consequences. May we be men of God and take our wives' counsel to the Lord and His Word for confirmation (God may not confirm it, but we must take it ever so seriously). When God does take us to the woodshed, may we be men about it and humble ourselves to our family, admit our failure, and share what we learned from it.

God bless each of you as you endeavor to be a man of God and lead your family in His ways.

# Do Real Men Ever Become Fearful?
## by Steve

In the spring we went through some difficult times. I have no doubt it could have been worse. I imagine that had it been years earlier, I would have lost many hours of sleep.

Christopher, my twenty-two-year-old son who works with me, was heavily involved in publishing a yearbook for foreign Army officers. We ended up spending extra time on the layout because one section in particular was not provided to us as we had requested (and in the manner on which we had based our cost estimate). That led to overrun on the design estimate. Then when it was printed, the yearbook pages began falling out—in the customer's hands! We had to work with the customer and our printer to get the books repaired and redistributed before the officers left for countries around the world. During these challenges, I was extremely busy on another project that consumed my thoughts and time. In addition, we had several other problems that surfaced, plus I had a presentation I needed to complete, and it was not coming together. I don't remember ever feeling such pressure—it was awful.

Then, fairly recently, we faced another time of intense pressure. There were no clear-cut answers to the numerous challenges that we faced. It easily could have become more than I could bear.

In Matthew 8:23 we read about Jesus and His disciples entering a boat to depart to the other side of the lake. The disciples were obediently following Christ's direction. Verse 24 reads, "And, behold, there arose a great tempest in the sea, insomuch that the ship was covered with the waves: but he was asleep." Several of the men were fishermen and would not have been surprised by a storm. However, this day it was a terrible storm. It was so bad that the ship was covered by the waves, and they thought they would perish. They would have been accustomed to storms; however, this one was so severe they feared for their lives. (It occurs to me that my petty problems were not life threatening and nowhere near the severity these men faced in the storm.)

The disciples were helpless. There were no flares to be shot, distress signals to be radioed, or life vests and boats to be relied on. It was grave, and they had every reason to believe they were about to drown. What could they do?

The disciples did exactly what I would have done. In their terror, they went to the Lord Jesus, Who was asleep. They were deeply afraid and likely had no preconception concerning how Jesus could help them out of their crisis, yet they still went to Him. (This lack of preconception is obvious by their amazement after He stills the storm.)

There have been many times when bad news has arrived, and the only thing I could do was go to our bedroom, lie on the floor, and pray. I can now see that usually my prayers were motivated by fear. I know men aren't supposed to be fearful, but often I respond to outward pressure with fear. It may be fear of failure, of being embarrassed, of financial loss, or of conflict. I may call that fear many things such as uncertainty, concern, worry, or doubt, but I think if I were to strip away everything else and ask God to examine my motives, most often fear is at the root.

Consider the difficulties we had with the yearbook. When we exceeded the estimate, there was fear of a confrontation with the customer. When the pages fell out, there was fear about not being able to deliver a quality product and our customer being upset. A disgruntled customer produces fear of financial loss. On and on it goes, with fear being at the heart.

Let's look at Matthew 8:26 and read, "And he saith unto them, Why are ye fearful, O ye of little faith? . . ." By every appearance they were about to drown while Jesus slept. They were at the point of losing their lives. Jesus didn't ask them why they woke Him up or why they weren't baling water. While the wind raged in their ears, Jesus asked them, "Why are ye fearful?" Jesus knew exactly why they were fearful. He had a teachable moment and wanted them to think. Clearly, they were afraid to die, but the deeper cause was their lack of faith that Jesus was God.

I worked for a company that was laying off their employees. It is an awful thing to see the fear that runs rampant in men's lives when they are faced with losing their job. It is very sad indeed. It would seem reasonable for a man to fear losing his job. However, in Matthew 6:30-34 Jesus says a man has little faith if he worries about what he will eat and wear. Worry and fear are closely related; they go about as co-conspirators, hand in hand to trouble us.

My heart aches when I hear of brothers and sisters in Christ who are facing persecution. It would be natural to be afraid of persecution. In Matthew 10:22-26 Jesus told His disciples not to fear persecution because of Him. He continues to tell them not to fear those who would kill them.

You and I are going to encounter problem after problem in life. How we respond to them is very important as it can have a significant effect on our children's belief in a sovereign God. May we be bold encouragers of their faith and not fuel the fear that is so natural in children.

So where might we begin? The commands, truths, and promises of Scripture are what I often cling to. We see from Matthew 6:30-34, 8:26, and 14:27 Jesus' admonitions not to fear under difficult circumstances. Then we read, "For God hath not given us the spirit of fear; but of power, and of love, and of a sound mind" (2 Timothy 1:7).

Next, we are to run to Christ. We should not approach with a doubting spirit, wondering, "Can the Lord deal with the situation?" as the possessed young man's father did in Mark 9:22. He said to Jesus, ". . . but if thou canst do any thing, have compassion on us, and help us." We are not to be like the disciples in the boat. Jesus did not rebuke them for coming to Him. He rebuked them for not having faith. If we lack faith, then like the possessed young man's father may we cry out, ". . . Lord, I believe; help thou mine unbelief" (Mark 9:24). Our Lord is so merciful and understanding that He will help even our unbelief if we will ask.

I don't know of anyone who enjoys difficulties. However, there is a big difference between enjoying them and being at peace in them. God has a purpose in those pressures. Problems are going to come, and they will be used by the Lord in our lives. Jesus used the situations to teach the disciples. We need to look at the problems and challenges we face as opportunities to deepen our faith in the Lord. It is easy to trust Him when things are great, but when a child is ill, business is slow, or there is great pressure, our faith is being refined.

"Take away the dross from the silver, and there shall come forth a vessel for the finer" (Proverbs 25:4). It takes intense heat, much greater than just the heat to melt silver, to burn the dross away. The problems we face can be extremely uncomfortable for us, so much so that we cry out to the Lord to "turn down the heat." Even though we don't see Christ or we think He may be sleeping, we must believe that He hears our prayers and is at work in our life. "Trust in the LORD with all thine heart; and lean not unto thine own understanding. In all thy ways acknowledge him, and he shall direct thy paths" (Proverbs 3:5-6).

The disciples could have sat down and said, "Jesus is with us, if we die we die." But that wasn't the answer. They were to go to Him, not in fear, but in faith. Isn't that what He was teaching them when He fed the four and five thousand people?

We must encourage ourselves that the trials and refining of our faith will result in greater challenges as we grow in the Lord. First the disciples had Jesus in the boat when they were in the storm. The next storm they encountered was with Jesus not in the boat with them. They were doing exactly what Jesus told them to, and yet they were encountering severe difficulties. When it was time, the Lord came to them. Maybe their fear was the reason they did not recognize Christ.

I would like to know if they were crying out to Him. My guess is that they probably weren't; otherwise, they would not have been so surprised to see Him.

Fear is a terrible master. It robs our joy and prevents us from properly responding to situations. It is likely we will never react to a situation correctly when fear is the stimulus. However, may we welcome—yes, welcome—our difficulties as opportunities for the Lord to refine our faith. It is with pressure that He conforms us to the image of His Son (Romans 8:29).

May we be men of God and leaders of our families. "Fear thou not; for I *am* with thee: be not dismayed; for I *am* thy God: I will strengthen thee; yea, I will help thee; yea, I will uphold thee with the right hand of my righteousness" (Isaiah 41:10).

# Aspects of Being a Leader — Part 1
## MAKING WISE DECISIONS
### by Steve

For months Sarah had been looking forward to visiting very special friends in New York State. Then, with the heartbreaking events of September 11th on the East Coast, Sarah's air travel became an item in serious question. I needed to decide whether she should go or not.

Recently, we had three windows replaced. Unfortunately, the windows all had a manufacturing defect that was discovered after they had been fully installed. The windows worked, but they were very noisy when they were raised or lowered. I really struggled with whether to accept them "as is" or call to see if they could be fixed.

We received an e-mail from a mom who was very unhappy that her post on one of our message boards was not approved. She had promoted something that was unacceptable according to the board's guidelines, and therefore, her post was not approved. She questioned us by saying it is a free country and why couldn't she, as a Christian, voice her opinion and spark a good, "healthy" discussion? She had "loaded both barrels" and aimed them at us. What should my response be?

I don't know about you, but I would rather not have to make difficult decisions or face confrontation! I want for people (especially my family members) to like me and for all my decisions to be good ones. Yes, my family is supposed to follow me even when I make stupid decisions, but it is much easier for them to trust in my leadership if I am making wise choices.

Answers to the above issues I faced would have come far easier had my father taught me how to make a godly decision. I suspect there are a few of you dads whose fathers did teach such things, but I don't believe too many have had that blessing. Just think if husbands had training in decision-making, how much better we would be prepared to lead our families.

At some point in a career, most of us have probably had a boss who struggled with making wise decisions, and as a result, the department/company suffered. If we will reflect back for a moment on how it felt to be under the authority of someone like that, it should help us understand how the quality of our decisions make our wives and children feel. When we make good (godly) decisions, our families will rejoice (although not always at the very moment), and when we make bad ones, they will be tempted to complain and criticize.

Making wise decisions is an important part of being a good leader. So how can we learn to make wise decisions and, in turn, teach our children how to do so? I can only share what I observe in Scripture and what God has taught me through failures.

First, everything must have a beginning, a point of reference, a foundation. What is yours? Is your beginning at the foot of the cross?

Those who are saved can look to their Lord for direction with confidence that He will direct their paths. "I will instruct thee and teach thee in the way which thou shalt go: I will guide thee with mine eye" (Psalms 32:8). "For this God *is* our God forever and ever: he will be our guide *even* unto death" (Psalms 48:14). "Thou shalt guide me with thy counsel, and afterward receive me *to* glory" (Psalms 73:24). Look at what confidence a believer can have when needing to make a decision.

Imagine being able to ask the God of creation, Who knows the beginning from the end, how you should make a decision. That is so amazing; all believers have the same opportunity. All have been granted access to the King to lay their petitions at His feet. Brothers, what good news that is for our families!

Imagine for a moment what navigation was like immediately following the invention of airplanes. A pilot was on his own when he was flying. There were no radar installations, no radio navigation aids such as instrument landing systems or Vortac transmitters. A pilot could not even radio someone for directions. If he wasn't good at following roads, then his passenger was in trouble.

Now think of the assistance that a pilot has today. Most have on-board radar, radio navigation, flight tracking computers, radar on the ground, radio communications with flight controllers, and probably even global positioning system equipment that pinpoints their position. Never has it been easier for a pilot to decide his flight path and what the conditions will be like en route.

The assistance a pilot has from technology and air traffic controllers is similar to what we have available from the Father through the Lord Jesus Christ. When a pilot takes off toward a certain destination, he does not worry about how he is going to get there. He has a flight plan, and he is counting on certain externals to help him make the trip. That is the way it is for Christians. We have a destination plotted out for us, but there are storms and unforeseen challenges that tend to blow us off course, appearing to threaten progress. We must rely on the One Who is sovereign to direct us according to His will and good pleasure. Men, there is such peace in that for us and those who are "traveling with us."

A while ago we had a difficult decision to make. I had brought it before my Lord on a daily basis and felt I understood the direction He would have us go. I remember telling Teri about it, knowing she might have some concern about the ramifications. She looked at me and said, "I have seen you seek the Lord and how the Lord has directed you previously. He has never steered us wrong, and I want you to know that I'm trusting you." I can't tell you how that made me feel. I think of that fairly often, and even now it is such a blessing to me.

The problems we face are wonderful tools in the hands of our Lord that He uses to draw us closer to Him. They also are great training opportunities for us to use with our children as they see us encounter difficulties and then observe how we respond to them. The three problems I mentioned at the beginning were excellent vehicles to draw me closer to Christ as I sought His will. "But of him are ye in Christ Jesus, who of God is made unto us wisdom, and righteousness, and sanctification, and redemption" (1 Corinthians 1:30). Jesus is wisdom personified. May we embrace Him Who is able to give us the direction we need to lead our families.

# Aspects of Being a Leader — Part 2
## MAKING WISE DECISIONS
### by Steve

Last month I shared that being a good leader of the home involves making wise decisions. The most critical aspect of how to make a wise decision is being "plugged into" the One Who is wisdom personified, and that is Jesus Christ. Since He has a plan for each of our lives, we must seek Him to find out how He would have us lead our families. "Before I formed thee in the belly I knew thee; and before thou camest forth out of the womb I sanctified thee, *and* I ordained thee a prophet unto the nations" (Jeremiah 1:5).

There is a trap that is easy to fall into when leading our families. This trap caused a man to make one of the worst decisions ever recorded in the history of mankind. This man was warned not to make his bad decision, but because of his pride he would not listen. He knew what he should do, but he just couldn't make the final decision properly. It was his pride that caused him to make this poor choice.

Pilate sentenced the innocent Lamb of God, Jesus Christ, to die a cruel and torturous death on the cross. God used a bad decision for our good as it was necessary for our salvation. God foreknew which decision Pilate's pride would lead him to make.

Pilate's wife had warned him. "When he was set down on the judgment seat, his wife sent unto him, saying, Have thou nothing to do with that just man: for I have suffered many things this day in a dream because of him" (Matthew 27:19). In His mercy God gave Pilate a second chance to avoid making this horrible decision. Because of his pride, he would not listen to his wife.

Pilate himself knew that Jesus was innocent, ". . . saying, I am innocent of the blood of this just person: see ye *to it*" (Matthew 27:24). Pilate called Jesus just! He had rendered the proper evaluation of Jesus, yet Pilate still made the wrong decision.

Pilate's position of power was the most important thing to him, and the Jews knew it. "And from thenceforth Pilate sought to release him: but the Jews cried out, saying, If thou let this man go, thou art not Caesar's friend: whosoever maketh himself a king speaketh against Caesar. When Pilate therefore heard that saying, he brought Jesus forth, and sat down in the judgment seat in a place that is called the Pavement, but in the Hebrew, Gabbatha" (John 19:12-13). Pilate's love for himself and his position is what finally caused him to pronounce a death sentence on Christ, even though he knew Jesus was innocent and being falsely accused because of the Jews' jealously. You see that in our pride, others are expendable for our selfish motives.

Pride is such an awful thing. It causes us to worry about what others are going say about us if we make a decision they don't like. Pride is what makes us want to take a poll before we make a decision so we can keep our families happy. Unfortunately, we want them happy so they won't cause us any trouble.

This is such a terribly sad thing to see in families. For example, what if the children want to watch TV and worldly movies? What if your children decide they no longer want to be homeschooled? What if a daughter wants to dress in tight, seductive clothes? What if the teens want to participate in youth group? I believe we are in agreement that our children can put a tremendous amount of pressure on us. Our pride, thinking of ourselves, may lead us to make the wrong decision. I wonder how many parents of a pregnant, unwed daughter have later regretted decisions they felt they were pressured into.

Please don't misunderstand. Love for others and wanting them happy is a good thing. But if we are in a position of leadership, that is not to be the basis for a decision. We must be committed to make the right decision regardless of whether people like us for them or not.

All three of the decisions I mentioned last month could have produced people who were unhappy (ranging from disappointed to irate) with me, depending on what I chose. It would have been a safe decision, and easiest on the family, to have Sarah stay home. She would have been disappointed, but she was at peace with whatever I chose. Certainly I knew she would be thrilled to go. I felt God telling me she was to go. I rejected the windows, and as a result, the company discovered an easy cure for the manufacturing defect. Not only am I pleased, but others will benefit as a result. Lastly, I chose to stick to what I believe God's leading was regarding the message board post. Yes, the woman was exceedingly displeased and expressed it with no little passion. However, it was the right decision.

The Jews would have been extremely upset with Pilate had he released Jesus. This would have been a real test of what kind of man Pilate was. I find that it is an incredible test for me, too, when I make an unpopular decision. About six years ago, I decided we were going to change churches, and the family was not pleased with my choice. I had agonized over the decision and believed the Lord was saying we needed to change, but the family was involved and comfortable where we were attending. I made the decision that we needed to change, and we did. Time has a way of proving decisions, and soon the family all saw that it was God's plan for us.

I have also made poor decisions in the past because I struggle with pride. Two decisions in particular come to mind, and both had to do with one of my children. This child is very skilled at applying emotional pressure. Instead of dealing with the root cause, I gave in on both decisions. Over time my heart convicted me, and I asked that child's forgiveness. In addition, the child and I jointly chose to reverse those decisions.

Pride will also lead us to make stupid decisions. "And Hezekiah hearkened unto them, and shewed them all the house of his precious things, the silver, and the gold, and the spices, and the precious ointment, and *all* the house of his armour, and all that was found in his treasures: there was nothing in his house, nor in all his dominion, that Hezekiah shewed them not" (2 Kings 20:13). Hezekiah's pride caused him to want to show those representing the king of Babylon everything of value. In return, the king of Babylon would later attack and carry away all of the treasures Hezekiah had shown the Babylonian emissaries.

Pride may lead a father into purchasing a bigger house or a fancier car just so he might feel good about himself. We have also heard of wives who say that their husbands want them to dress immodestly to show off for other men. Those types of decisions can lead to situations that might be regretted in years to come. Severe money problems and moms who feel used are recipes for divorce. Just like Hezekiah's poor decision, our decisions prompted by pride may not have immediate consequences, but the consequences will come nonetheless.

There is so much more that could be said about how our pride will cause us to make terrible decisions. However, we can see the serious danger our family is in when we make decisions that are influenced by our pride. *"When* pride cometh, then cometh shame: but with the lowly *is* wisdom" (Proverbs 11:2). Our Lord will give us the right decision if we will humble ourselves.

May we be men of God and pray, "Lord, may I cling to You and know Your mind so I may serve those You have called me to serve. May I protect and lead them in the way You would have them to go. Lord Jesus, enable me to be a man of God."

# Aspects of Being a Leader — Part 3
## MAKING WISE DECISIONS
### by Steve

I wonder how many decisions a dad is faced with each day. The more children in the family, the more decisions will need to be made. Last month we saw how a dad's pride can negatively affect his ability to make the right decision. This month we will look at one area that can have a great positive effect on our decisions.

It is an area that parents profess to have a passionate bias toward, and yet in practice, we may struggle just as much as our children. Because it is critical for a Christian, we work hard to train our children in it.

This concept is so important that Scripture promises special blessing for children who embrace it since it is foundational to reaching Christian maturity. "Children, obey your parents in the Lord: for this is right. Honour thy father and mother; (which is the first commandment with promise;) That it may be well with thee, and thou mayest live long on the earth" (Ephesians 6:1-3).

Learning obedience is critical for children because it is an essential part of adulthood. Adults must know how to obey. We must obey the laws of our God and our land.

Based on observation of my family and others, I believe that many, if not most, decisions a dad faces boil down to simple obedience. If that is the case, then why is there such turmoil when trying to decide what to do?

This morning one of my children made a bad decision. He saw one of his sibling's shoes lying near the top of the basement stairs. Since the shoes obviously did not belong there, he graciously decided to help his brother by delivering at least one of the shoes a bit closer to the basement bedroom. This was a good decision. However, the bad decision came along in the delivery method. This child thought the easiest way to get those shoes in the basement was to kick them, one at a time, down the stairs.

Exercising great caution, he listened for a moment to make certain no one was about to come up the stairs before giving the shoe a mighty kick. Off it sailed into the air. The trajectory carried the shoe so that it was still over five feet in the air at the bottom of the stairs. Unfortunately, my quietly walking wife was just rounding the corner and starting up the basement stairs where her face was on a collision course with the projectile. To everyone's relief, her reflexes were good, and her hand was able to intercept the flying shoe just prior to facial impact. Her hand was sore, but the wound would have been worse had it been her face.

Now, this child knew he wasn't to throw or kick things like that. If he had obeyed, there would not have been a problem.

On Christmas Eve I was cooking Mexican meat for the family. It still had quite a bit of juice to cook off in the crock pot, so I thought I would help it along. I overruled the check in my spirit that told me I was about to violate the rules of crock pot use. I wrapped a couple towels around it so it would hold more of the heat in and boil off the juice more quickly. It worked great, as I had hoped it would, but as I removed the towels I saw something I hadn't counted on. The towels were actually scorched, and the crock pot's plastic feet had melted. The cutting board I had placed it on was split from the intense heat, and the counter top was too hot even to touch. Could it have ignited? I don't know for sure, but I do know it was one of the dumbest decisions I have ever made.

It all could have been avoided had I "obeyed" the instruction manual. In my heart I knew I was doing something outside of the design of the appliance. Why is it so difficult to follow instructions?

God gave us His Word to instruct us in how to live our lives. Many, if not the majority, of the answers we are looking for are clearly addressed in Scripture.

Then why do we struggle with decisions? I believe there are two primary reasons. One is we don't know what His Word says. The second is that, even when we do know, we often don't want to follow it.

To make wise decisions, we must know the Scriptures well. Friend, there is no shortcut. We must be in the Word every day. Read it, study it, and love it! It will guide you. "Thy word *is* a lamp unto my feet, and a light unto my path" (Psalms 119:105).

I recently dialogued with someone who said that modesty was only a matter of the heart. They explained their thinking: that God looked on the heart, and if they were modest in heart, that would please God. "In like manner also, that women adorn themselves in modest apparel, with shamefacedness and sobriety; not with braided hair, or gold, or pearls, or costly array" (1 Timothy 2:9). Even a quick reading of the above verse would indicate that modest apparel means modest clothing. Otherwise, after Adam and Eve sinned, God would not have clothed them in animal skins; He would have just looked at them and seen that their hearts were modest and left them alone.

One reason we occasionally hear from a wife who doesn't wear dresses is that her husband likes to see her in jeans. It is not difficult to discern why a husband might like to see his wife in jeans; however, the dad needs to evaluate the decision in relation to obedience of Scripture. If the choice is to be made between what appeals to the flesh and what is in obedience to God's Word, we must choose obedience.

Often we will hear of wives who are troubled by the types of things their professing husbands are viewing on the TV or computer. Proverbs 6:25: "Lust not after her beauty in thine heart; neither let her take thee with her eyelids" is very straightforward. It is not a suggestion, but a command. "But I say unto you, That whosoever looketh on a woman to lust after her hath committed adultery with her already in his heart" (Matthew 5:28).

"Mortify therefore your members which are upon the earth; fornication, uncleanness, inordinate affection, evil concupiscence, and covetousness, which is idolatry" (Colossians 3:5). We are not just to avoid these things, but we are to make these activities dead and play no part in our lives.

Next time we tell one of our children not to do something, we should ask ourselves if we are applying the same standard in our life. Are they supposed to obey us while we don't have to obey our Lord? Of course not!

So often I hear from others that all kinds of questionable activities are simply a matter of being free in Christ. That may have a catchy ring to it, but there is no basis for it in Scripture. Would you agree with your child if next time you tell him to do something, he says to you, "I would like to Dad, but I'm free in Christ. I really don't have to do that"?

Galatians addresses our freedom clearly. We are to be free from the bondage of sin so we may serve one another. We are not free to live as we choose. Galatians 5:13 sums it up well: "For, brethren, ye have been called unto liberty; only *use* not liberty for an occasion to the flesh, but by love serve one another."

Obedience makes the decision process simple. God calls me to obey. "By this we know that we love the children of God, when we love God, and keep his commandments. For this is the love of God, that we keep his commandments: and his commandments are not grievous" (1 John 5:2-3).

Obedience points the way to how we spend our time. It enables us to know how to lead our family. It makes the decision process much easier.

There will be times when our flesh is hesitant to obey God's Word, but there is blessing with obedience. The decisions will be easier, your family will flourish in the Lord, and your wife and children will bless you. May we be obedient servants of our Lord Jesus Christ.

# Aspects of Being a Leader — Part 4
## OBEDIENCE
### by Steve

The Thursday night prior to Nathan and Melanie's wedding, we had a "friends of the groom" fellowship. At one point in the evening, two brothers in the Lord were discussing a bit of their common past, while several of us were listening.

They are both West Point graduates and were reminiscing about some of their experiences there. In particular, they were sharing several of their more distressing situations. One told how on occasion he was given orders to do things that were impossible. The one giving the order knew it was impossible but did it to hone the young cadet's obedience. Both brothers confessed they had wanted to quit many times, but they would not allow themselves to do so. Isn't it interesting that the military believes that to be a good leader, you must be obedient?

Our neighbor, who is a city police officer, had just finished his dinner break when he walked across the ice-covered street to comment on Nathan and Melanie's wedding the previous Saturday. He said he appreciated being invited and how much it meant to him. I told him we weren't sure whether to invite him. Because of his busy schedule, we were concerned the wedding invitation might be an imposition. He said that he loves watching our children grow up, and when he is old, he wouldn't miss one of their weddings even if he had to be pushed in a wheelchair. He went on to say how he takes great pleasure in our children, as he is involved with children every day who don't know how to obey.

Not only do the lives of those in the military depend on their ability to be obedient, but our children's lives do as well. I doubt anyone would question the truth of that statement. However, how aware are we that the lives of those in our family are greatly affected by our ability to obey as well. Drive at speeds exceeding the law, and your family is in danger. If you choose to cheat the government and lie about your taxes, you may go to jail—now that will affect your ability to provide your family with food and housing! If a dad won't obey his boss, he is at risk of losing his job. Men love their freedom, but often the family suffers consequences if Dad doesn't obey those he should.

It is impossible for a dad to be a good leader if he isn't obedient. First, his family knows he is a hypocrite if they see Dad being disobedient while he tells his family to obey him. He may get away with it for a while, but he will eventually lose his children.

Saved dads are both children and soldiers. We are children of God and soldiers of Christ. "The Spirit itself beareth witness with our spirit, that we are the children of God: And if children, then heirs; heirs of God, and joint-heirs with Christ; if so be that we suffer with *him*, that we may be also glorified together" (Romans 8:16-17). "Thou therefore endure hardness, as a good soldier of Jesus Christ. No man that warreth entangleth himself with the affairs of *this* life; that he may please him who hath chosen him to be a soldier" (2 Timothy 2:3-4).

It was no accident that the Holy Spirit led Paul to refer to those saved as both children and soldiers. There should be no doubt about the importance of obedience in our lives as we endeavor to lead our families. However, do you also get the feeling that obedience is a "dirty" word in Christian circles these days? Begin talking about obedience, and freedom fighters will start crying, "Legalism, legalism!" I hear much talk about freedom in Christ and very little about obedience. Has political correctness neutered God's Word in the church?

Those who are saved are to obey the Lord Jesus and His Word. "Not every one that saith unto me, Lord, Lord, shall enter into the kingdom of heaven; but he that doeth the will of my Father which is in heaven" (Matthew 7:21). "And he answered and said unto them, My mother and my brethren are these which hear the word of God, and do it" (Luke 8:21).

Just to be certain there is no misunderstanding, obedience does not earn us salvation in any way, shape, or form. It is, however, evidence of our salvation and love for the Lord. The verses just read confirm that obedience gives evidence of our being saved. The point that the freedom fighters miss is that we obey because we love the Lord Jesus. We don't obey to earn salvation, but we obey out of love for our Lord. The One Who is our Model and Lord was obedient unto death, and He expects our obedience (Luke 17:10). Jesus said in John 14:15, "If ye love me, keep my commandments." That is really very simple, isn't it? Those who love Him little, obey little.

A father's level of obedience will affect how he leads his family and how his family follows him. First, Christ said obedience reveals one's love. If we love Christ, we will obey Him, but if we don't obey Christ, we reveal our love for ourselves. The family knows Dad better than anyone, and as soon as they know anything about Scripture, they are looking to see if Dad is obedient. If Dad isn't obedient, he will be seen as a hypocrite, and his family will not want to follow what he says. They will tend to follow his example.

A father's obedience to Christ gives the family confidence in his decisions. They will see that Dad makes decisions based on his obedience to his Lord and Scripture. They will respect Dad as a man of God.

Unfortunately, the disobedient dad's family will not have confidence in his decisions. Dad's self-love will cause the family to suspect his motives when he makes decisions. Selfish decisions are easy targets for whining, complaining, and arguing against. If the family member can make Dad miserable enough, then selfishly, Dad may reverse the decision to give himself a little peace.

Obedience makes leading a family much easier than disobedience. Decisions based on the Bible and God's direction are pointless to attack, as those assaults would have to be directed toward God. It changes the whole attitude in the home.

Obedience will protect your family from sin. In Exodus 24, Moses, Joshua, and the elders went up Mount Sinai as the Lord instructed them. God told the elders to wait at one place while Moses and Joshua climbed higher. Then Moses left Joshua alone and completed the climb to the Lord.

Moses was with the Lord for forty days! I find that absolutely incredible. There is so much more I would like to know about that time. They weren't told to bring any food, and we can only assume that God intended to somehow sustain them for that long. Moses fasted the entire time and so did Joshua.

But what about the elders? "And he said unto the elders, Tarry ye here for us, until we come again unto you: and, behold, Aaron and Hur *are* with you: if any man have any matters to do, let him come unto them" (Exodus 24:14). The elders were told clearly to wait for their return. Yet they did not obey (Joshua did obey and look how God later used him). As a result they turned to idolatry by worshipping the golden calf, were immoral, and many were slain. There are tremendous blessings with obedience and chastening with disobedience.

It is likely that many reading this Corner are experiencing discipline from the Lord as a result of disobedience and thereby causing the whole family to suffer. Brothers, repent of the disobedience and wrong choices, and God will pour out His blessings.

Each of us dads, who is a child of God, must take the Bible seriously and obey Him out of love for the Lord Jesus. May we say, "Lord, I will do whatever You tell me to, when You tell me to do it."

May each of us pick up our Bibles and prayerfully read them every morning as we begin our days. Then we should obediently apply the lessons to our lives daily. It will make leading our families so much easier, and it will cause each of us to strive to keep our lives clean and pleasing to the Lord.

"These things I command you, that ye love one another" (John 15:17). "According as he hath chosen us in him before the foundation of the world, that we should be holy and without blame before him in love" (Ephesians 1:4).

# Aspects of Being a Leader — Part 5
## PROTECTING OUR FAMILIES
### by Steve

I had to drive to Kansas City this afternoon to deliver some software to a client. I invited Teri to accompany me. We were enjoying our ride as we traveled down a four-lane section of highway that had a sixty-five mile per hour speed limit and several traffic lights.

I could see the light ahead of me turn red and along with the two cars behind me, we began bleeding off speed as we came to a stop. I glanced in my rearview mirror and saw a burgundy car still traveling at the speed limit, or more, bearing down on the intersection in the left lane next to us. I quickly glanced ahead and saw two cars beginning to pull into the intersection, on their green light, in a collision path. Just then, the burgundy car's driver slammed on the brakes, and the car began skidding. There was absolutely no way that car was going to stop or even reduce his speed enough to matter.

I quickly looked forward, and the two cars were now approaching the same point on the pavement as the "red-light runner." The two legal cars hit their brakes and were able to stop before venturing into the path of the speeding car. Obviously, they had seen this car flying down the road and were entering the intersection much more slowly than they might have under other circumstances.

Thankfully, I have never witnessed a fatal accident, but I came as close today as I would ever care to come. Tragedy was averted because the lead car was being observant, looking ahead for danger as he proceeded. Had the driver not been attentive, it likely would have been terrible for all those involved.

What kind of driver are you? I'm not talking about your skills behind the wheel, but your methods as leader of your home.

Old Testament Lot was a man who reminds me of the person driving the burgundy vehicle. If it hadn't been for God's grace, he would have reaped more serious consequences than he actually did.

In Genesis 13 we read that there was strife between Abram's herdsmen and Lot's. Abram asked Lot to pick where he wanted to live, and Abram would go somewhere else. "And Lot lifted up his eyes, and beheld all the plain of Jordan, that it *was* well watered every where, before the LORD destroyed Sodom and Gomorrah, *even* as the garden of the LORD, like the land of Egypt, as thou comest unto Zoar. Then Lot chose him all the plain of Jordan; and Lot journeyed east: and they separated themselves the one from the other" (Genesis 13:10-11).

Lot chose the best for himself. He was a selfish man. Because of decisions like this one, his family would know that most of his decisions would likely have a selfish motive to them. This would cause them to question his leadership of their family. We see this questioning clearly when the Lord was about to destroy Sodom. Lot tried to convince his sons-in-law to leave the city. However, since Lot had not demonstrated real leadership, they would not listen to him or follow him. Instead they thought he was joking.

I believe we see that Lot was also lazy. He was a shepherd, but he ended up living the easy life in Sodom. His motives are later confirmed when the angels tell him to flee to the mountains, but Lot wants to live in another city of his choice. Because of Lot's laziness, he was willing to raise his family in the morally corrupted environment of Sodom. He knew it was a wicked place; that is why he wanted to protect the angels from sleeping in the city square. Yet, Lot would not take his family away from there for their own good.

May we not be of a like mind with Lot. I struggle with laziness, and that is one small reason why we don't watch any TV. I know my own sin nature and how tempted I am to watch what is a snare to my soul and would corrupt my family. Sure, a dad can justify the desire to be entertained by feeling he deserves a mindless break and that he will be careful about what he watches. However, regardless of your efforts to avoid damaging shows, you will still be bombarded with lewd and inappropriate commercials. Even news bites present things done in darkness, which Scripture says are not to be spoken of: "For it is a shame even to speak of those things which are done of them in secret" (Ephesians 5:12). Watching television will have an affect on the dad's soul and the children's. Dads, which are we more concerned with: our pleasure and entertainment or the purity of our families? What other harmful influences may there be that we have been too lazy to protect our family from?

Lot was willing to sacrifice his daughters for others. At first that may seem noble, but is it? A noble act would have meant being willing to sacrifice himself for others. That is our example in Christ. (Certainly, Christ would have us sacrifice our selfish entertainment and pleasure to keep our family pure as we serve Him.)

Often parents tell us how they desire to reach the lost by using their children to evangelize in different places and activities. Frankly, as I observe their decisions and listen to the justification, it sounds much like the excuse I believe Lot would use for being willing to send his innocent daughters out to appease a lust-incensed mob. Dads, the result will be the same. I believe you will either lose your children, or they will be corrupted by others' influence and never be what they could have been. We are to evangelize, but we are to be the ones doing it. May we not sacrifice our children, but protect them as a father should (John 10).

God's priorities were not Lot's priorities. In the morning the angels urged Lot to arise, hurry, and flee the city. (How many of us think we would be in bed if we knew our city was about to be destroyed?) In Genesis 19:16 we read that Lot "lingered," and the angels took hold of his hand and those of his family members, bringing them out of Sodom. If Lot had been in tune with the Lord when he was told to leave all the angels would have seen was his dust. Lot was not a godly leader of his family. We also see this confirmed when his wife looks back after having been told not to. They both loved the easy life, but she was not strong enough to only look forward.

I wonder if this isn't analogous to dads who choose not to spend time with the Lord Jesus in the beginning of their day. Most often the "reason" is they are too busy. That just isn't true; we all take time to do what is important to us. Most of us will not go without eating, because we feel it to be important. If our time with the Lord were seen as critical to our walk with Him and leading our family, then we would do it every day regardless of our circumstances. The truth is that we consider other things more important than spending time with our Lord. We are relying more on ourselves than we are the Lord, otherwise we couldn't bear not to spend time with Him. May we not be found in bed (like Lot) when we have the urgency of meeting with our Lord first thing in the morning.

When the angels had brought them outside the city, they instructed Lot to flee to the mountains. Next, an amazing thing happened. Lot argued with them by saying, ". . . Oh, not so, my Lord" (Genesis 19:18)! This absolutely floors me! He had just been delivered by God's mercy, after he lingered, and now he wanted to go to another city. What a picture that is of what it takes to pry sin out of our grasp. It cost him most of his family and everything he had. God had given him clear instructions, and he didn't want to follow them. AUGHHHHH!

I wonder if that isn't a major reason so many dads really don't want to begin their day with a quiet time with the Lord. Could it be they don't really want to hear what the Lord is telling them? Could it be that they don't want to get too close to the Lord in case He might give them instructions they really don't want to hear or obey? What price, men, are we willing to pay to have it our way? It may cost us our family as it did Lot.

May we be men of God and not live after Lot's selfish and lazy example. Whatever it costs us, may we lead our family in paths of righteousness, protect them from evil, and obediently follow God's direction for our family. May we not endanger our families like the driver of the burgundy vehicle and Lot did theirs.

# Aspects of Being a Leader — Part 6
## Trusting God
### by Steve

Last month we looked at Lot's life to see what insight we could glean from it. We saw that Lot was a selfish man who made decisions based on what was good for him. Yet, Lot was referred to as a just man and was still better than the pagans around him. But, was he God's man?

Based on observation, I find many professing Christians who seem to have a saving faith, yet their walk bears great similarities to Lot's. We must each ask, "Is it I, Lord?"

The man we are going to look at this month was quite different from Lot, yet he had similar circumstances. Let's look briefly at Abraham's life and compare our life to his.

In Genesis 12:1-4 we read, "Now the LORD had said unto Abram, Get thee out of thy country, and from thy kindred, and from thy father's house, unto a land that I will shew thee: And I will make of thee a great nation, and I will bless thee, and make thy name great; and thou shalt be a blessing: And I will bless them that bless thee, and curse him that curseth thee: and in thee shall all families of the earth be blessed. So Abram departed, as the LORD had spoken unto him. . . ."

What a promise of incredible blessing that was! I find it tempting to think, "How could anyone not act on that?" But let's look at this more closely, and see if we think we would have obeyed like Abram did.

First, God is telling Abram to leave the security of his extended family. In those days, living by your family was much safer than living by yourself in a foreign country. The men in the family would join together in opposing those who might attack them. By leaving, Abram no longer had that security. Abram trusted God with his life.

God didn't even tell Abram where He was sending him. Abram was told not only to leave the security of his family but also to go someplace unknown. Most of us would ask ourselves, "What if I don't like it there? Is this really God's direction?" There is just something unsettling about not knowing. Oftentimes, we can handle good or bad news; it is the not knowing that "kills" us.

Years ago, at a training clinic for marriage enrichment leaders that Teri and I attended, each spouse blindfolded the other and led him or her around the building. I remember how uncertain I felt (okay, I'll admit it, even a little fearful at times) as Teri enjoyed leading me on a very strange journey, up and down stairs, in circles, and through different rooms. It was natural for me to want to know where each step was being placed and where I was going to end up. One aspect the exercise demonstrated was how important it was to be able to trust the person leading you. It was much easier to blindly be led about because I trusted Teri and knew she would not take me anywhere that wasn't good for me, yet because I couldn't see, I still had an emotional response. Abram not only trusted God, but his expectation was in Him. Abram was not told where, but he went.

What an incredible beginning to Abram's walk with God. It reminds me of the old saying where one says, "Jump!" and the recipient of the command says, "How high?" However, with Abram, he didn't even ask how high. He simply obeyed. It is the desire of my life that if God says to do something, I will do it.

Abram traveled to the land of Canaan. Then in Genesis 12:7, God spoke to Abram again and said, ". . . Unto thy seed will I give this land. . . ." God did not give the land to Abram right then, but He said He was giving it to Abram's seed. I wonder how many of us would be happy if all the blessings God was going to give us were to go only to our children's children. We would not be able to enjoy them ourselves but would have to be content knowing they were coming. Are we willing to make decisions that will reap a harvest of righteousness only for our children and our children's children?

As we read about Abram's life, we are surprised twice by decisions of his that are not representative of a good leader. In fact, we would expect Lot, not Abram, to have made these decisions. God records these events for our benefit. What can we learn from them to help us be good leaders of our families?

In Genesis 12:13 and 20:2 Abram (now Abraham), like a good leader, was "looking down the road" ahead of their travels and thinking about situations they might encounter. Sarah was very beautiful, and Abraham was concerned in his heart that Sarah would be taken to be part of a king's harem. It must have been fairly common that if the woman was married, the husband was killed and the wife taken. Therefore, Abraham reckoned that he was going to be in serious danger, and he asked Sarah to deceive them by not admitting that she was his wife, but to say that Abraham was her brother (he was her half brother). Deception is not God's plan.

A good leader should be alert to danger, but he must seek the Lord for the right solution. Abraham's plan of deception was not of the Lord. God "stepped in" and protected Abraham and Sarah, and there appeared to be no consequences for the deception.

We may be tempted to think the lesson Abraham learned through these situations was to trust God for protection. I believe, though, that an even greater lesson would have been to ask God first before proceeding. I could find no mention in Scripture of where Abraham sought God's direction prior to traveling to those two areas that got him into trouble. Look how those failures could have been avoided if Abraham had prayed before he went down those roads.

"And he entreated Abram well for her sake: and he had sheep, and oxen, and he asses, and menservants, and maidservants, and she asses, and camels" (Genesis 12:16). We read how Pharaoh gave Abraham gifts in exchange for Sarah. Then we read in Genesis 16:1, "Now Sarai Abram's wife bare him no children: and she had an handmaid, an Egyptian, whose name *was* Hagar." Then we read how Sarah gives Hagar to Abraham as his wife so Sarah can claim Hagar's children as her own. Here is another creative human plan laden with consequences. Yes, it was Sarah's plan, but Abraham agreed to it and, therefore, owned the consequences.

Now we see that had Abraham not decided to go to Egypt, Hagar would not have been given to them, and she would not be part of Sarah's scheme for children. Had Ishmael not been born, is it possible that the Arab-Israeli conflict through the centuries could have been avoided? Only the Lord knows, but it is an interesting question. How bitter the fruit we may serve our family when we aren't following God's direction.

Do you ever neglect to ask God for direction and then cry out to Him to fix the situation when the road leads to trouble? How much better for us and our families if we cry out to the Lord for direction prior to going down a certain road.

Abraham was God's man and did so many things right. He had incredible faith in God, and it was counted unto him for righteousness. He was obedient to God to the point of being willing to sacrifice his only son, Isaac. He was satisfied with his descendants receiving the blessings of a homeland, instead of having the blessing himself.

May we be like Abraham in his good points and learn from his failures. May we seek God every morning and at every decision. May we be totally dependent on the Father to direct our lives.

# Aspects of Being a Leader — Part 7
## ANGER — RELATIONSHIP POISON
### by Steve

I was looking for my glasses in the kitchen when I realized and then said that they were still in the van. John immediately headed for the door to the garage, announcing that he would get them for me. I was grateful for his desire to serve, but told him that I had better retrieve them because I didn't want them dropped. He assured me that he would be careful, and off he went.

Seconds later John came flying back into the kitchen with the glasses in hand. As he closed the door with the hand holding the glasses, the handle caused him to loosen his tender grip on the glasses, and they headed for the floor. The speed at which he was coming in the door gave the glasses momentum. I watched with no little distress as they went sliding across the tile floor—lens down.

I have been working at laying down anger in my life. Therefore, when I felt anger welling up inside of me, I turned to the wall behind me. I raised my hand and placed my palm against the wall. I didn't smack the wall, but it was obvious that I would have liked to. With my anger now under control, I turned to face a sweet eleven-year-old who had tears brimming in his eyes. He apologized and said he didn't mean to do it. He was very sorry.

I told him that was why I didn't want him to get the glasses as he is always in a hurry and prone to accidents like that. I said it was okay and thanked him for his desire to help. He had something to do after that and went off.

Most would say I did a great job of controlling my anger. I was not harsh, and I didn't discipline him. Yet, I was angry. Teri observed the situation and could tell I was angry. Several days later I spoke to John about it. I asked him if he thought I was angry. He said, "Yes," and that was why he started to cry, because he was afraid. Ughhh! How that broke my heart.

Dads, that is why if we want to be good leaders of our homes, we must, "Let all bitterness, and wrath, and anger, and clamour, and evil speaking, be put away . . ." (Ephesians 4:31). Our children know when we are angry, and it drives a wedge between them and us. They are afraid of us when we are angry, which is not conducive for having them turn their hearts to us.

The fact is, at that moment, I thought more of my glasses than I did of my son. That is something to repent of before God. Doesn't that sound ridiculous to you? Yet I wonder how often that happens with other dads as well.

What causes you to respond angrily? Maybe it is a glass of spilled milk, the refrigerator door left open, tools lying in the yard, bikes in the middle of the driveway, lots of screaming and yelling, toys left out and tripped on, doors slammed, a child hurting another child, a child being disrespectful to you or your wife, a child not obeying you, a child mocking you, or any of a limitless list of ways a child could make us angry. We need to step back and ask ourselves, "Does anger achieve God's results and make us good leaders?" "For the wrath of man worketh not the righteousness of God" (James 1:20).

There was a time when I allowed myself to be visibly angry because the children responded so much better when I told them to do something. But it soon became apparent that I was driving a wedge between their hearts and mine. If we desire to raise up godly seed (Malachi 2:15), then anger—visible or invisible—must have no part in our lives.

I expect if we were to put our heads together we could write down a fairly lengthy list of ways our spouses can make us angry. I have noticed that when I'm angry with Teri, it does nothing to improve our relationship. Have you experienced that in your marriage as well? There is something about anger that causes the other person to pull back. They don't want to open up and become close, because they don't know that they can relax and not be on the defensive. Anger, even a spirit of anger, will cause the one receiving the anger to put up a shield of emotional protection.

My controlled anger with John that night was as harmful to our relationship as if I had yelled at him. He sensed the internal anger and admitted to me that he was afraid. He had no reason to be afraid as I was calm on the outside, but he sensed my spirit. It was angry. We have everything to win and nothing to lose if we will purpose, by God's grace, to put away all anger.

Scripture is very clear about putting away anger. Read the following verses.

"Cease from anger, and forsake wrath: fret not thyself in any wise to do evil" (Psalms 37:8).

"But I say unto you, That whosoever is angry with his brother without a cause shall be in danger of the judgment . . ." (Matthew 5:22). Even if there was to be a cause, we need to consider Romans 12:19, "Dearly beloved, avenge not yourselves, but *rather* give place unto wrath: for it is written, Vengeance *is* mine; I will repay, saith the Lord."

"Let all bitterness, and wrath, and anger, and clamour, and evil speaking, be put away from you, with all malice" (Ephesians 4:31). Notice all anger is to be put away.

"But now ye also put off all these; anger, wrath, malice, blasphemy, filthy communication out of your mouth" (Colossians 3:8). Again, all anger is to be put away.

"Now the works of the flesh are manifest, which are *these*; Adultery, fornication, uncleanness, lasciviousness, idolatry, witchcraft, hatred, variance, emulations, wrath, strife, seditions, heresies, envyings, murders, drunkenness, revellings, and such like: of the which I tell you before, as I have also told *you* in time past, that they which do such things shall not inherit the kingdom of God"

(Galatians 5:19-21). Look at the other qualities that wrath (anger) is listed among. Would we excuse any of the others in our home?

"I will therefore that men pray every where, lifting up holy hands, without wrath and doubting" (1 Timothy 2:8). Do we want to pray effectively?

"Wherefore, my beloved brethren, let every man be swift to hear, slow to speak, slow to wrath: For the wrath of man worketh not the righteousness of God" (James 1:19-20). Our anger will not lead to righteousness in our life or those to whom our anger is directed at.

Out of all the verses in the Bible telling us to put away anger, some will still cling to Ephesians 4:26, "Be ye angry, and sin not: let not the sun go down upon your wrath," as giving them freedom to be angry. Yet, they ignore that five verses later we are told to put away ALL anger. When we look at the above verses, it makes it extremely difficult to justify any anger.

As I said earlier, I have purposed to put away all anger by God's grace. If there is such a thing as anger, with a cause that the Lord would approve of, I can't imagine experiencing it. I can see what Scripture says about anger and how anger destroys intimacy in the home. It is difficult enough to win the hearts of my family members; I do not want to allow something in my life that will destroy what I've worked so hard for.

How about you? What place does anger have in your life? Have you seen anger's harmful effects on relationships in your family? One resource that was very helpful in my life was Dr. S. M. Davis' audio, titled *Freedom from the Spirit of Anger*. (It can be purchased from our website: www.Titus2.com) Dads, this really is a serious issue. Will you ask the Lord to search your heart and discover how He might remove anger from it? Will you trust Him to give you the grace needed?

# Aspects of Being a Leader — Part 8
## No Critical Spirit!
### *by Steve*

A short time ago while Teri and I were on our morning walk, she said, "I'm feeling like you have a critical spirit toward me lately. Is that true?" I didn't enjoy hearing her question because that told me she was not feeling loved. Even worse, she was sensing a negative, critical spirit on my part.

"No, I don't think so," I responded, and the conversation drifted onto other things.

I'm not sure of the exact chain of events, but over the next few days the Lord started speaking to my heart. He convicted me of times when I had allowed negative, judgmental thoughts in my mind about Teri. Yes, I finally had to admit it; I did have a critical spirit toward her!

"Mr. Webster" defines critical as "inclined to criticize severely and unfavorably." Criticize "implies finding fault especially with methods or policies or intentions." It was true. I was looking at Teri with the predisposition of finding fault. I was allowing myself to criticize certain actions and behaviors of hers in my mind. When I was looking at what Teri did through a magnifying glass, was she able to do anything to my satisfaction? Was she hearing praise and gratefulness for all she did in our home? Clearly not!

Perhaps some might wonder what is wrong with having a judgmental spirit, as long as the negative thoughts aren't expressed. If you are going to be critical, might it not be acceptable to do it secretly? I suppose in a similar way we might justify being angry on the inside or having secret lustful thoughts, as long as we don't outwardly show them. The problem is that we can't be one thing on the inside and another on the outside. We truly are what we are in our hearts. If we lust in our hearts, we are adulterers. If we are angry in our hearts, we are angry men. If we are critical in our hearts, we are critical people. "But I say unto you, That whosoever looketh on a woman to lust after her hath committed adultery with her already in his heart" (Matthew 5:28). "For as he thinketh in his heart, so *is* he: Eat and drink, saith he to thee; but his heart *is* not with thee" (Proverbs 23:7).

Just like Teri noticed something was wrong, the person our judgmental spirit is directed at will not feel loved. It poisons our thoughts about them. It will affect our words, actions, and attitudes towards them. "Out of the same mouth proceedeth blessing and cursing. My brethren, these things ought not so to be. Doth a fountain send forth at the same place sweet *water* and bitter? Can the fig tree, my brethren, bear olive berries? either a vine, figs? so *can* no fountain both yield salt water and fresh" (James 3:10-12). What is in our heart directs our speech. "O generation of vipers, how can ye, being evil, speak good things? for out of the abundance of the heart the mouth speaketh" (Matthew 12:34).

Harboring secret, negative thoughts will damage a husband's love for his wife. If you have been struggling with loving your wife deeply from your heart, evaluate whether you have a critical spirit. A judgmental spirit will also put up a barrier between you and your child. As loving as we may try to be to them, our spirit will be shouting even louder that we don't accept them the way they are, we aren't happy with them, and they'd better change.

Think of a possession that you have that means a lot to you. It very likely isn't perfect, as few things are. However, for some reason or other, you really like it. Maybe it is your car since men often have some attachment to their vehicles. When you think of it, why is it pleasing to you? What aspects of it come to mind? When you are thinking pleasant thoughts about it, are you thinking about anything negative concerning it?

For example, I spend a great deal of time with my computer every day. I appreciate it, and I am very pleased with it. I seldom think about its negative aspects. It is fairly slow by today's standards because it is only 450 MHz. It doesn't have a large hard disk so I have to be reasonably careful with what I store on it. The display has a very large footprint and takes up a great deal of desk space as opposed to the sleek new flat panel displays that are out. It's in my office in the basement where I don't have any windows, and it gets quite stuffy in there with the door closed.

Now, what if I started thinking about how slow my computer is, the small hard disk, the clunky display, and how stuffy it is in my office? Would I still have pleasant feelings toward that computer? Of course not! That is the way with anything we allow ourselves to think negatively about. Concentrating on what is not pleasing will erode positive feelings.

We may think we are doing this in secret, but just like hidden anger or lust, it always shows. It comes across loud and clear, as I realized when the spirit of love that Teri normally felt was being dissolved away.

So what do we do if we have a judgmental spirit? How can we stop it? I will share what I did to be free from it. First, I was convicted that it was sin. I am to love and cherish Teri, to die for her if need be (Ephesians 5:25). I am not to sit in continual judgment of her. I confessed this to my Lord Jesus and asked His forgiveness. Next, I went to Teri and confessed that she was right and asked her forgiveness. Then, I asked the Lord to convict me of judgmental thoughts when I was allowing them into my mind. I also asked that He might give me an attitude of gratefulness. I purposed to cast every negative thought down. Not only has Teri not had a husband who is looking at her with faultfinding eyes lately, but she now has a husband who has found a new sense of appreciation for her.

A critical spirit is a cancer that will destroy your ability to delight in the one it is focused on. It isn't healthy, and it certainly isn't enjoyable. Do you want to rejoice in the wife of your youth? Purpose to love her and not judge her. What if instead of loving me, Teri were to concentrate on my faults? Now that is a scary thought!

# What's Your Excuse?
## *by Steve*

I have an audiocassette of a sermon by David Ring that he preached during a Moody Bible Institute's Founder's Week. He wove the testimony of what Christ did in his life throughout the message. What set his message and life apart from any I've heard is that Brother Ring has cerebral palsy.

He shared the tremendous struggles he has had in life. He talked of how the children made fun of his stammering speech and his difficulty in walking. Most of us have had others tease us at some point in our life, but it is likely that very few reading this have ever experienced the mockery that David endured. Children can be cruel and can delight in making fun of anyone, no matter how "perfect" they may be. But let children see someone who has a real physical challenge, and they will swarm to attack like killer bees or sharks in a feeding frenzy. Can you imagine what it would be like to be around children and have great difficulty speaking clearly? What about not being able to run and play like the other children, but instead to have a leg that hinders you from walking normally?

If that wasn't bad enough, both of David's parents died when he was a child. I believe his father died first, and David was all the more dependent on his mother. When his mother died, he was devastated. One of his sisters loved him deeply and took him in. She showed him incredible kindness and patience as he was struggling greatly with the loss of his mother and the way others treated him.

School was awful for him, and he wanted to give up. His sister kept encouraging him that he could do it, while others said that he would never amount to anything. I'm not sure of the exact sequence, but he was finally saved. God began working in his life, even giving him the desire to be a preacher. He shared, to my amazement, that other men studying to be preachers would tell him he would never make it. He completed college, married (and now has several children), and travels the U.S. as a full-time evangelist.

Religion may provide some degree of outward conformity, but Jesus Christ not only saves a person from hell, He also changes lives. Jesus Christ can take ashes and make something beautiful. Jesus Christ did a wonderful work in David Ring's life. He took a man who was full of despair and bitterness and made a new creation. Jesus Christ took a man who was predisposed to a life of failure and rejection, and appears to be using him as a powerful instrument to glorify Himself and challenge others in their walk.

There were several things I noticed in particular from his message that encouraged me as a father. First is the influence we can have on those around us when we are encouragers. It is easy to point out every time our children fall short. The Lord used David's sister in a mighty way. She believed in her brother and conveyed that to him over and over. When I'm not with my children, will their thoughts "hear" me correct them or tell them they can succeed at something? Are they likely to see Dad as the one who most believes in their ability to succeed? When they think of Dad, does it give them a feeling of assurance? Those are my desires for my children.

Along similar lines are the voices of those who told David he would never amount to anything. Have you ever heard yourself say, "You always . . . ?" I sure have, and I wish I could take back every one of those times. The positive affirmations we make to our children can be quickly forgotten by our negative global statements. If we are going to make a universal statement, may it be one of blessing. "Son, I want you to know that every time I see your face my heart rejoices."

Everyone on the face of the earth has areas of weakness. As I listened to David Ring, I realized the great need to be extra patient and understanding with the mental and physical limitations of my children. It is easy to let their weaknesses become irritants instead of stimulants for us to bless them more. These are the areas in which they need us most. Yet, those are often the areas where we will lose patience first. "Charity suffereth long, *and* is kind; charity envieth not; charity vaunteth not itself, is not puffed up" (1 Corinthians 13:4).

I suppose the greatest challenge I received from David was his desire to be used of God despite any difficulties he faced. "But we have this treasure in earthen vessels, that the excellency of the power may be of God, and not of us. *We are* troubled on every side, yet not distressed; *we are* perplexed, but not in despair; Persecuted, but not forsaken; cast down, but not destroyed; Always bearing about in the body the dying of the Lord Jesus, that the life also of Jesus might be made manifest in our body" (2 Corinthians 4:7-10). David Ring longs to be used by God for His glory. In David's physical limitations, God gives grace. David is willing to receive God's strength and be used as an instrument of righteousness.

For those who are saved, we have been bought with a price, the precious blood of the Lord Jesus Christ. "For ye are bought with a price: therefore glorify God in your body, and in your spirit, which are God's" (1 Corinthians 6:20). We are no longer our own, but His. We are not on this earth for our pleasure and entertainment, but to serve our Lord. "Ye are bought with a price; be not ye the servants of men" (1 Corinthians 7:23). We have daily opportunities to serve our families. The needs of our wives and children are to come before ours. "Husbands, love your wives, even as Christ also loved the church, and gave himself for it" (Ephesians 5:25).

May each of us take a sincere appraisal of our life. One way might be to review how we spend our time each day. Who or what is it spent on? Are we being obedient to the Lord? Are we serving Him in gladness of heart? Are we serving others outside the church? Are we responding with peace and patience to the tribulations that come our way? Are we welcoming them as opportunities for God to show Himself strong? If not, what is our excuse? David certainly had a good excuse, and yet he chose to be used of God. May we be men of God and let Him be glorified through our willing, cheerful obedience. What is our excuse for not being used of God?

# Lawn Care:
# How Is Your Lawn?
## by Steve

I am able to go for a walk six mornings a week, four days with Teri and two days with her father. We walk roughly the same route every day. Strolling week after week along the same path gives me the opportunity to observe the yards we pass by.

It is amazing the variance in people's lawns. Some are beautiful, lush, green yards; then there are those that look quite nice. Others could use improvement. Finally, there are yards that are complete disasters. They look absolutely terrible!

I'm thinking of one appalling lawn in particular. It is on the corner so you can see both the front and back yards. In the spring I noticed clover lightly scattered around the yard. Over time the clover spread like wild fire and finally took over the whole yard. From a distance the lawn looked pretty good, but as you drew closer it became obvious that it was all clover rather than grass. When the summer heat came, the clover died. That would be good, except the clover had already totally killed the grass. Then the homeowners didn't have to mow (not that they did much before) because nothing was growing in the bare dirt except a few low weeds.

"I went by the field of the slothful, and by the vineyard of the man void of understanding; And, lo, it was all grown over with thorns, *and* nettles had covered the face thereof, and the stone wall thereof was broken down. Then I saw, *and* considered *it* well: I looked upon *it, and* received instruction. *Yet* a little sleep, a little slumber, a little folding of the hands to sleep: So shall thy poverty come *as* one that travelleth; and thy want as an armed man" (Proverbs 24:30-34).

The above verses tell me that I have the opportunity to learn a great deal from observing others. We try to take advantage of this in the Maxwell home. I don't know about you, but I would much prefer to learn from someone else's mistakes. "Smite a scorner, and the simple will beware: and reprove one that hath understanding, *and* he will understand knowledge" (Proverbs 19:25). I don't mind identifying with the simple if it means I can avoid a trip to the woodshed.

Over the months as I observed that lawn, I was struck with how similar it was to some aspects of raising children. First, I never looked at clover as a threat to my lawn. As a matter of fact, in some ways I have always liked clover. I have fond childhood memories of summer play times in fields of clover. Clover hasn't seemed like a weed to me, and it isn't ugly like many weeds. Maybe that was the initial attitude of the homeowner whose lawn was destroyed by clover.

It doesn't matter whether it is a new or old yard, clover still presents a danger when you are trying to grow healthy, beautiful grass. In the same way, whether our children are young or old, there are situations for which we must keep our eyes open. I think most of us will notice recognizable weeds that sprout up in the lives of our children. What about those things that appear innocent, just like that clover? Will we spot areas that have negative impact on our children, perhaps ones that the world (and even the church these days) calls good and beneficial? There are certain harmful behaviors and activities, innocent in appearance that our children may take up. By the time we become concerned, they are much more difficult to address.

Let's see what Scripture says. "Flee also youthful lusts: but follow righteousness, faith, charity, peace, with them that call on the Lord out of a pure heart" (2 Timothy 2:22). Paul was warning Timothy to flee youthful lusts and replace them with righteousness, faith, love, and peace. Many would quickly recognize youthful lusts as being immoral lusting for the opposite sex, pride, and the desire to be in control. There may be others, but there is one in particular that most would not put in the category of youthful lusts.

In 2 Timothy 3:2-5 Paul describes evil men in the end times. "For men shall be lovers of their own selves, covetous, boasters, proud, blasphemers, disobedient to parents, unthankful, unholy, Without natural affection, trucebreakers, false accusers, incontinent, fierce, despisers of those that are good, Traitors, heady, highminded, lovers of pleasures more than lovers of God; Having a form of god-liness, but denying the power thereof: from such turn away." As you read that list it should be pretty obvious how harmful most of those listed "weeds" are. However, if you reread the list, you should spot some "clover." What about those who are "lovers of pleasures more than lovers of God"?

Look at the company "lovers of pleasures" is keeping in the list: lovers of their own selves, covetous, boasters, proud, blasphemers, disobedient to parents, unthankful, unholy, without natural affec-tion (sodomites), trucebreakers, false accusers (liars), incontinent (no self-control), fierce, despisers of those that are good (they love evil), traitors, heady, highminded, LOVERS OF PLEASURES more than lovers of God. How many Christian parents do you know who are as concerned and careful that their children don't become "lovers of pleasure" as there are parents concerned that their children don't become sodomites? Raising a child who is a "lover of pleasure" (or being one ourselves) is very serious and should not be taken lightly. Then why is it not even questioned or rebuked in Christian circles?

"Lovers of pleasure" so characterizes our society. Billions and bil-lions of dollars are spent each year on seeking greater thrills, chills, excitement, and fun. Why? It is pleasurable! Movies, automobile races, football, baseball, soccer, hockey, a myriad of other sporting activities, alcohol, and drugs—to name only a few—all produce pleasure of sorts. In our area, when there is a Kansas City Chiefs game, even the professing Christians dawn their red apparel. It isn't because they are trying to relate to the other fans with the hope of winning them to Christ; it is because the excitement of the game is pleasurable.

So what does one do about clover? Some (the world) let the clover take over. I read how a Canadian group actually promotes clover lawns. Many take that approach with pleasure. "Why fight it? Embrace it!"

For our family, we take "clover" very seriously. I'm careful what types of fun our family enjoys. The children ride bikes and have wholesome toys and healthy play (less as they grow older).

There are certain things we just don't do. For example, we would not even consider going to a movie theater, a professional sporting event of any kind, or amusement parks. For us, there is nothing redeeming about any of those activities, and much that is negative (that is for another Dad's Corner). In addition, there is the potential if we participate in those areas of creating the intense appetite for more. Please don't get me wrong; we have fun as a family, and much laughter is heard in the Maxwell home. However, it is the desire of my heart to raise children who are "lovers of God" far more than "lovers of pleasure."

We would all do well to treat pleasure as the dangerous drug that it is. Yes, God did give us the ability to enjoy pleasing things, but Satan is the one who wants us to take pleasure in nonprofitable things. "But seek ye first the kingdom of God, and his righteousness; and all these things shall be added unto you" (Matthew 6:33). "If ye then be risen with Christ, seek those things which are above, where Christ sitteth on the right hand of God. Set your affection on things above, not on things on the earth" (Colossians 3:1-2). How's your lawn?

# Spiritually Healthy Children
## by Steve

Reflecting back on all the places Teri and I have lived during our twenty-eight years of marriage, I realized there was one thing consistent with each place: they all had "needy" lawns. I always mowed the lawns on a regular basis, but I had no clue as to what it took to have a truly healthy lawn.

There were times when I would get inspired and think, "If my neighbor can have a reasonable looking lawn, then so can I." I would go buy a bag of fertilizer and a new drop spreader (the old one had rusted to a point of uselessness by that time) and painstakingly attempt to apply the chemicals to the yard. Then, with significant anticipation, I would watch for the lawn to green up. I can remember the satisfaction of seeing beautiful, green grass. Unfortunately, that satisfaction was always tempered by the disappointment of seeing lush green stripe, pale green stripe, lush green stripe, then pale sickly-looking stripe.

No matter how careful I was to overlap each pass with the drop spreader, it seemed like I missed as much as I covered. At each turn, I would even put a stake in next to the wheel and aim for the opposite stake across the yard. I just couldn't get it right. I wasn't sure which was worse, a uniformly pale, anemic yard, or one with deep green stripes accenting the pale stripes, sort of a drop-shadow affect.

Then, eleven years ago when we moved into this house, I decided it was time to do it right. By combining my lawn with my father-in-law's lawn (he lives next door to us), I could get the chemical treatments applied professionally for less than I could buy them over the counter. With the volume discount, a rich, green lawn was on the horizon. No more striped lawn! A pro was going to be applying the treatments, and all I would have to do was mow. I was so pleased!

I greatly enjoyed seeing the lawn green up as the chemical plan started. I began to take even more notice of the lawn than I ever had. The lawn-treatment company always said that if you weren't pleased with the results, just to give them a call. They would come back out and take care of whatever they needed to do. So for the first time ever, I had hopes of not only a green lawn, but a weed-free lawn as well.

I wish I could tell you those six years of professional lawn treatments revolutionized our yard. Unfortunately, I can't because we didn't have one successful year. My only explanation is that the Lord obviously had a lesson in it for me.

Each year there was always some sort of problem with the lawn. I would discuss it with the lawn-treatment company, and they always had a reason why the yard wasn't improving. For several years it was because it was a wetter-than-normal year. They told me the fertilizer and weed control were being washed away. Then there were the years when it didn't rain often enough. They said I needed to water the lawn so it received at least an inch of water every week. Do you have any idea how much an inch of water over the whole yard each week costs? It made what we were paying for the chemicals seem like chicken feed. Then there was a year when they had to treat for grubs two or three times. By the time the grubs were finally conquered— well, actually, "conquered" probably isn't accurate—I think there was nothing left to eat so the grubs moved on.

After several years, I finally could see that having someone else responsible for fertilizing and weed control was not the answer either. What needed to happen was for me to learn what should be done to properly care for the lawn, and then do it myself.

The first rule I discovered was that a healthy lawn—one that is well-fed and well-watered—will resist weeds. Unfortunately, my lawn was in such sorry condition that it needed much more major work.

The first thing we did was to verticut the yard, reseed it, and apply starter fertilizer. After applying large amounts of daily water, the grass seed sprouted and began growing. It took several years of fertilizing, watering, and some more over-seeding to achieve our current lawn. It has grass that looks nice—not beautiful, but acceptable, by my standards.

In giving you that much detail of my lawn history, I didn't want to bore you or brag about what little I know regarding lawn care. I felt the background was important in laying the foundation for what I wanted to share.

Brothers, I am deeply grieved by my observation of how many dads are doing nothing to maintain healthy children's hearts. It is as if, just by giving them a place to grow, these dads believe their children will turn out all right. To me that is like giving grass a place to grow and then expecting it to be a beautiful lawn. I don't think either will happen.

The next wrong assumption I see is that it is best to turn our children over to the professionals to be properly trained. The experts are supposed to know exactly how to raise children, just like the guys who spray chemicals on the yard are to have your "lawn's best interests" in mind. However, even if some professionals have more knowledge than a typical dad, they don't have the heart attachment that a dad has for his own children.

Deuteronomy 6:6-9 is clear in stating that the responsibility for discipling children rests on fathers. "And these words, which I command thee this day, shall be in thine heart: And thou shalt teach them diligently unto thy children, and shalt talk of them when thou sittest in thine house, and when thou walkest by the way, and when thou liest down, and when thou risest up. And thou shalt bind them for a sign upon thine hand, and they shall be as frontlets between thine eyes. And thou shalt write them upon the posts of thy house, and on thy gates."

The temptation is to let others give our children their spiritual training. We cannot, though, expect Sunday School teachers, youth group leaders, or even our pastors to be responsible for our children's spiritual growth and nurturing. Notice the key word in that last sentence: responsible. We are the ones who will be held responsible for how our children have been spiritually fed. Others may supplement what we are feeding our children, but we will not stand before the Lord and say, "It was his fault that my children weren't discipled." As long as the chemical "pros" were responsible for my yard, I was hardly even willing to water it. That was my fault and not theirs! Just because we take our children to church does not mean they are being trained in the way the Lord wants them to be.

The chemical "pros" give every lawn the same treatment. That is why it took three treatments of increasing-strength chemicals to deal with the grubs that one year. Even within a family, each child needs individual care and nurturing. There are times when I'm choosing to give one child much more attention than others, because that is what the child needs at that time. I wish we were able to train each child in the same way as it sure would make raising children easier, and we wouldn't have to work so hard. That is my preference, though, and not the Lord's. "And he said unto me, My grace is sufficient for thee: for my strength is made perfect in weakness. Most gladly therefore will I rather glory in my infirmities, that the power of Christ may rest upon me" (2 Corinthians 12:9). The fact that we feel inadequate and uncertain about how to raise our children is a good thing and will motivate us to pray. Then God gets the glory for everything that is done.

The essence of having a healthy lawn is to nurture it. That means, at a minimum, we give it proper food, water, and cutting. Weather will always be a factor in how much we do of each of the basics, so we have to be observant. In the same way, we must be observant of our children's needs. The storms of life will come and go, and they have an effect on how we are going to care for each child. This will vary from year to year, and maybe even day to day, as needs will be different depending on the conditions.

One thing is certain: food and water are a must. Dads, that is why we must be serving our family a healthy portion of the Word daily. It may be a larger serving at some times, but they need God's Word every day. If you don't want them to grow in the Lord, not leading your children in a daily time of family worship will accomplish that goal. Your children will not grow and mature spiritually if you don't spiritually feed them! Are we relying on the experts to feed our children? Please don't if you really care about your children!

In John 21:17 Jesus said to Peter, ". . . Simon, *son* of Jonas, lovest thou me? Peter was grieved because Jesus said to him the third time, Lovest thou me? And he said to him, Lord, thou knowest all things; thou knowest that I love thee. Jesus saith unto him, Feed my sheep." Men, if we love our children, we must feed them. May we not stand before the Lord someday admitting we didn't feed His sheep.

# Trust
## *by Steve*

Buddy was cutting my hair while the owner of the barbershop was giving a twenty-year-old young man a haircut. The man's wife and six-month-old baby were watching "daddy" get a major overhaul. There was some teasing going on as six inches worth of hair was being moved from his head to the floor.

Blake, the barbershop owner, has had this shop for many years. I suppose when you stand there all day cutting hair, you find ways to make time a little more enjoyable. Blake had just put shaving cream around the young man's ears and on his neck. Then, with a straight razor in his hand, Blake pointed at the wife and asked her husband, "Do you trust your wife?" This question not only peaked my curiosity, but I saw that she quit bouncing the baby, becoming quite interested in what her husband was going to say.

The husband thought just a moment and said, "I sure do!" With that admirable reply, his wife smiled, put a kiss on the baby, and began bouncing him again.

On hearing the words Blake was hoping for, he held out the straight razor to her and said, "Great! Come on over here and shave around his ears with this."

I'm not sure I can adequately describe the emotions that husband and wife began to exhibit. Both of them were repeatedly saying, "No!" with enough zeal that Blake was feeling very rewarded.

After the couple relaxed again, Blake said he recently did the same thing to a couple about to be married. The groom-to-be had answered, "I'd trust her with my life." (Good answer, if true.)

However, when Blake tightened the noose that the groom-to-be had just stepped into, the future bride saw her "prince charming" do such a U-turn that she was crushed. Blake chuckled with a little satisfaction as he said, "It really turned into quite a squabble."

Trust is an amazing thing. It is the foundation for the depth of a relationship. You can have a relationship without love, but if there is no trust, then there is no real relationship. *Merriam-Webster* defines trust as: "assured reliance on the character, ability, strength, or truth of someone or something, one in which confidence is placed." The more we trust someone, the more open we will be with him and the closer the relationship becomes. David trusted Jonathan and shared information that could have cost David his life if Jonathan had betrayed that trust by telling his father, Saul. That was an example of a friendship between two young men that had a deeper level of trust than the relationship between the son and his father. How sad, and yet that is common today, even in Christian homes.

As the straight razor in my barbershop story put into perspective, trust is only a word until it is tested. David's trust in Jonathan wasn't meaningful until Jonathan proved he could be trusted. Our children's trust in us is a measure of our trustworthiness through the years. We need to guard it zealously.

The issue of whether my children trust me is critical to my effectiveness as a parent. What is their level of confidence in me? A little child initially has deep trust in his parents, but often as he grows that trust is eroded. This can happen throughout childhood, as the child perceives that his parents are making some bad decisions. "Then said Jonathan, My father hath troubled the land: see, I pray you, how mine eyes have been enlightened, because I tasted a little of this honey" (1 Samuel 14:29). With the strength of Jonathan's criticism of his father, this was obviously not the first time that Jonathan felt his father, the king, had made a wrong decision. Likely, he had watched his father's pride lead him to make many other bad decisions.

There are times we, as dads, make bad decisions. There may be other times when we make the best decision, but our children's understanding is not sufficient to see the decision properly. When this is the case we receive "credit" for a bad decision.

This is one reason I choose to have a weekly private meeting with each of my older children (eleven and up). I cherish that time on Sunday while lunch is being prepared and then cleaned up. The time I meet with each child varies according to what we have to discuss. It has proved to be critical in maintaining and deepening their trust in me. We discuss decisions that have been made and why they were made that way. It gives the child a chance to understand why I did what I did and why I felt the Lord leading in that direction. There also have been times when I confessed to them that I made a wrong decision and asked their forgiveness if it affected them. That way they are able to see that dad can make mistakes, but when he does, he makes it right with them. Both situations are so very important in ensuring confidence in me.

In the area of trust, think about what our poor wives go through. You and I know that no wife would make every decision perfectly if she was responsible for making the decisions. However, there are times when she would have made the correct choice, when her husband made the wrong one. Even if she doesn't remember the times when she would have chosen wrong, she is likely to remember the times when she was right.

If any wife had reason to distrust her husband, it was Sarah. Abraham betrayed her twice out of concern for his own safety (Genesis 12:11, 20:2). Twice! Yet, she did not rebel against Abraham's leadership and appeared to continue to trust him (1 Peter 3). She was commended for her faith in God in Hebrews 11, and that is probably the secret of her confidence in Abraham. (All moms would likely learn a powerful lesson in how to have faith in a husband, and that is by trusting in their Lord.)

A wife's trust in her husband is to be treasured. Husbands can easily damage that trust, and it is difficult to regain. Frequently, we hear of a mom who has discovered her husband is into pornography. Why does it hurt a wife so badly? It is because porn is mental adultery.

The husband into pornography or lusting after other women "drives a knife" into his wife's heart, and she cannot trust him. She knows her husband is driven by lust and therefore can't be trusted. Once an adulterer, will he ever really stop, and to what lengths will he go?

Repentance is the only way to begin rebuilding trust. The father who reacts defensively when questioned by his wife has not repented. He is only sorry he got caught. But the man who truly hates his sin, is repentant, and wants to change will accept any boundaries and accountability necessary. A man who is repentant will embrace boundaries as an opportunity to show those who love him he realizes his sin. He will gladly avoid all appearances of evil. He will be willing to spend the rest of his life trying to rebuild what he does not deserve. What do you think? Was the young man showing prudence in not letting his wife use the razor, or did he simply not trust her? I believe he didn't trust her. If he had, he would have thought, "I trust that she loves me so much she wouldn't do anything to hurt me. I believe that if she doesn't have the skill to use that razor, then she won't, because she doesn't want to take a chance of cutting me." In the same way, do we love our families so much that we choose to do nothing that may hurt them?

Trust is priceless. Do you want the hearts of your family members? It isn't possible without trust. Have you damaged trust? Be committed to rebuilding it. We can't demand it, but we must covet it and seek to always build it.

# Can Dads Influence Their Children's Spiritual Outcome?
## PART 1 — YOUR EXAMPLE
### by Steve

Recently, a father wrote about a number of issues that should be near and dear to the heart of every father who wants to raise children to love and serve the Lord Jesus. I thought I would share some thoughts on the first part of what he wrote this month and then discuss the last part next month.

*We live a pretty controlled life. We dress plain. We built ourselves a small cabin to live in, in order to "Owe no man any thing, but to love. . . ." My wife homeschools, and we keep our kids with us constantly. (We can't even trust either set of grandparents to maintain our level of protection.) No TV, etc., although we do take the kids shopping and to church (only three families in the church, including us [and no other children]).*

*The brethren in the church we fellowship with believe that you can't really guarantee that your children will be saved. Both of them, godly men, have children that don't follow the Lord (one of them had all his children slip away). They even have a grandson who was homeschooled, but went away when he got into the work world. A dad (To be continued next month.)*

Praise God for the heart of this dad! Did you sense the love he has for his children and that he is willing to live any way necessary to raise men and women of God? No wonder he is concerned by what he is being told.

I, too, have heard a number of others, including Christian men in leadership, imply that you can't guarantee how your children will turn out. They indicate that no matter what you do, a child may still rebel. Those types of statements can be so discouraging to dads who have hearts for their children. Personally, the guarantee I am putting my trust in comes from God's Word—that He Who is faithful and begun a good work in my children will complete it (Philippians 1:6). Look at 1 Timothy 3:4-5, where one of the qualifications for a bishop (elder) is listed. "One that ruleth well his own house, having his children in subjection with all gravity; (For if a man know not how to rule his own house, how shall he take care of the church of God?)." Next, look at Titus 1:6, where the bishop's (elder's) children again determine his qualification for office. "If any be blameless, the husband of one wife, having faithful children not accused of riot or unruly." God said if someone is to be an elder then his children can't be rebellious, and in Titus 1:6 we read that they must be faithful. The idea is that if an elder can't raise his children to love the Lord, he won't be able to lead a church either. I don't believe God would have made that a requirement if it weren't a reasonable thing to expect.

First, let's evaluate carefully those from whom we hear these kinds of negative statements. It is always reasonable to cross-examine a witness bringing testimony. In court, under cross-examination, a testimony may be discredited, or thrown out, if there is reason to doubt the accuracy of what is being reported. The purpose in this case is not to condemn those who have "lost children," but rather to understand and learn from them. My experience has been that upon careful scrutiny there seems to be justifiable reasons why a child might rebel in his teens and not serve the Lord as an adult.

Just because the men (mentioned at the beginning of the Corner) making those statements appear to be godly, this doesn't mean they (who said children can go astray) actually raised their children in a godly home. It doesn't mean the men were godly when they were raising their children. It doesn't mean that the men's hearts were turned toward their children. And even if the children were raised by godly men in a godly home, it doesn't mean the children weren't exposed to harmful influences that drew their hearts away.

This has been a subject of great interest to me through the years. As such, when I have met someone with wayward children, I will gently ask the father some subtle questions while we talk. My questions will vary depending on how well I know the person, but the following are representative of what I try to discover.

How was the Lord Jesus lived out in the home? Did they have a daily family worship time? Was it a time the children enjoyed? Did Dad lead it? Did he like leading it? Did they eat together as a family? Did they worship together? Did Dad, Mom, and the children have personal devotions each day? Was it a good or a dreaded time?

What influences were there to pull the hearts away? Did the dads feel like they had their children's hearts and, if not, who did? How much time did Dad spend with the children? Did he have two jobs requiring long hours out of the home? Was there a TV in the home? (I believe this was less of an issue 30 to 40 years ago, but is a critical issue now.) Did they go to movies? How important were friends in their children's lives? What did the family do when Dad wasn't working? What did they do for entertainment and recreation? Did they minister to anyone as a family or individually? Two important questions nowadays: are the children homeschooled, and are they in a youth group?

Another big issue is to sense if the dad has an angry spirit. Children will not draw close and trust a parent who is angry or even has a spirit of anger. I believe that this alone can drive children away.

These questions aren't to condemn anyone, but I think they can be very indicative of how the child will do as an adult. I hope that the "right" answers don't bring to mind an unattainable, perfect family. If they do, it is only because the drifting of the current "church" in our country sees what should be normal life for a Christian as extreme. The answers to my questions present a picture of whether Deuteronomy 6:6-8 was being lived out in the home, whether Dad's heart was lovingly turned toward the children, and what harmful influences were pulling at the children.

Also, I don't want you to think for a moment that I believe that if you follow a simple list of do's and don'ts, your children won't rebel. I'm not saying that at all. James said, ". . . I will shew thee my faith by my works" (James 2:18). The essence of what I try to find out is just how the love for (and of) the Lord Jesus Christ and His Word is lived out in a home. I believe that is an indication of how real a presence the Lord Jesus had in the home and whether the children will want to live for Him themselves.

Now, to understand the basis for my questions, let's take a brief look at Deuteronomy 6:6-8. "And these words, which I command thee this day, shall be in thine heart: And thou shalt teach them diligently unto thy children, and shalt talk of them when thou sittest in thine house, and when thou walkest by the way, and when thou liest down, and when thou risest up. And thou shalt bind them for a sign upon thine hand, and they shall be as frontlets between thine eyes."

Notice that the words of God's commands must be in Dad's heart. What we treasure and love is in our hearts and is the essence of our very beings. "For where your treasure is, there will your heart be also" (Matthew 6:21). What is in our hearts will come out in our words and actions. No one knows Dad like those living in the home.

The Lord shall be taught diligently to the children. Have you noticed how it is almost impossible to train a bad habit out of your children that you haven't personally conquered in your life? Our children observe how we live out our faith. Our life must affirm what we are teaching them. If we don't live it as we teach it, then we shouldn't be surprised if they don't choose to live it either. If we live a life of hypocrisy, our children will want nothing to do with our "religion."

My heart is deeply grieved by how many professing dads don't live Christ out in the home. "Thou shalt talk of them" conveys that we will so love the Lord Jesus that our talk is seasoned with Him. He is the salt that flavors and adds real meaning to what is being discussed. Those topics that are being discussed will not be the things of the world with a little religion added in once in a while.

In the original language, the word for "diligently" carries the picture of how one sharpens swords and arrows. It is far more than just casual discussions of the Lord during the day. It is a purposeful decision to do something that is important. It takes effort and care. You don't put an edge on a sword or a point on an arrow carelessly. It takes determination, skill, and careful observation of the progress being made with each sharpening stroke. We are to continuously, skillfully, and methodically share Jesus with our children.

I have "spoken" with some who believe they can't fulfill Deuteronomy 6 unless the dad is working from the home and has his children with him. I would encourage any father who feels this way to question whether he is doing everything he can with his family life in his current vocation. Is Dad having a personal time with the Lord each day? Is Dad gently coaxing each child to spend time with the Lord each day? Is Dad leading the family in a time of Bible reading and worship each day in the home? If not, I don't believe coming home is the answer.

Why not find another man and hold each other accountable? Ask each other specific questions each week while remembering it is not a list of do's and don'ts that determine how your children will turn out. How much do you love the Lord your God, and how are you living that out in the home? The questions are merely an attempt to catch a glimpse of what is going on.

A dear brother and I were discussing the difficulty of a father keeping the hearts of his children. We wholeheartedly agreed. There is nothing more difficult, time consuming, and worthwhile than a father striving to keep the hearts of his children while directing them to Christ. Dads, it is a tall order, but we can't quit and assume "we have arrived" for a moment. The enemy seeks our children.

# Can Dads Influence Their Children's Spiritual Outcome?
## PART 2 — THE FLESH
### by Steve

Last month we looked at the first part of what a dad wrote, and this month we will continue. To recap, we saw what God calls fathers to do in discipling their children. Now we begin evaluating whether/how children should be exposed to the world. This topic was going to be two parts, but it is such a critical subject, it will take longer.

The dad continues: *What I am seeking is good, practical advice on how and at what age to expose my children to the world. And how to keep from losing them to the world. (I've got a seven-year-old daughter, four-year-old daughter, two-year-old son, and one on the way.) This isn't the first time that I have heard people speak of sheltered kids getting out and "going nuts." It seems to me that it would be best to expose them to the results of sin (chapel for recovering addicts, jail, etc.), as compared to them seeing "all of the pleasures and none of the guilt," such as is seen at the mall, etc. Maybe even working this into some kind of a family ministry (although my children may be too young now, that is part of my question). This recent comment about the backsliding grandson has got me seriously considering self-employment and some kind of family businesses.*

This is a problem as old as sin itself. We are to be in the world but not of it (John 17:11-16). We are to live around sin, but not be pulled into it. I believe that one of the most critical aspects of protecting ourselves and our children from the world is for them (and us) to see the dangers of it and how powerful it is. The poor person who feels he is stronger than the pull of sin is a likely victim.

The types of sinful temptations will vary between young men and young women. I couldn't cover each one, but I think by using one as an illustration you will get the idea in general. So for the sake of example, let's use men and the lust of the flesh as the basis for discussion.

With that introduction, what do Solomon, a pastor in his fifties, and a young man of twenty have in common? First, they all are men with male hormones. Second, they are all prone to falling prey to the lust of the flesh. Solomon, the wisest man in the world and given that wisdom by God, could not contain his lust. He disobeyed God when he sought wives of different nationalities. His lust brought him down below the level of a twenty-year-old, hormone-driven young man. Of all people, Solomon knew better and should have been faithful to his God, yet he failed miserably.

"But king Solomon loved many strange women, together with the daughter of Pharaoh, women of the Moabites, Ammonites, Edomites, Zidonians, *and* Hittites; Of the nations *concerning* which the LORD said unto the children of Israel, Ye shall not go in to them, neither shall they come in unto you: *for* surely they will turn away your heart after their gods: Solomon clave unto these in love. And he had seven hundred wives, princesses, and three hundred concubines: and his wives turned away his heart. For it came to pass, when Solomon was old, *that* his wives turned away his heart after other gods: and his heart was not perfect with the LORD his God, as *was* the heart of David his father. For Solomon went after Ashtoreth the goddess of the Zidonians, and after Milcom the abomination of the Ammonites" (1 Kings 11:1-5).

Solomon was a man who heard God speak to him. He was the wisest man on the earth, but Solomon loved many strange women in spite of God telling him not to "go in to them, neither shall they come in unto you; *for* surely they will turn away your heart after their gods." Yet parents will say, "Your son is an adult now that he is eighteen, and you need to let him go his own way." Ughhhhh. That may be true if you don't love him, but if you do, there must be MUCH more that goes into the decision than just how old he is.

You may say, "My son is very spiritually mature, and I have full confidence in him being able to resist moral temptations." My question for you is, "Do you think your son is more spiritually mature than King David, a man after God's own heart?" David saw that ". . . the woman *was* very beautiful to look upon" (2 Samuel 11:2), and in essence, David lusted after her beauty. Oh what danger "we" are in when it is readily accepted among Christians to "appreciate" the beauty of other women. Had David realized the trouble he was in right then and taken action—the sin, the separation, the consequences—most likely, none of these would have happened. "But I say unto you, That whosoever looketh on a woman to lust after her hath committed adultery with her already in his heart" (Matthew 5:28). The level of sin we will accept has great bearing on what will be acceptable to our children.

David, the author of most of Psalms, was not spiritually above temptation or failure. So it would appear that just because a man loves the Lord with all his heart and has a heart after God's, that isn't enough to keep him from lust, adultery, and murder.

Have you ever heard of a pastor or man in spiritual leadership running away with a young woman and leaving a wife of many years behind? Most everyone has. Could it be that the pastor wasn't aware of the consequences for such actions? Not likely. Most men in any form of ministry have observed others suffering due to their sin. Don't they know better? Of course, but once the lust of the flesh kicks in, all reason goes out the door. Likely, this man tolerated an "acceptable" level of lust in his life thinking he could control it without consequences.

Have you seen photos of bomb squad members who were handling explosives in the attempt to disarm them or move them to another location? I imagine the protective gear and shields they use to protect themselves make Goliath's armor look like a loin cloth. If you think about it, aren't the bomb squads being overly cautious? When was the last time you heard about a bomb squad having a suspicious item blow up and injure some of them? So why does the bomb squad dress like they do and take all of those precautions? Could it be that they are aware of the serious danger they are in, and they are protecting themselves in the event something were to happen? Their cautions don't appear to be because they don't have confidence in themselves or their procedures. Rather, they know that you can't ever be too careful and that, if something happens, the consequences can be disastrous.

Every man who desires to remain morally pure should have the same attitude of caution that a bomb squad has. The key to acquiring that attitude is understanding what Jesus said in Matthew 15:19: "For out of the heart proceed evil thoughts, murders, adulteries, fornications, thefts, false witness, blasphemies." In the Greek, the phrase, "For out of the heart," refers to where these sins originate. Until we lose this body of flesh, we have to come to grips with the fact that we are our own worst enemy. We have to realize what we are capable of because it is bound up in our flesh. We have to understand it isn't our great wisdom or our lofty spirituality that keeps us out of trouble. It didn't work for Solomon or David or countless other mighty men that have failed through the ages, and it won't work for you, our children, or me.

A young man (or father) will not take steps to protect himself if he doesn't understand what is in his heart and how easily he can fall. If he thinks he is above falling, he doesn't understand his own heart. I wonder if the main reason many men don't flee lusts is because they are pleasurable. Could it be like the cute little wolf pup that is found by a man in Alaska? He brings it home, cares for it, and raises it to an adult, only to have it one day suddenly turn on him and kill him. That is one reason why our family doesn't watch TV. With the programming and commercials that are broadcast these days, television can easily stir up sinful lusts. That is also why we don't go to movies, many summertime activities, and even the circus any more. They are designed to entertain, but one of the ways they do that is to stir up lust in the men who are watching.

Our children must be taught the depravity of their hearts and not to trifle with sin. Do they have a father who walks as close to the line of sin as possible or a dad who desires to walk as close to the Lord Jesus as possible? I've heard some say, "I'm just appreciating her beauty." But in Proverbs 6:25 we read, "Lust not after her beauty in thine heart; neither let her take thee with her eyelids." Jesus was clear in making the connection between lusting in one's heart and committing adultery. It is sin. What are we teaching our children by word and example?

If the children see Dad condoning, by his viewing entertainment, the things of the world, we should not be surprised to see them "going nuts" trying to embrace the real thing when they finally have a chance. If sin is not called sin, what is to stop them? If they don't understand the mighty fire that the flesh contains, will they want to protect themselves?

Our children must be raised in a home where Christ is alive and Deuteronomy 6:6-9 is lived out. They must see that they cannot have confidence in their spiritual maturity or wisdom to keep them from being drawn in by the world. The world "knows" how to stir up a person's desires and then what to offer to feed those desires. Our children should understand that they are capable of being drawn. "But every man is tempted, when he is drawn away of his own lust, and enticed" (James 1:14).

How about you? The Lord Jesus sees your heart and knows what goes on there. Are you playing with fire? Have you accepted that which is unacceptable to your Lord? If so, you will likely offer little counsel to your children in helping them avoid being ensnared by the world. Prayerfully ask the Lord these questions until next month when we will continue with this critical topic.

# Can Dads Influence Their Children's Spiritual Outcome?
## PART 3 — WILL YOU FAIL AT THE FINISH?
### by Steve

If you are like Teri and me, the issue of how children are exposed to the world is critically important to you. This topic is where the rubber meets the road in parenting: we either win or we lose after years of raising the child. We can do what appears to be a wonderful job in raising our children, and when we are close to the finish line, all can be lost.

We'll re-look at part of what the father wrote in the second part of the series: *What I am seeking is good, practical advice on how and at what age to expose my children to the world. And how to keep from losing them to the world. (I've got a seven-year-old daughter, four-year-old daughter, two-year-old son, and one on the way.) This isn't the first time that I have heard people speak of sheltered kids getting out and "going nuts." It seems to me that it would be best to expose them to the results of sin (chapel for recovering addicts, jail, etc.), as compared to them seeing "all of the pleasures and none of the guilt," such as is seen at the mall, etc. Maybe even working this into some kind of a family ministry (although my children may be too young now; that is part of my question). This recent comment about the backsliding grandson has got me seriously considering self-employment and some kind of family businesses.*

Last month I shared what I believe to be a critical attitude for our children and ourselves and how important it is in regard to our association with the world. I discussed how I believe that we would all benefit from the attitude that any one of us can fall into sin. We must own the fact revealed in Matthew 15:19: "For out of the heart proceed evil thoughts, murders, adulteries, fornications, thefts, false witness, blasphemies." This is just as important a truth for us as it is for our children. If we accept the fact that any of us can fall, and if we don't really want to, then shouldn't we welcome something that will help us avoid falling?

This month I want to share about something that I believe is at the center of parenting, although there is far more than can be written in one or two Corners. In a way this is a mini reflection of the essential element in our relationship with the Father. "Jesus said unto him, Thou shalt love the Lord thy God with all thy heart, and with all thy soul, and with all thy mind" (Matthew 22:37). The Lord wants our hearts because He loves us and desires fellowship with us. Also, when He has our hearts we are far less likely to be drawn away by the idols of this world. The blood of Jesus enables us to enter into a heart relationship with the Father. When we are born again (John 3), we become the children of God (John 1:12-13). Notice how God uses "family" terms so we will understand heavenly truths.

This is a beautiful picture of, ideally, how our relationship should be with our children. In the Bible, we see a God Who loves His children so much He died for them. The Father desires, more than anything, fellowship with His children. He wants to spend time with them, listen to them, teach them, guide them and—in return He wants our hearts. The more we give Him our hearts, the more wonderful that relationship becomes.

This is true for the parent-child relationship as well. As parents we are called to sacrifice for our children, love them, spend time with them, listen to them, teach them, guide them and . . . We may be tempted at times to think we will be satisfied with mere outward conformity, but we really want their hearts. When we have our child's heart, the older the child becomes, the sweeter the fellowship.

I was talking to a good friend a while ago and discussing the importance of keeping our children's hearts. We agreed that we both believe it is the most important and most difficult challenge before a father. If only dads would become passionate about their children's hearts, we would not see so many "children" being lost to the world.

Why is it that more dads aren't concerned about keeping their children's hearts? First, I think many would say that they are. Unfortunately, there seems to be a disconnect. It is impossible for a father to spend his time and mental focus on a number of other things (outside of work time) and have anything left for his children. There is no substitute for time, and we are lying to ourselves if we think we can just spend quality time because we aren't willing to give quantity. It takes time and effort.

Why is having a child's heart so important? Aren't they going to grow up anyway? Yes, they are going to grow up whether you have their hearts or not. However, if you don't have your child's heart, you miss out on the tremendous blessing of your children as they grow up. You stand the very significant chance, I believe, of losing them. Keeping a child's heart is like the shepherd who is constantly inspecting his flock. He knows the danger that comes if disease or pestilence takes root. The toll to restore the flock to health will be high, if the shepherd is even able to accomplish it. If you have your child's heart you can quickly tell if something is drawing his heart away. You will sense a heart change and know something is wrong.

There was a time when I felt that the heart of one of my children was slipping away. During our weekly discussion times, there were more issues of increasing difficulty to work through. Instead of being able to share my concerns and know this child was receiving them, I could see this child was struggling. I was perplexed and couldn't figure out what was going on. I began crying out to the Lord and seeking Him for answers. The Lord was faithful and showed me what the cause was. I shared this with the child, who was able to receive it. Soon, the sweetness was back in the relationship and our hearts were close again.

If I hadn't had my child's heart, I would not have noticed the drifting of the child's spirit. I would have thought that it was a normal separation, due to growing older, and believed the lie that you should accept it and not worry about it. If you believe the lie, as it gets worse and you see changes in your child, you cry out to the Lord because you are concerned about the direction the child is heading. The more concerned you are, the more desperate and fearful. Finally, resignation sets in, and you now believe that everyone was right and rebellion is normal.

I don't believe that having our children's hearts means they instantly receive everything we tell them. At times I wish that were the case, but it hasn't been my experience. However, I do think it means that we can talk on a very deep and intimate level, and they will listen carefully to what we say. It means they value what we say, and what comes from our hearts will weigh heavily on their souls. Isn't this true of our relationship with the Lord as well?

There are things the Lord brings to us that we do not receive with open arms. When the Lord started telling me that I was wrong to have had a vasectomy, and He wanted to be in charge of when we had children, I was not thrilled. However, because of my relationship with Jesus and spending time with Him, I began to see why I was wrong in getting the vasectomy. However, I was not ready to accept Him determining how many children we were going to have. My spirit was troubled because I wanted to resolve the issue about more children. Finally, one day when I was home ill from work, I said in my heart, "Okay, Lord. Today is the day. I'm going to find out what you really think about children." So I got out my Bible and concordance and began to look up what God had to say about children. I don't remember how long I was at it, but I do remember finally being broken. With tears in my eyes, I said, "Lord, I now see how precious children are to You and that they are the best gift You can give, next to our salvation." It appears that in a similar fashion those things that are on our hearts from the Lord will find acceptance by our children if we have their hearts.

Dads, I encourage you, no matter what the state of your relationship with your children may be, to make having and keeping your children's hearts your highest priority next to your relationship with your Lord and your wife. If you feel it is too late and your children are rebels, there is still hope. (If that is your situation, one resource we would recommend is Dr. S. M. Davis' audio, *Changing the Heart of a Rebel,* www.Titus2.com) Years down the road you may well have deep remorse that you didn't invest what was necessary to win and hold your child's heart. Whatever it takes, do it. There is no sacrifice too great. You will never regret it.

There is another very important aspect to having our children's hearts, and I will share about that next month as we continue to look at how to avoid losing our children to the world.

# Can Dads Influence Their Children's Spiritual Outcome?

## PART 4 — WHAT ARE YOU DOING WITH THEIR HEARTS?

### by Steve

How deep is the sadness when parents lose their young adult children to the world. To lose them at a time when the sweetness of the parent-child relationship should be close to its peak makes this a high fall. To lose one's child after years of investing heavily into his life through homeschooling makes the fruit of the loss all the more bitter. To most of us, it would make more sense to lose our children if they weren't homeschooled. How is it that some homeschooled Christian children are being lost to the world? Is there nothing that we can do as fathers to train up God-fearing children who will love and serve the Lord? We continue with this heavy subject.

I've copied that last half of the message the father wrote again for reference.

*What I am seeking is good, practical advice on how and at what age to expose my children to the world. And how to keep from losing them to the world. (I've got a seven-year-old daughter, four-year-old daughter, a two-year-old son, and one on the way.) This isn't the first time that I have heard people speak of sheltered kids getting out and "going nuts." It seems to me that it would be best to expose them to the results of sin (chapel for recovering addicts, jail, etc.), as compared to them seeing "all of the pleasures and none of the guilt," such as is seen at the mall, etc. Maybe even working this into some kind of a family ministry (although my children may be too young now, that is part of my question). This recent comment about the backsliding grandson has got me seriously considering self-employment and some kind of family businesses.*

First, I would like to make a comment to answer the implied question this father asks, "How and at what age should I expose my children to the world?" Scripture would provide direction if that were the primary issue. However I believe the real question is, "How do I prepare my children to be in the world but not of the world?" Scripture has much insight on this subject, and that is the essence of what I have been sharing.

Initially, we saw that the starting point is an awareness that within our hearts is the potential for each of us to be ensnared (Matthew 15:19). The child who does not have a healthy respect for and fear of fire will likely get burned. The Christian who doesn't have a healthy respect for and fear of what his heart is capable of will likely fall.

Next comes the whole issue of having and keeping our children's hearts. If we have their hearts, they will listen to us and receive instruction from our hearts. That is why Solomon said, "My son, give me thine heart, and let thine eyes observe my ways" (Proverbs 23:26). Solomon was instructing his son to give him his heart. He wanted his son to entrust the center of his very being to the care of his father. "Let thine eyes observe my ways" might be restated to, "Be attentive to the way I live life and be favorably drawn to it."

Therein lies the tremendous responsibility that goes with having our children's hearts. What have we done with the most precious trust we have received? Have we tenderly cared for their hearts or lashed out in anger at them? Can they trust Dad more than anyone else in the world and go to him when they have any sort of problem that needs to be shared?

Our children will give their hearts to someone or something, and that is what will have the greatest shaping effect on their life. "For where your treasure is, there will your heart be also" (Matthew 6:21). The person whom your child perceives as valuing him the most will have his heart. Does your child know that you care for him more than anyone else in the world? Do you tell him how much you love him and how special he is? Do your actions confirm your words? Do you spend time with him?

We communicate value in many ways. I think one of the most obvious and immediate is by our facial expressions and the tone in our voices. A person's face brightens when speaking with someone who is important to him. This is especially obvious when a young man or young woman is speaking with someone in which they have an emotional interest. It is true of dads as well. Do the expressions on our faces indicate the delight we have in our children?

I'm not saying that we should put on false faces. We need to "tell" our faces how important our families are to us because our faces will communicate to them. Once the Lord convicted me of this and I became aware of it, I found it natural to smile at my children. When I saw them first thing in the morning, it was easy to brighten my voice, smile, and cheerfully greet them. I delight in my children. They are my greatest treasures. However, I had gotten lazy in communicating this to them. My face now tells them how much they mean to me.

I think that is why anger is so damaging. Next time you are around an angry person, watch his face. It looks awful and indicates such dislike of the person that the anger is directed toward. Is it any wonder that the child of an angry father is quick to give his heart to someone else? The child "knows" the parent does not love or value him, and he is going to find someone who will. Brothers, may we not justify ANY anger in our lives at all. Anger alone may drive our children away.

Solomon told his son to watch his ways with the goal of favorably influencing the child's life. Unfortunately, even though Solomon was the wisest man in all the earth, his life had serious problems. Eventually he was disobedient, had out-of-control lust as evidenced by hundreds of wives and concubines, and allowed idol worship. We can see that Solomon's children were watching his ways by observing the results in his children's lives.

Our children know us better than anyone else (except maybe our wives), and they see what sort of Christians we really are. They know whether Jesus is more exciting to us or whether a sports event is. They know whether we are more inclined to want to read the Bible, spend time with them, read a magazine or newspaper, or watch TV.

The first priority for us is winning and keeping our children's hearts. The second issue is what we are doing with those hearts as they will be drawn to what draws us. They will want to emulate their dad if there is any measure of heart attachment. The things that are important to you will likely be important to them. That is the power that having their hearts involves. I encourage you to ask yourself if your children are seeing a father who is sold out to the Lord or one who is living for the world.

My ultimate goal in having my child's heart is to transfer his heart from me to his heavenly Father over time. It all begins when he comes to a saving knowledge of the Lord Jesus. Then over time, I want my child to grow steadily more dependent on Him and less on me. The emphasis is on a relationship with Christ—loving God with all of his heart, soul, and mind. Children aren't born with that love for Christ, but God does give them a natural love for their parents. We are to use that relationship to lead them into a relationship with God. It is to be a process of transferring their hearts from us to their Lord.

I love what God said about Abraham in Genesis 18:19. "For I know him, that he will command his children and his household after him, and they shall keep the way of the LORD, to do justice and judgment; that the LORD may bring upon Abraham that which he hath spoken of him." With all my heart I want the Lord to say that about me, and I want my children to benefit from that blessing. I desire to raise children who love God with all their hearts and want to serve Him. Brothers, if you have your children's hearts, what are you doing with them?

# Can Dads Influence Their Children's Spiritual Outcome?
## PART 5 — WELCOME, MR. WOLF?
### by Steve

Teri and I have had our hearts broken to see parents close to finishing the job of raising a child then lose the child to the world. I have to admit that quite a few years ago I actually said, "Homeschooled children don't have problems with drugs, alcohol, immorality, and rebellion." From the large group of homeschoolers we interact with, I can't say that is true anymore. Now my thoughts run this way: "Homeschooled children don't have to have problems with drugs, alcohol, immorality, and rebellion." I don't believe it is a matter of whether you "get a good one or a bad one." The issue is this: "Dad, what are you doing with what God has entrusted you?"

We continue with this heavy subject. The topic was originally broached by a father, and we've been looking at what he wrote. I've copied the last half here again for reference.

*What I am seeking is good, practical advice on how and at what age to expose my children to the world. And how to keep from losing them to the world. (I've got a seven-year-old daughter, four-year-old daughter, two-year-old son, and one on the way.) This isn't the first time that I have heard people speak of sheltered kids getting out and "going nuts." It seems to me that it would be best to expose them to the results of sin (chapel for recovering addicts, jail, etc.), as compared to letting them see "all of the pleasures and none of the guilt," such as is seen at the mall, etc. Maybe even working this into some kind of a family ministry (although my children may be too young now, that is part of my question). This recent comment about the backsliding grandson has got me seriously considering self employment and some kind of family businesses.*

Space no longer permits revisiting all we have already covered in previous Corners. However, each piece is critical to our parenting.

I firmly believe that if you do everything else and not this next area we will discuss, your children are at great risk. Please don't think that I'm exalting my opinion to such a high place that you need to follow it. Read this Corner, and study the Bible passages to which I refer, to see if it is true. May the Holy Spirit confirm in your heart truth.

"Verily, verily, I say unto you, He that entereth not by the door into the sheepfold, but climbeth up some other way, the same is a thief and a robber. But he that entereth in by the door is the shepherd of the sheep" (John 10:1-2). "Then said Jesus unto them again, Verily, verily, I say unto you, I am the door of the sheep" (John 10:7).

In verse one, we see that all who don't enter the sheepfold by the door are thieves and robbers. Then in verse seven we see that Jesus is the Door. The Middle-Eastern shepherd was so concerned about his sheep that after bringing his sheep into the fold for the night, he would sleep in the doorway. The shepherd, literally, became the door. Nothing could get through the doorway that the shepherd didn't allow. He would give his life for the sheep. Therefore, a thief knew the only other way to get to the sheep was by climbing over the wall. In doing so, he was still likely to be confronted by the shepherd as he entered the fold.

The protection of the sheep was of utmost importance to the shepherd. He would have carefully constructed his fold so that the sheep would be safe. I can picture him building the walls so that nothing could easily steal away those who depended on him for safety. Even though the sheep knew his voice and not the voice of the stranger, he still took great care in protecting them. Was it because he didn't trust the sheep? Of course not. Scripture says that they knew his voice and wouldn't follow a stranger. He knew, however, that others presented danger to the sheep.

This example is critical for dads who love their children. We are the shepherds of those God has entrusted to our care. We are to be the door to the family. No one gets by us to our children. Is it because we don't trust our children? Absolutely not. It isn't a matter of not trusting our children. Rather, it is a matter of our responsibility to protect them from others.

Recently, a dad was telling me that he didn't have a problem sending his children off for further training because they had proven themselves trustworthy. Unfortunately, I believe, he is basing the future of his children on his evaluation of their being trustworthy. Their trustworthiness is important, but maybe as important is the issue of WHO they will encounter.

It doesn't matter whether it is a school or religious organization of stellar credentials. I'm not even assuming there is evil intent on the part of the other person. However, something happens when the right two people get together. Suddenly all logic and self-control are gone. I expect that most have heard of pastors who have become involved in an immoral relationship. Likely those who have been ensnared like this never thought it would happen to them. It is contrary to everything for which they had lived. It is just that they found themselves in a situation that soon was out of control. If it can happen to those who are highly respected and have proven themselves "trustworthy," then how is it parents think it can't happen to their young adult children?

Even if the child isn't "lost to the world," but only fallen and morally scarred, is it worth the risk? I expect most parents of children that this has happened to don't even know about it. We have heard many a Christian mom share how she failed when out from under her father's protection. Might their fathers have done more to protect them? Could it be that their fathers trusted them when they should have protected them?

That is why the shepherd isn't content knowing that he has his sheep's "hearts." He knows there are others out there who may cause him to lose the ones for which he is responsible or who may actually cause them harm. He values his sheep so much that he is not willing to take any chances with them. No matter how confident we are that we have our children's hearts, they are still flesh and blood. They have to deal with the appetites of the flesh. Is it a matter of trust, or is it a matter of prudence and responsibility?

Remember what Jesus said was in the heart of EVERY person. "For out of the heart proceed evil thoughts, murders, adulteries, fornications, thefts, false witness, blasphemies" (Matthew 15:19). If we ever think our child is strong enough and cannot fall, I believe we have put him in great jeopardy.

Remember the pastors or other people I referred to earlier—the ones in high spiritual positions who ran away in an immoral relationship, often leaving a wife and family? These are people who "had" proven themselves to be of certain moral character and spiritually trustworthy—enough to earn the positions they held. They wouldn't have been given their positions if others hadn't had confidence in them. Not only had they given their hearts to their spouses in marriage, but they also had made a covenant before God to be faithful to that spouse. That was not enough to stop them. No matter what explanation is given or what warning signs there were, trust was breached, testimonies blackened, and lives shipwrecked.

Then how is it that, if pastors and others in high spiritual positions fall, parents can so easily "trust" their children putting them at such risk? I challenge you to evaluate whether it is really a matter of trust or value. Teri and I trust each other completely. However, we value our relationship so much we are not going to put it at risk. That is one reason why I don't have business lunches with women. There are more safeguards that we have put in place, but those are sufficient examples. We believe what Jesus said about the depravity of the human heart and that if we can fall, certainly our children can. May we value our children so much that we take our responsibility to protect them seriously. How is it that parents who have poured out their lives into their children and homeschooled them to protect them from the world will put them in situations where they are at great risk? If they were going to lose their children anyway, wouldn't it have been much easier on the mother to have sent the children to public school in the first place and spared herself the years of great effort homeschooling them? By putting our children in situations that may lead to their falling, I believe the parents have become their own enemies. Their actions have betrayed their goals. Instead of the father being the door, he has invited the wolf in to spend the night with the sheep. Oh, dads—may it not be!

To prevent any misunderstanding, let me give you some examples. If your desire is that your children would remain pure until they reach the marriage altar, then is it wise that they date or have friends who are dating, and should they spend time with others (of the opposite gender) to whom they may be drawn? Youth groups, ministry projects, short-term mission trips, joining the military, anything that involves young men and young women spending time together will likely stir up emotions. May each of us carefully evaluate the activities are children are involved in as to whether they are consistent with our goals. If you let your young adults participate in any of those activities even while you claim to be committed to courtship, do not be surprised if your children don't court. We hear too many tragic stories from people who have let their young adult children go down those roads and have experienced great disappointment.

If you don't want your children to rebel, then is it wise to let your children associate with rebels? Where might you find rebels? Youth groups, friends (even from great "Christian" families), sports teams, vocational technical schools, junior colleges, and colleges (Christian or secular) should all be viewed with great caution. Even if someone uses the word "Christian" to describe the organization, this does not mean that everyone there is a Christian living for the Lord. As the one called to protect our families, may we be able to look our wives in the eyes and say, "God is telling me that I must send my son/daughter there." If God isn't telling you clearly, do you really want to send them? Just because everyone else "is doing it" or your son or daughter really wants to, this is no reason to let them. "Foolishness *is* bound in the heart of a child . . ." (Proverbs 22:15). Often we hear the excuse that the child REALLY wanted to do something, so the parents let them. Dads, that is no reason. We are the ones who are accountable to the Lord for our decisions. Our children should only do what we are convinced is God's best for them—nothing less!

Being the "door" is not a very popular position. There will be times when some of the sheep want out, and the door is stopping them. There are other times when a wolf wants in, and the "door" has to mount a defense. However, the Lord didn't ask us to do it because it is fun. It is our responsibility.

May I encourage you to get alone with your Lord and determine what His goals are for your family. Then critically evaluate your decisions in light of those goals. You may be surprised to see that you have invited Mr. Wolf to spend the night. Evict him before it is too late. May we be the men God has called us to be.

# Can Dads Influence Their Children's Spiritual Outcome?
## PART 6 — WHAT'S FOR DINNER, DAD?
### by Steve

There is a wonderful elderly man we know at the nursing home, and we love him dearly. We have known him for close to ten years, but I'm afraid he won't live much longer. The biggest problem seems to be that he doesn't eat and therefore is wasting away. I don't see how such a thin person can continue to lose weight. The food seems to be good there, but I'm told he just sits in front of his food, picks at it for a while, and then quits. He will die without nourishment.

I recently had a very engaging discussion for about an hour with a young man in his early teens. He was strongly opinionated, and I was enjoying asking him questions in trying to understand what the basis was for the decisions he was making. He was intelligent and articulate, and yet there was a major disconnect in his reasoning. I then asked him about personal and family devotions. He said he was having personal time with the Lord, but his family didn't have a time when they would look at Scripture together. After hearing himself say that and realizing how that appeared, he thought for a moment and said, "Well, I guess I'd have to say, that our family devotion is sort of all day. It is the way we live."

Have you ever thought about the fact that God did not have to make our bodies to need food? God could have easily created us never to require food, but He had a purpose in it. "Give us day by day our daily bread" (Luke 11:3). We require continued sustenance to keep our focus on our Provider.

The reality of physical food is used by the Lord to teach us about our need for spiritual food. In John 21:15-17 we read, "So when they had dined, Jesus saith to Simon Peter, Simon, *son* of Jonas, lovest thou me more than these? He saith unto him, Yea, Lord; thou knowest that I love thee. He saith unto him, Feed my lambs. He saith to him again the second time, Simon, *son* of Jonas, lovest thou me? He saith unto him, Yea, Lord; thou knowest that I love thee. He saith unto him, Feed my sheep. He saith unto him the third time, Simon, *son* of Jonas, lovest thou me? Peter was grieved because he said unto him the third time, Lovest thou me? And he said unto him, Lord, thou knowest all things; thou knowest that I love thee. Jesus saith unto him, Feed my sheep." Jesus was not talking about Simon Peter physically feeding sheep but rather spiritually feeding the flock.

Notice how Jesus related Peter's love for Christ with Peter's feeding those for which he would soon be responsible. Peter would soon be leader of the church in Jerusalem, and if Peter loved Jesus, Peter was to feed them spiritually. If Peter loved the Lord, he could demonstrate that love by feeding the flock. In asking the question three times with slight variations, Jesus was making His point very clear. "Peter, if you love Me, you will feed My sheep." That is true of us dads as well, if we love the Lord Jesus, we will spiritually feed those He has entrusted to our care.

In John 10:3-4 we read, "To him the porter openeth; and the sheep hear his voice: and he calleth his own sheep by name, and leadeth them out. And when he putteth forth his own sheep, he goeth before them, and the sheep follow him: for they know his voice." The shepherd leads the sheep out to find good pasture. He is careful that the sheep only eat what is beneficial for them. He cares about the sheep and wants to see them grow and be healthy. A shepherd may be negligent in several areas and still not devastate the flock, but if he is not feeding them, they will suffer. That is so true for our families. We may fail our families in many ways, but if we aren't feeding them spiritually every day, they will suffer.

"The LORD *is* my shepherd; I shall not want. He maketh me to lie down in green pastures: he leadeth me beside the still waters"

(Psalms 23:1-2). What a beautiful picture of a caring Shepherd Who pastures His flock in lush green fields where they will eat well and then may rest. Do we fathers make our daily family devotion time appetizing? Does our family look forward to dining on God's Word together? Is it something we are excited about like a hungry man with a steak dinner, or do we force ourselves to take a few bites when we really aren't interested? If we aren't interested in God's Word then we need not expect our families to be excited.

Ezekiel 34 is amazing as God blasts those shepherding Israel. ". . . Woe *be* to the shepherds of Israel that do feed themselves! should not the shepherds feed the flocks? Ye eat the fat, and ye clothe you with the wool, ye kill them that are fed: *but* ye feed not the flock" (Ezekiel 34:2-3). "Thus saith the Lord GOD; Behold, I *am* against the shepherds; and I will require my flock at their hand, and cause them to cease from feeding the flock . . ." (Ezekiel 34:10). God harshly judges the shepherds who will not nurture their sheep.

Can we be serious about our desire to raise children who will be men and women of God without feeding them the spiritual food that they will need to grow spiritually strong and healthy? How can they resist the world if they are not spiritually strong?

A homeowner who says he is working hard to grow a nice, healthy lawn and never feeds it is only fooling himself. All his neighbors know the truth by merely observing his lawn and what steps he is taking. They can see that his actions aren't consistent with his words. In the same way, those around us who observe our children and who visit our home will soon come to understand what emphasis we place on spiritually feeding our family.

Feeding those we are responsible for is critical. Just as we can expect repercussions from the government if parents don't physically feed their children, there are consequences when parents don't spiritually feed their children. Why is it so many dads don't lead their family in daily Bible reading when this is such a serious matter? There are probably a myriad of answers, but NONE of them matter. I believe if dads realized the consequences they will experience (and observe in the lives of their children) for not spiritually feeding them, they would get serious (and excited) about daily feeding their family God's Word.

The Lord is our example. He says, "I will feed them in a good pasture, and upon the high mountains of Israel shall their fold be: there shall they lie in a good fold, and *in* a fat pasture shall they feed upon the mountains of Israel. I will feed my flock, and I will cause them to lie down, saith the Lord GOD" (Ezekiel 34:14-15). Men, we must feed our families. I would encourage every dad not to eat a meal the day following a missed family devotion. Let your physical hunger spur you on to feeding your family's spiritual hunger.

When I started leading the family devotion, I knew Teri could have done a far better job. But that was okay because I knew I needed to do it, and God would enable me to improve over time. The Lord has been so faithful through the years in teaching me how to lead my family. He will do the same for you if you will begin (if you aren't currently). So Dad, what are you feeding your family tonight?

# Can Dads Influence Their Children's Spiritual Outcome?
## PART 7 — A MIGHTY MAN'S BREAKFAST
### by Steve

I was sitting in the car doing some work while Teri was inside the dentist's office having her teeth cleaned. There was a large, nicely mown tree-shaded lot in front of me. I glanced up, and my eyes caught sight of a black bird walking through the grass. His head disappeared for an instant, and then with his beak, he began flinging leaves into the air. He would take another step, and more leaves would explode into the air. After every leaf or two, he would find a bug or worm; I couldn't tell which. I would see him eat it and begin looking under more leaves.

A short distance away, a robin was looking for breakfast. I was much more familiar with the way a robin finds his food. He would take a few steps, tipping his head to listen. Then he would either jab his beak into the ground, trying to spear a worm, or he would take a few more steps.

Both birds were gathering food the way God had directed them, even though their technique was quite different. I wonder if that might be a fitting analogy to a man's personal time in Bible reading and prayer—a quiet time or, as some might call it, devotions. We all should have spiritual nourishment from the Bible, yet we have different needs based on what is going on in our lives and where we are in our spiritual walk. Therefore, God will direct us to various places in Scripture. Then our study may involve individual methods of hunting for the tasty morsels that we need to grow and lead our family.

From the informal questions that I regularly ask men, I'm confident that less than 10 percent of conservative Christian men read their Bibles each day and pray. I believe one reason is that many need a brother who loves them enough to get in their faces to confront them. This brother would tell them that they can't live without a daily quiet time and give them some idea how to have one. The purpose of this Corner is for me to be the brother in your face. I want to give dads an idea of what they can do for their personal devotions and stress again how critical it is. 1 Corinthians 3:11 tells us, "For other foundation can no man lay than that is laid, which is Jesus Christ."

First, I pray that no dad ever senses a spirit of judgment or condemnation from me if he isn't spending time in the Word and prayer. I want him to sense a great amount of my passion as I plead with him to meet with his Lord daily. This Corner should be immensely practical, as I will try to be very specific in giving some ideas about how to have a quiet time. Just like the different techniques of those birds, there are many ways to spend daily time with the Lord. However, to make it simple, I'm suggesting you try it this way until you are comfortable, and then ask the Lord Jesus to direct you.

How often should you have your personal devotions? "Yet they seek me daily, and delight to know my ways, as a nation that did righteousness, and forsook not the ordinance of their God: they ask of me the ordinances of justice; they take delight in approaching to God" (Isaiah 58:2). If we would delight to know God's ways, then we must seek Him daily.

When in the day should we read our Bibles and pray? I believe you can never go wrong by doing it first thing in the morning when you get up. If we have our personal devotions first, they will always get done. We know how the urgent often crowds out the important. That doesn't happen with your Bible reading if you choose to do it first. Set the alarm so you will have time to get up and have your devotion before other daily scheduled commitments. DON'T CHANGE YOUR ALARM. That way if you want your sleep, you will go to bed on time.

If spending time with the Lord Jesus is important to you, you will make yourself go to bed at night in order to get enough sleep to get up with the alarm. If babies will wake you in the night, then go to bed earlier so you can still get up and meet with the Lord. I would encourage each of us to treat ourselves like men and not children. If we want sleep, we go to bed earlier, but we don't move the time we get up. Soon you will see how easy it is to consistently wake up and have your devotions. What would we think of a co-worker's frequent excuse of being late to work, or missing work, because he was tired and slept in? We would say, "If work is important to you—get up!"

How long is good for your time with Jesus? That is like asking someone, "How much gold would you like?" However, we must deal with reality in that there are limits. I would encourage no less than twenty minutes per day no matter what—ten minutes reading the Bible and ten minutes praying. There was a time when I took an hour and a half, but currently I'm spending forty minutes. The time investment will pay such dividends in your walk with the Lord. Give as much time as you can.

Where should you have your Bible reading and prayer time? "But thou, when thou prayest, enter into thy closet, and when thou hast shut thy door, pray to thy Father which is in secret; and thy Father which seeth in secret shall reward thee openly" (Matthew 6:6). Jesus suggested you go into your closet when you pray. The word "closet" means an inner chamber or someplace hidden away. The idea is that we are to get alone with the Lord. We can't effectively concentrate on Him when there are distractions around us. That is another advantage of getting up early when everyone else is asleep. It is easier to find a quiet place.

Currently, I go to the living room since I can be alone there. Find a quiet place, and if need be, ask others not to come in during that time. If there are sounds from elsewhere in the house, then I would recommend foam earplugs to reduce the ambient noise. I'm easily distractible, and I use earplugs fairly often when I need to concentrate. Whatever it takes, for the good of your soul—do it!

Where in the Bible should you read? If a person isn't very familiar with the Bible, I would encourage him to first read the book of John. I ask the Lord where He wants me to read. Lately I've started back through the four gospels. When I am close to finishing them, I will ask the Lord where He wants me to go next. There was a time when I read Jeremiah three or four times in a row. Ask Him during your prayer time, and He will show you.

A number of times I have been led to read the Bible from Genesis to Revelation. There are many read-through-the-Bible-in-a-year programs out there, but I have come to where I don't encourage my family to do them. Don't misunderstand me, reading through the Bible in one year is great, but often it requires a person to hurry through their reading to complete the assignment. I want my family to read slowly during this time because the goal is to grow in intimacy with the Lord. If a person has an extra hour a day when he could read the Bible, going through it in a year would be great. However, don't let the goal crowd out a time of savoring the Word. The purpose of our quiet time is to experience the Lord Jesus, grow in greater intimacy with Him, and apply His Word to our lives.

A side note I feel important to share is that I would not suggest that anyone read the short daily devotionals for their primary Bible time. I wonder if reading them isn't like eating something that someone else has chewed first. I desire that God would speak to me directly through His Word and that I would learn it more and more. I don't believe either of those goals is accomplished by reading some warming anecdote and two verses of Scripture each day. That is fine for reading while you brush your teeth, but I would implore everyone not to consider that a substitute for spending quality time with the Lord Jesus.

After "where" to read is "how much" to read. I would not necessarily read a given amount each day. Read with an open heart. There are days when I read a chapter and other days when I read a handful of verses. I read slowly so I can understand what I'm reading. At the same time, I don't get bogged down if I can't understand a verse. I may continue on and return when I can study it further.

Lastly, what am I trying to get from my time in the Word? I want to know the Lord and how I can apply His Word to my life. I ask myself questions about what I'm reading. "Why might Jesus have said that?" "Why did they do that?" "Lord, how do You want me to apply this to my life?" Questions, questions, questions! Why, why, why, why, and why? Through the years I have seen the Lord answer so many questions. I love it when He gives new and fresh insight to a passage I have wondered about for years.

"Blessed *are* they that keep his testimonies, *and that* seek him with the whole heart" (Psalms 119:2). "With my whole heart have I sought thee: O let me not wander from thy commandments. Thy word have I hid in mine heart, that I might not sin against thee. Blessed *art* thou, O LORD: teach me thy statutes" (Psalms 119:10-12). The blessings, the wisdom, the protection, and the promises that are buried in the Bible are critical to our spiritual health and our ability to lead our family. Dads—we can't afford not to have a daily time in the Word and pray. Won't you begin today?

# Can Dads Influence Their Children's Spiritual Outcome?
## PART 8 — WILL IT BURN?
### by Steve

Sitting on my desk in front of me is a "gold brick" with the words "Outstanding Performance" engraved on top. I was awarded this treasure in 1983 for my many hours of "meritorious" work at my corporate job. My gold brick has become very meaningful to me, but not, perhaps, in the way you might think. The brick is actually solid brass, even though it has the look and feel of gold. Funny what a striking analogy it is, being as deceptive in its true value as my hours to earn it were deceptive in their true (eternal) value.

For me, it has become a symbol of how my normal daily work is about as worthless as a fake "gold brick." It has become a frequent reminder of how easy it is to have misplaced priorities. When it comes to eternity, the hours we men spend at work are basically wood, hay, and stubble. "For other foundation can no man lay than that is laid, which is Jesus Christ. Now if any man build upon this foundation gold, silver, precious stones, wood, hay, stubble; Every man's work shall be made manifest: for the day shall declare it, because it shall be revealed by fire; and the fire shall try every man's work of what sort it is. If any man's work abide which he hath built thereupon, he shall receive a reward. If any man's work shall be burned, he shall suffer loss: but he himself shall be saved; yet so as by fire" (1 Corinthians 3:11-15).

Just think, the work we believe is so important that we spend eight hours a day on (and then some) is all going to be consumed in eternity. This work, which becomes most men's identity, will burn. It won't even give off bright colors and fancy sparks that dazzle the eye like we have just seen on the Fourth. The flames will simply devour all our precious effort, and nothing will be left of eternal value as we stare at the ashes. Of course, it is our responsibility to provide for our families, so the real work of eternal value can be carried forth. Plus the money we earn can be used to further the Kingdom of God. In general, however, the work we spend so many hours a day doing will count for nothing in eternity.

How easy it is to be deceived into thinking our important work occurs during the for-pay job, but the work we do at home isn't as important. That is backwards! Finally, when we come home to our family, that is when we have the opportunity for gold, silver, and precious stones. The question is—are you creating more wood, hay, and stubble when you come home, or is it gold, silver, and precious stones? We each have a choice with our hours at home with our families.

I have come to realize that the time I spend with my family, leading them in the ways of the Lord Jesus, is when something of value is produced. Discipling my family for the few hours I have available in a day is the primary investment I have for something that will last for eternity. I feel that even if I were in the ministry full time rather than having a secular job, my time with my family would still be my opportunity to spend those minutes on something of the greatest value.

I would have to put high on my list of time spent well, with an eye on eternity, as our family altar. I absolutely love those moments and look forward to them. I know that when I'm discipling my family and washing them in the water of God's Word, instead of a fake gold brick, I'm building using gold, silver, and precious stones.

I believe a lot of dads want to lead their family in evening worship, but next to misplaced priorities the greatest roadblock is that they don't know how to do it. I would like to make this Corner practical and share how we have ours. I'm sure there are other, better ways, but for the sake of being brief, I will tell you what I am familiar with doing.

I will usually have our family worship time right after dinner is cleaned up. That way I know nothing else will get in the way. We do first what is most important to us, and so it makes sense that devotions occur in our first available time after dinner. However, the main point is to find a time that works for you and to which you can be consistent.

We only use the Bible for family altar even though we have a wide range of ages. I have come to realize through the years that even the young children will learn a great deal from Bible reading although some of it is beyond their understanding. Whatever book of the Bible we are in, I purpose to do my best to make it interesting. I constantly try to reveal Jesus Christ to my family and show them how Scripture applies to our everyday lives.

When we first began family worship almost twenty years ago, I would read the chapter we were going to read during my personal Bible reading time, before our common worship. I would jot some notes down and think about the verses so I was prepared. I used a study Bible with comments, and they helped me feel more comfortable in understanding what we would be reading as a family. Even now there are times I won't know an answer. I think that is something we dads have to come to peace with and share with our family. We don't have all the answers. However, I am willing to do some study and see what I can find. Even then, with some questions, I may have to wait a few years, or perhaps even until heaven, before I finally get an answer.

Frankly, if you are at all unfamiliar with the Bible, don't let that stop you from leading family devotions. Go out and buy a good study Bible. Ask around for recommendations, and then buy one. It is worth the investment. Just do it.

Where to read is simple. Start at the beginning of the New Testament and read a chapter a night. I prefer to go slowly and have everyone enjoy it, rather than to race through several chapters. We come away with new understanding rather than plowing ahead simply to cover more ground.

Everyone reads two verses as we take turns around the room. For fun, Jesse, our youngest reader, always gets to start, and Anna reads the last verse. It is a little silly, but when it works out perfectly that the last verse falls in sequence where Anna is sitting, visitors have been surprised to hear the word "perfect" being uttered around the room as we realize it has come out perfectly for Anna to get the last verse. There is nothing real spiritual about that; we just have a good time in the Word of God.

As we read, everyone is supposed to be looking for a special verse that they would like to apply to their life. For variety, we cycle through the family, starting with the youngest, so that each night someone different gets to share his verse first. Then, after telling everyone his verse and application, he gets to pick which way we go around the room for the others to share their verses.

After everyone has had his turn, I ask if there are any confessions. It is my desire that when we wrong another during the day, we would confess that sin to the other person right away, but that doesn't always happen. This provides an opportunity to confess sins, forgive each other for sins committed (Matthew 6:14), and avoid bitterness in the home.

Finally, the person who shared his verse first is the one who gets to pick a hymn for us to sing. We sing that song, and our family altar is over. Many families will pray during family worship, but we have chosen to have our time of prayer when we put the children down for bed. However, that is the beauty of it. Do what fits your family and is pleasing to the Lord.

Do you love the Lord Jesus and His Word? If so, then a daily family time in the Word is just a natural extension of your love. It is not difficult, but it does require consistency, which will come from proper priorities. What are you creating with your time—wood, hay, and stubble, or gold, silver, and precious stones?

# Can Dads Influence Their Children's Spiritual Outcome?
## PART 9 — TURNING YOUR HEART
### by Steve

Teri and I were eating dinner with another couple earlier this year at a homeschooling event, when a sixteen-year-old young man asked if he might sit in the empty seat next to me. I said, "You are welcome to as long as you don't mind me asking you a ton of questions." He told me that was fine as long as I didn't mind him eating. I chuckled as I thought about what he said while looking at his plate. It was what you would expect of a young man with an appetite, lip-lopping full without a square inch of empty room. As Randy sat down, I observed in him a young man with a confident smile, who looked accustomed to working hard. True to our words, he commenced to eat, and I began launching questions his direction. How old was he, how many in his family, how did he spend his time, what did he like to do, what sort of friends did he have? As soon as he answered one, I had another one for him.

His replies were not just courteous but also full of respect. The more I listened to his answers the greater appreciation I had for his parents and what they were doing in his life. I could hear how much he enjoyed his family. He truly loved his parents and his six brothers and sisters. The average sixteen-year-old young man would feel his siblings were a nuisance, to be avoided at all costs. Randy clearly loved his family.

His favorite person to be with in all the world was his father. He had one friend outside the family, a young man in his twenties who had a construction business. He really enjoyed working with his friend and learning the trade.

He was always busy. Most boys his age would be on every sports team they could find. Not Randy. His time was filled with working with his friend, helping, and being with his family.

I told him I really wanted to meet his father. He pointed with his chin and said he was sitting right behind me. Unfortunately, as soon as I was finished and ready to meet his dad, he had already moved on to some responsibilities. I was disappointed but hoped I might run into him before we had to leave.

God is so good. The next morning as I was on my way to check out of the hotel, I saw Randy's dad having breakfast. I went over, introduced myself, and asked if I could visit for a short while. He smiled and welcomed me to sit down.

I told him about my conversation with Randy and how impressed I was with him. From my brief time of discussion, Randy really seemed to be a godly young man of character who enjoyed his family and working. Was this really the case, how long had Randy been like this, and what was this father doing to have such success with his son?

His dad then shocked me by what he said. Just four years ago, Randy was a very angry boy such that, those who knew him were well aware of his problem with anger. Over the last four years God had done a mighty work in Randy's life. He isn't perfect, but he is a young man who dearly loves his God and his family and enjoys working.

I asked Tom, Randy's father, how the Lord had worked in Randy's life. Tom said that one of the first things that changed was that he was shown that his (Tom) focus needed to be on his family and not himself. The principle that the family applied to how they spent their time had become (aside from Tom's job), "If we can't do it as a family, we won't do it."

Tom said his golf clubs have about four years' worth of dust on them now. He loves to golf and did quite well in tournaments. Even now some have encouraged him that they could golf as a family, but he knows that the passion would be rekindled. It wasn't worth pulling his heart away from his family again.

I expect their family would have been a very typical "religious" family. The children were in private school and in all the normal activities. Besides school activities, Randy was on basketball and baseball teams like all his friends.

However, God started working in Randy's parents' lives. They decided to homeschool the children and made other changes. They sought solutions to Randy's anger and were willing to do whatever was necessary. The parents continued to be obedient to the Lord's leading and over the past four years have seen God do a mighty work in their family.

I interrupted Tom a few times as we talked with an exclamation of praise for the Lord's goodness and mercy. These parents responded to the Lord's leading and what a marvelous work is in process. Tom is quick to say they aren't perfect and still have some consequences from their earlier lifestyle, but the change is welcome and continuing.

This home is a wonderful example of Malachi 4:6: "And he shall turn the heart of the fathers to the children, and the heart of the children to their fathers, lest I come and smite the earth with a curse." How the futures of so many children could be positively changed if only the father's heart would be turned toward his children. I believe that the parent usually thinks it is his child's problem. "He just won't listen to me," or, "I've told him a hundred times, and he won't obey me."

It all begins with dad and mom's hearts. Are they turned toward their children? I asked Tom what he would have said if someone had asked him years ago if his heart was turned toward his children. He said he wouldn't have known what that meant. I then asked him if he had his own activities and the children had theirs. He said, "Yes, that was true."

I wonder if many dads think their hearts are turned toward their children, when in fact they aren't. If I were to ask you right now, "What has your heart?" what would you say? If you said, "my children," do a reality check on that. Aside from Dad's work time or Mom's daily responsibilities, how do you spend your time?

"Lay not up for yourselves treasures upon earth, where moth and rust doth corrupt, and where thieves break through and steal: But lay up for yourselves treasures in heaven, where neither moth nor rust doth corrupt, and where thieves do not break through nor steal: For where your treasure is, there will your heart be also" (Matthew 6:19-21). Face it. There are a myriad of "important," or fun, things that can take every minute we have. Then we toss our children the scraps of time that are left over, when it should be the opposite.

Even as I write this, I'm convicted of some things that need to be reworked in the way I allocate my time. I feel that I need to make better use of the way I'm spending my time after our evening family altar time and before the children go to bed. I can't tell you what is going to change, but I know I need to pray about it and see how the Lord will direct me. I cherish these years of raising my children, and I desire to have no regrets when I look back on these years.

I delight in spending time with my children. Next to Teri, they are my best friends. The time I am with my children is a treasure that doesn't rust and can't be stolen. I have a passion for flying private planes, and yet I haven't flown for over twenty years. I laid that use of time and money aside for something of far greater value—time with my children and a heart focused on them. So many things will creep in to steal away our time and attention.

A daddy's heart focused on his children is an amazing thing. God used Tom's change of heart direction in a mighty way in Randy's life. The promise in Malachi is real. If we will turn our hearts toward our children, they will turn their hearts toward us. Families all around are experiencing awful consequences due to not having hearts turned toward each other. Are you? If so, are you willing to turn your heart toward your children?

# Pride — Part 1
## WHO SAID IT'S HOPELESS?
### by Steve

It would be quite revealing if we took a survey and asked how many dads have a struggle with pride. I expect most dads who have either read the Bible much or heard many sermons would say they wish they were less proud. Although I know one dad who seems to be somewhat proud of his pride, most everyone else I know (if it has come up in conversation) would prefer not to be proud.

So why would most Christians want to be less proud? Maybe we could go so far as to ask why would some desire to be humble and not proud at all? Let me list a few verses about pride and let them speak for themselves.

Proverbs 6:16-17, "These six *things* doth the Lord hate: yea, seven *are* an abomination unto him: A proud look, a lying tongue, and hands that shed innocent blood."

Proverbs 16:5, "Every one *that is* proud in heart *is* an abomination to the Lord: *though* hand *join* in hand, he shall not be unpunished."

Proverbs 21:4, "An high look, and a proud heart, *and* the plowing of the wicked, *is* sin."

Proverbs 21:24, "Proud *and* haughty scorner *is* his name, who dealeth in proud wrath."

These verses seem to come on pretty strongly against pride. After reading them, I find myself wondering how I could ever have thought, "I really don't like my pride, but thankfully it isn't a big problem for me." I wonder if that attitude isn't similar to being willing to drink a glass of milk with only two drops of sewage in it. Just two small drops—that isn't much, is it? Okay, what if we cut it down by 50 percent and make it only one drop of raw sewage in a nice big glass of cold milk. Who would drink it?

Why am I willing to live with just a little pride when God's Word calls it an abomination? An abomination is something that is an abhorrence, or is disgusting, to God. Proverbs 16:5 says that a proud heart makes God sick, and He loathes it.

I think there are two reasons why I have allowed a "little" pride to be justifiable in my life. First, I have always seen Scripture as if it was talking about having too much pride. This was an incorrect assumption. Surely I didn't have too much. The second reason is even a bigger issue; I've not seen Scripture telling how to remove pride from a person's life. If there is no way to remove it, then we can't be held accountable for it, can we? That's another incorrect assumption.

Maybe there is some threshold of pride we can't exceed. What is it going to hurt the average dad with the average amount of pride? Unfortunately, if pride being an abomination to God isn't enough, there is the practical issue that we really aren't able to love our family and others as 1 Corinthians 13:4-7 instructs us. We can see that pride is the root cause that keeps us from loving others. ("Charity suffereth long, *and* is kind; charity envieth not; charity vaunteth not itself, is not puffed up, Doth not behave itself unseemly, seeketh not her own, is not easily provoked, thinketh no evil; Rejoiceth not in iniquity, but rejoiceth in the truth; Beareth all things, believeth all things, hopeth all things, endureth all things.")

If we open up our minds, it isn't too difficult to see that pride is the main reason why we struggle with being good fathers. It keeps us from being loving because:

Pride says our time is more important than anyone else's.

Pride says why be kind? Everyone is here for our benefit as we are the most important.

Pride says everyone delights in hearing all about the wonderful things we have done, and so why listen to anyone else.

Pride is rude because our feelings are the only ones that matter.

Pride is selfish because our pleasure is most important.

Pride is easily angered because our rights come first, and everyone must put us first.

Pride thinks the worst of everyone because no one is as good as we are, and frankly, thinking the worst of others makes us feel better.

As I began thinking about pride and how serious it is, I found myself asking the Lord a question in my heart. "Lord, if pride is so terrible, then why isn't it very clearly dealt with in Your Word?" It would have been so easy for the Lord to have devoted a whole book to removing pride from our lives. If not a whole book, why not a whole chapter?

God is so merciful in answering prayers. I think in some ways I would have preferred to remain ignorant about pride in my life and how to deal with it, yet I believe God showed me the answer in His Word. It may not be as revolutionary to you as it was to me, but it sure was amazing as I have studied it. I challenge you to read further.

"For from within, out of the heart of men, proceed evil thoughts, adulteries, fornications, murders, Thefts, covetousness, wickedness, deceit, lasciviousness, an evil eye, blasphemy, pride, foolishness: All these evil things come from within, and defile the man" (Mark 7:21-23). Look at the company pride keeps—evil thoughts, adulteries, fornications, murders, thefts, covetousness, wickedness, deceit, lasciviousness, an evil eye, blasphemy, and foolishness. We look at most of these, and we can see that no "good" Christian would allow these in his life. Why not? He wouldn't tolerate them, because they are just too bad. He couldn't allow it. How much murder, adultery, and fornication have you allowed in your life lately? Hmmmm.

Now read, "Hear ye, and give ear; be not proud: for the LORD hath spoken" (Jeremiah 13:15) and, *"Be* of the same mind one toward another. Mind not high things, but condescend to men of low estate. Be not wise in your own conceits" (Romans 12:16). Here we read two clear, direct commands regarding pride. In essence, we are told not to be proud. God never tells us not to do something if we aren't able not to do it. If He tells us to stop doing something, then we can and should stop it.

Frankly put, pride is an abomination to God, it is sin, and He has told us to put it away. How much is acceptable? The answer is clear—none! The reason we don't commit the other sins I mentioned above is because we choose not to do them. Plain and simple. That means that pride is also a choice.

There is something that makes ridding our lives of pride especially difficult. Not only is it a choice, but unfortunately, it is a habit in varying degrees. The greater the habit, the more difficult it is to cast off. God shows no sympathy toward our pride. It is an abomination. There is nothing to feel sorry for ourselves over. Truly, what we need to do is repent over our pride.

Would you like to see real revival break loose in your home? I know I would. Would you join me in focusing on pride in our prayers and daily Bible reading? May we cry out to the Lord and ask Him to examine our hearts. May we memorize several verses on pride. As we go to sleep, let the truth of those verses cut deep into our hearts, bringing true repentance.

May our hearts be prepared for next month when we look at what I believe God has set as the cure for pride. Will you join me and see what the Lord Jesus will do with hearts that are surrendered to Him?

# Pride — Part 2
## THE ANSWER TO PRIDE
### by Steve

I wonder if pride isn't the number-one accepted sin in Christian circles. A church may discipline men for using alcohol or being immoral, but I have never heard of a man being disciplined because of his pride. Pride is an abomination to God. Pride is what cast Satan from heaven and brought hell to earth. We will tolerate it in our lives but react to it in others. It is at the root of all contention and an abomination to God. It often destroys marriages and can be a tremendous factor in losing the hearts of our children. Yet, if God hates it, why don't we? I wonder if one reason we don't hate pride is because we feel so helpless to kill it in our lives.

In September's Dad's Corner we discussed pride. This month we will finish with some further thoughts on it. Let's briefly look over the verses that were listed in a previous Corner.

Proverbs 6:16-17, "These six *things* doth the LORD hate: yea, seven *are* an abomination unto him: A proud look, a lying tongue, and hands that shed innocent blood."

Proverbs 16:5, "Every one *that is* proud in heart *is* an abomination to the Lord: *though* hand *join* in hand, he shall not be unpunished."

Proverbs 21:4, "An high look, and a proud heart, *and* the plowing of the wicked, *is* sin."

Proverbs 21:24, "Proud *and* haughty scorner *is* his name, who dealeth in proud wrath."

For the man who despises pride in his own life, there is hope. For the man who tolerates it, there is a fall coming. "Pride *goeth* before destruction, and an haughty spirit before a fall" (Proverbs 16:18).

As I shared previously in Part 1, one night in frustration I prayed, "Lord, if pride is so awful, then why don't You plainly tell us how to put it away?" Since humility is the opposite of pride, why didn't He tell us step-by-step how to be humble? Soon after that, as I was studying a section of Scripture, I was thrilled as I realized that He has told us. Frankly, it is about as close to step-by-step instructions as I could have hoped for.

I believe that 1 Corinthians 13:4-7 is key in overcoming pride. "Charity suffereth long, *and* is kind; charity envieth not; charity vaunteth not itself, is not puffed up, Doth not behave itself unseemly, seeketh not her own, is not easily provoked, thinketh no evil; Rejoiceth not in iniquity, but rejoiceth in the truth; Beareth all things, believeth all things, hopeth all things, endureth all things."

Looking at these verses, one can soon see that the focus is on the other person. Every aspect of each verse requires a choice on the part of the person who loves the other. We are not at the mercy of some emotional feeling that catches hold of us and propels us toward loving the person more. The love being shared here is a choice based on a rational decision to place value on the other, and then express it in a tangible way.

Jesus said, "A new commandment I give unto you, That ye love one another; as I have loved you, that ye also love one another. By this shall all *men* know that ye are my disciples, if ye have love one to another" (John 13:34-35). Notice it isn't by our humility that all men will know we are His disciples, but by our love. In time, humility will be a by-product of our love, but choosing to love is where it begins. Is that really it? Is it that simple? All we have to do is love others according to 1 Corinthians 13.

When pride brought sin into the world, what was God's answer? His answer was Christ Jesus and His atoning work on the cross. Jesus said, ". . . as I have loved you, that ye also love one another" (John 13:34). What was God's motivation? "For God so loved the world, that he gave his only begotten Son . . ." (John 3:16).

Love is the answer to pride. Pride is focused on self, and love (agape) is focused on others. We can't focus on ourselves and still be able to love others. We really can't be proud and love others in accordance with 1 Corinthians 13. Look how simple it is to get rid of our pride!

Unfortunately, as soon as we begin in earnest to love as we are told to, we discover a problem. At least I have discovered a problem when I tried to love according to 1 Corinthians 13. It seems impossible!

Charity is patient. Charity is kind. Charity does not envy. Charity does not boast. Charity is not proud. Charity is not rude. Charity is not self-seeking. Charity is not easily angered. Charity keeps no record of wrong. Charity does not delight in evil. Charity delights in truth. Charity always protects. Charity always hopes. Charity always trusts. Charity always perseveres.

At the same time, pride is impatient. Pride is unkind. Pride envies. Pride boasts. Pride is rude. Pride is self-seeking. Pride is easily angered. Pride keeps record of wrongs. Pride delights in finding evil in others. Pride rejects truth about oneself. Pride only protects self. Pride can't hope because it trusts in self. Pride quits when it gets too uncomfortable.

I think these next two verses present a further explanation of the relationship between love and pride. In Matthew 22:40 Jesus says, "On these two commandments hang all the law and the prophets." If we love the Lord with all our heart, soul, and strength and our neighbor as ourself, we fulfill all the law. Paul explains that "Love worketh no ill to his neighbour: therefore love *is* the fulfilling of the law" (Romans 13:10).

The law was meant to show the Jews they could not fulfill it themselves by their own goodness and efforts. I believe God is showing believers the same thing. We can't fulfill the law of love in our own strength and character. Without His power and intervention, we are helpless to love as we are commanded. The more we try to love, the more we are humbled as we see we are unable to love others in our own strength. As hopeless as it is for any lost person to earn salvation by doing good or keeping the law, it is impossible for a Christian to love as we are commanded to love. (I'm not saying that if we fail to love others we will lose our salvation. Christ has purchased that fully for us.)

I believe that what we will find is that love for others will lead us down a path to the cross. It did for Christ, and it will for us as well. Brothers, pride dies on the cross. "And he said to *them* all, If any *man* will come after me, let him deny himself, and take up his cross daily, and follow me" (Luke 9:23). As Christ surrendered His will to the Father and only did and said what the Father showed Him and told Him, may we surrender to the Lord and let Him simply work through us. We become vehicles for Him to love through us.

I don't believe focusing on pride is the answer. Killing pride is simple, just not easy. The Jews had to humble themselves because they couldn't fulfill the law in their own strength. We will be humbled as we take up our cross of love. We need to make the choice to love, and God provides His grace if we will surrender our will. If we will surrender, our homes will be transformed. May we be committed to loving as God has called us to, all the while crying out to the Lord to use us as a channel for Him to love through us. "And being found in fashion as a man, he humbled himself, and became obedient unto death, even the death of the cross" (Philippians 2:8).

# He Could Do No More.
# What About Us?
### by Steve

His son was his joy. He loved to hold him and take care of him. The weeks passed and so did the months, until his son finally began to walk. What a delight to have his little boy follow him around the house. Each day was better than the previous. Then one day he was told that he and his wife, with their son, must appear in court. They went as commanded. At the conclusion of the proceedings, someone picked up his son, walked across the courtroom and out a door. That was the last time he ever saw his son. A large portion of his heart was ripped out of his body at that moment. The anguish he has experienced not many have known.

It has probably been six months that he has been attending our church at the nursing home. He has amazed us with his love for the Lord Jesus and knowing so many of the old hymns. I'm guessing he is in his seventies. Tall and thin, he still gets around quite well with a walker or cane. It might be that those size-twelve boots add to his stability, but if not, he keeps himself upright through sheer determination.

He has trouble speaking, and you have to listen carefully to understand him. That doesn't seem to bother him, though, even if I ask him to repeat something. He has a room to himself, and it is quite full with furniture that the county brought over from his house.

Several weeks ago he was telling me about how he had set his room up, so I walked down the hall with him to look at it. The couch was strategically placed at one end of the room. He went on to tell me about how he moved his two dressers and his reasons for placing them just so. I cautioned him about moving such heavy things alone. With a twinkle in his eye, he said how the staff didn't want him to, but he could do it just fine by himself.

He has a picture of his wife and him on the opposite wall from his bed. He will tear-up just about every time he speaks of her passing away. They didn't have much, but they had each other and the Lord Jesus.

One Sunday coming home from church, I was telling the family about my conversation with him, just minutes earlier. I shared about our discussion and that at the end, he said how he prays every day for his son's walk with the Lord. He has no idea where his son is, but he also prays that someday he will be able to see him again. As I tried to finish telling the family what he had told me, that he has trusted God . . . I just couldn't get all the words out without breaking down. I finally sort of squeaked out that he was trusting God with his son.

I almost can't even write this because my heart feels like it is in a vise. This man of God has suffered so deeply for all these years. He has been able to deal with his grief through his faith in God. I detect no bitterness. I think if there were any, it would have killed him by now.

I share this story because I felt there was a powerful lesson for each of us. He had his son taken from him many, many years ago. He has not been able to do anything for his son except pray—and pray he has. He would have given everything he has to exchange places with any of us dads. He wanted to have children around him—to love them, hold them, and teach them. I'm convinced that no matter what your circumstances, he would gladly change places with you in a heartbeat.

Dad, how do you look at your wife and children? Are they your delight or a burden? Are you excited to be able to spend time with them? Do you spend time with them, and what do you do with them?

My friend could do nothing to disciple and shape his son. What are we doing to disciple our children? Are we leading our family in a daily Bible time? Are we spending meaningful one-on-one time with them? Have you gladly forsaken "your" time for time with your family?

When my friend stands before the Lord Jesus someday to give account for his life, with a clear conscience he will be able to say he did everything he could to raise his son in the nurture and admonition of the Lord (Ephesians 6:4). Will we be able to say that? While there is still time, may we turn our hearts to our children and have an active daily role in shaping their lives. "And he shall turn the heart of the fathers to the children, and the heart of the children to their fathers, lest I come and smite the earth with a curse" (Malachi 4:6).

# When the Boat Is Sinking, What Is Our Example?

## by Steve

The last two months have been absolutely incredible. Our family business, CCI, has had a major software project that had to be completed in January. Teri and I have been finishing our newest book, *Keeping Our Children's Hearts.* I have had a message to produce for our church each week. Plus we have had a myriad of other issues surface in our family and ministry that have required mental, emotional, and spiritual energy. All of that had to be kept in right priority in relation to my walk with the Lord and my time and attention for my family.

Pressure is something we all have to deal with. It is a fact of life. When you are dead, there is no longer any pressure, provided you are saved. If one doesn't know Jesus as Lord and Savior, then whatever pressure this life can muster is nothing compared to eternity in hell. "And fear not them which kill the body, but are not able to kill the soul: but rather fear him which is able to destroy both soul and body in hell" (Matthew 10:28). However, in keeping our thoughts on what we are facing day to day, I know that most dads are accustomed to facing pressure. How do you react to it?

My natural tendency is to convert pressure into stress—the greater the pressure, the greater the stress. When there is a long line of people requiring things from me, and the "shelves of time" are stocked very sparingly, stress begins to mount. Then when I'm feeling very stressed, I tend to be irritable and self-focused. To make matters worse, sleep can become more difficult with growing stress. Being tired introduces a whole new set of negative factors into the equation. Uggh! It is easy to understand the attitude of several men at the homeless mission. They don't mind being there because they have no responsibilities and nothing pressuring them. Life may not be easy for them, but it is simple.

A law of nature is that pressure tends toward equalization. This means that pressure must meet an opposite pressure to stabilize or it will dissipate on its own. It seems like this can be applied to us as well. If we are feeling a lot of pressure from the outside, instead of letting the pressure dissipate on its own, we will tend to ramp up the stress and worry on the inside to counteract the outside pressure we are feeling. However, is this the life Jesus desires for us? In calling us to be busy and fruitful, does that mean the Lord intends for us to live under constant pressure, with worry and stress?

What does Scripture teach us about this? We don't find the word "stress" in Scripture, but there are still verses that apply. Could it be that we are not to be stressed over small things, but it's okay to be stressed about big issues such as the needs of our family? "Therefore I say unto you, Take no thought for your life, what ye shall eat, or what ye shall drink; nor yet for your body, what ye shall put on. Is not the life more than meat, and the body than raiment?" (Matthew 6:25). "Take no thought" means do not worry. That seems to make it clear, doesn't it? We are not to worry. I believe the American equivalent of worry is stress. This verse is saying we are not to be stressed.

Jesus is not just suggesting we aren't to be stressed—He is commanding it. An uncomfortable way of saying this might be that worry is sin and feeling stressed is sin. If stress weren't bad enough, now we are adding the challenge of calling it sin. God did not intend for us to live our lives full of worry or stress.

To acknowledge we are stressed is no different from acknowledging we are angry or bitter. They are all sin. We need to confess worry or stress as sin and forsake it. Is not our God capable of dealing with any situation at hand? Yes, of course He is!

I have an analogy I share with the children in appropriate situations: "Anyone can rest in a hammock in the backyard on a beautiful spring day. To rest in a hammock that is tied between two masts on a boat in a storm is entirely something else. In the storm is where we really learn how to rest." If God didn't allow times like these, we wouldn't have the opportunity to learn how to rest in Jesus.

I often think about the disciples in the boat in the middle of the storm. "And, behold, there arose a great tempest in the sea, insomuch that the ship was covered with the waves: but he was asleep. And his disciples came to *him*, and awoke him, saying, Lord, save us: we perish. And he saith unto them, Why are ye fearful, O ye of little faith? Then he arose, and rebuked the winds and the sea; and there was a great calm" (Matthew 8:24-26). This was no little storm. The Greek word for tempest is seismos, and it means a gale or an earthquake. These men had every reason to be afraid.

Several of His disciples were fishermen and accustomed to storms, yet they were afraid of dying. Should they have been afraid? Weren't they in the boat with Jesus? Jesus had told them in Matthew 8:18 "to depart unto the other side." Had they believed His Word, they would have had confidence He would fulfill His Word to them. Yet, in the terrible storm, they were afraid and woke Jesus up. What was the first thing Jesus did? He rebuked His disciples for their lack of faith, and then He rebuked the wind and the seas. The terrible storm provided the opportunity for Jesus' disciples to trust in Him.

Which do you think would impart greater learning? For Jesus and the disciples to sit around a warm campfire on the beach while Jesus tells them they can always rely on Him, even during their greatest trial, or for them to be close to drowning and see Jesus command the wind and the waves to be silent?

As we neared the deadline for our software, we encountered what seemed to be a major architectural problem. New requirements had been added by the customer as we progressed, but there had not been time to step back to make the extensive changes required. Finally, a problem surfaced, and it looked hopeless. Our programmer and I were discussing the seriousness of what was just discovered. Just before hanging up, the programmer said something like, "It will be okay. God has always worked in one way or another in situations like these in the past."

That wasn't positive thinking on his part—it was fact. Over the years we have worked together, we have seen God do amazing things. Many times, a difficulty has arisen that was darker and more ominous than any previous problem. When that happens, we pray and do our best while we depend on His grace. Each situation has worked out for good. The problems are not always fixed like we intended, but in some way, there has always been an acceptable resolution. That isn't positive thinking. It is reliance on our Lord. If God didn't allow times like these, we wouldn't have the opportunity to learn how we can further depend on Him.

How do you respond to pressure and difficulties? Are you thankful for them? "And not only *so*, but we glory in tribulations also: knowing that tribulation worketh patience" (Romans 5:3). Do we desire to be conformed to the image of Christ? "And we know that all things work together for good to them that love God, to them who are the called according to *his* purpose. For whom he did foreknow, he also did predestinate *to be* conformed to the image of his Son, that he might be the firstborn among many brethren" (Romans 8:28-29).

The trials and pressures we face are not just for our own benefit, but for our children as well. Our children read us like a book. What sort of "story" are the children reading in our lives? Do they see that their dad has a real relationship with Jesus Christ, and He is at work in their dad's life? Does Dad depend on Him, and is Dad at peace in the middle of the storms that come? If the answer is yes, we are demonstrating the reality of a life based on Jesus Christ. That will speak volumes to them. More teaching will go on during difficult times than during any discussion.

I'm reminded again of a time when we were at a homeschool conference. A mother asked to sit in one of the chairs behind the table and attend to the needs of her young child. I watched in awe as this precious mommy gently took care of her child. She shared how her child would soon die, and she had to care for him in this way every hour around the clock. What a heartbreaking situation, and yet there was no bitterness or stress, just gentleness and patience to the glory of God. I will never forget what I observed in her life.

Do we desire that our family and others would observe the fruit of the Spirit in our lives? If so, may we look at the pressures and problems that come our way this next month as allowed by God to conform us to the image of His Son. If we will welcome them, they are opportunities to draw close to Jesus and see Him work in our lives. "And he arose, and rebuked the wind, and said unto the sea, Peace, be still. And the wind ceased, and there was a great calm" (Mark 4:39).

# Are You on a Collision Course?
## *by Steve*

Our family was returning home from a trip to Lawton, Oklahoma. Happy, enthusiastic talk filled the van as we rolled down the interstate. Ahead of us on the other side of the highway, I noticed a car that was just merging onto the other side of interstate headed the opposite direction from us. Suddenly, I saw the car abruptly make a sharp 180 degree turn and strike out toward seventy-mile-per-hour oncoming traffic—a nightmare scenario.

In horror I said aloud, "Oh no!" and I cried out, "Lord Jesus, help them!" As we passed the car now traveling the same direction as us, I saw a woman driving with several small children in the car. I glanced ahead. There were two cars bearing down on her. To the Maxwell family's relief, she pulled over and stopped on the median shoulder as the cars safely whizzed by her.

Our excited chatter had been replaced by a momentary deathly silence. Now everyone was voicing a similar thought. What if she hadn't pulled over then? We realized we had just narrowly missed being eyewitnesses to a freeway head-on collision. We could not fathom what possessed that woman to make a U-turn and head the wrong way down the interstate toward oncoming traffic. How could she have risked her life, the children's lives, and those of the people in the other cars?

Praise God that she realized she was heading in the wrong direction and took appropriate action in time to avert a disaster. How heartbreaking it would have been to watch something terrible happen had she struck one of the two oncoming cars.

For quite a while now, Teri and I have had heavy hearts as we read e-mails, read message board posts, and observe Christian families losing their children to the world. These families are busy with normal life until, all of a sudden, they are in the midst of a crisis. The child, who has been nurtured and taught for so many years, begins making choices that reflect the negative influence of the world.

Our sadness is nothing compared to what the parents of those children have experienced. The disappointment and anguish they suffer is horrible. But where is God in all of this? Does not His Word offer hope for the rest of us? Is it simply the destiny of a fixed percentage of families to have a child who will embrace the world?

It can be discouraging for parents when they look around and mostly see teens who are very worldly. Is there nothing that can be done, or do we just wait until they're grown to see how it will all turn out?

We have found encouragement in these verses. "A bishop then must be blameless, the husband of one wife, vigilant, sober, of good behaviour, given to hospitality, apt to teach; Not given to wine, no striker, not greedy of filthy lucre; but patient, not a brawler, not covetous; One that ruleth well his own house, having his children in subjection with all gravity; (For if a man know not how to rule his own house, how shall he take care of the church of God?)" (1 Timothy 3:2-5).

As we look at these verses, it is clear that they are intended to be the litmus test of a man to see if he qualifies to be an elder or overseer of the church. Let me briefly list the meaning of the requirements: blameless, have one wife (one marriage), vigilant (circumspect or temperate), sober (self-controlled), of good behavior, hospitable, able to teach, not a drinker, not violent, not greedy, patient, not quick to quarrel (peaceable), not covetous, rules his house well, and having reverent children. Also, in Titus 1:6, it is added that the children would be faithful.

As we look at those requirements, we see how none of them have to do with the color of the man's hair or how tall he is. Notice that the first thirteen all have to do with things that are affected by his personal choices of obedience to the truths of God's Word. For example, a man makes a choice as to whether he will be self-controlled or gluttonous, greedy or generous, patient or angry. In the same way, this man of God who is qualified to lead the church has made decisions that have allowed him to rule his house well and raise obedient children. The fruit of that man's walk with Jesus Christ are children who are reverent and faithful. His home is to be a miniature representation of the church.

The focus of the elder's heart and his efforts are on fulfilling his God-directed, God-given, and God-taught responsibilities. He is proving himself to be a follower of God, by walking in love and obedience, and therefore he is qualified to lead the church.

Frequently, we see families who are on a collision course with disaster. At first they aren't aware of it, but in time, they realize all is not well as they sense they have lost their children's hearts. Our prayer is that they will realize it before it is too late. They need to hit the brakes and get off the road they are traveling down.

The problem is that, often, those needing to change direction are comfortable because they are with so many others. Someone once told me he was okay going to hell because all his friends were going to be there as well. Unfortunately, when the results of that decision are realized, it will be too late, and hell will not be the party that he was expecting. "And fear not them which kill the body, but are not able to kill the soul: but rather fear him which is able to destroy both soul and body in hell" (Matthew 10:28).

Whether you are following the crowd or on your own, I plead with you, don't propel yourself into a similar situation as that woman we saw. Praise God she finally made the right decision before it cost her, her children, and others a horrible consequence. "Who then is a faithful and wise servant, whom his lord hath made ruler over his household, to give them meat in due season?" (Matthew 24:45).

# When We Feel Pressure, What Is Our Example?

## *by Steve*

In the February Dad's Corner, I shared that we can welcome stressful times so we can learn how to rest and not be stressed. Last week I had the opportunity to embrace those words. By the end of one particular day, I was so exhausted from the stress, I couldn't wait to go to bed. It hadn't been the restful, growing experience that I desired.

The situation that day involved demanding work with significant confrontation. I am trying very hard to learn how to remain calm inside when in a difficult and tense environment. Unfortunately, I have a long way to go. Following the meeting, I was exhausted because of the inner pressure and anxiety I had experienced.

I know I'm not alone in having days with stress "opportunities." Most dads (and moms) will encounter situations where stress is likely every day in various degrees. In some cities, simply driving to work can be very stressful. Is that just the way it is, living in fast-paced America? But what about the dad who farms? Would he ever have a reason to be stressed in a peaceful, country setting? Might there be days when it seems like all his equipment is breaking down and times when the weather is ruining his crops? What about the dad whose child is deathly ill, or the dad who is out of a job while the bills are piling up?

Look at how even the world defines stress. One definition from *Merriam-Webster OnLine* calls stress "a physical, chemical, or emotional factor that causes bodily or mental tension and may be a factor in disease causation." That seems to depict clearly what I was experiencing. The definition described stress as a factor in causing disease.

The world knows what stress is, but it can't offer any solutions other than what comes in a needle, a bottle, or a prescription. The world cannot offer real peace. Jesus said, "Peace I leave with you, my peace I give unto you: not as the world giveth, give I unto you. Let not your heart be troubled, neither let it be afraid" (John 14:27).

The word peace means quietness and rest. If I had been experiencing the peace of Jesus, I wouldn't have been exhausted by the end of the day. Because I wasn't resting in the Lord and trusting Him to work out the difficulties, I had nothing left for my family that evening. I was spent as a result of my work. It wasn't a good kind of exhaustion like that which comes from hard physical work. Instead, my exhaustion was due to the negative emotional turmoil going on inside me. It was a needless waste of energy.

Stress is akin to worry, and worry is sin. When I was in that meeting, I was thinking about how what was being discussed impacted our company. I had to carefully weigh my words when responding to questions. I didn't like it at all. "Let not your heart be troubled" is in the imperative mood. It is a command of Jesus that we are not to be troubled. That means it is a choice, and if we choose to be troubled, then it is sin. I was thinking more about how I was going to deal with the circumstances at hand than I was about the resources of my Lord Jesus. As a result, I was extremely stressed, and I was sinning.

I was also demonstrating my lack of faith at that point. As I have shared previously, we have seen Jesus work mightily in our business projects, time and time again. Who was I trusting in to deal with the situation? Myself. When I trust in myself I have great reason to be worried and stressed. Through the years, I've learned that the closer I'm drawn to Jesus, the more it takes to stress me.

In 2 Corinthians 4:8-9 we read, *"We are* troubled on every side, yet not distressed; *we are* perplexed, but not in despair; Persecuted, but not forsaken; cast down, but not destroyed."* Before I was saved, I went to a rock concert while I was temporarily stationed in Germany. There was a throng of people waiting for the iron gates to be opened to the concert. People kept crowding in toward those gates in anticipation of being let in. The press became so heavy that my friend and I literally picked our feet up one time and were held in place. Word passed by us that the people next to the iron fence in front were being injured by being pushed so hard against the fence. The pressure exerted by the crowd is what the Greek word thlibo means and is translated as "troubled" in verse eight. The difficulties of life can exert such pressure that we feel as if we are being crushed when we reject the peace of Jesus.

In the midst of the concert crowd, I had a very helpless and trapped feeling, as it was virtually impossible to be able to free myself from the midst of the press. If someone had fallen down (which I doubt they could have), it would have been impossible to get back up. That feeling is pictured in the Greek word apereo, which is translated as "perplexed." No matter how good one's reason for wanting to get out of there, it didn't matter. There was absolutely nothing that we could have done.

I wonder if that isn't what many dads frequently feel. They see themselves trapped in a difficult situation without hope of escape. Is there a solution? "And he said unto me, My grace is sufficient for thee: for my strength is made perfect in weakness. Most gladly therefore will I rather glory in my infirmities, that the power of Christ may rest upon me. Therefore I take pleasure in infirmities, in reproaches, in necessities, in persecutions, in distresses for Christ's sake: for when I am weak, then am I strong" (2 Corinthians 12:9-10).

Do you have stress induced by problems of the flesh? "Infirmities" refers to difficulties such as disease, sickness, and human weakness. "Reproaches" refers to bad treatment by others. "Necessities" refers to being in need. "Persecutions" refers to what our enemies may do to us. Finally, if the other words missed something, "distresses" completes the package, referring to calamities and anguish. Paul didn't say he simply endured these things. He said he would gladly glory in them.

I doubt any of us will ever "arrive" when it comes to eliminating all stress from our lives, but may we be committed to treating it as sin and not accepting it in our lives. May we treat it as an enemy of our peace and something that robs us of our ability to bless and enjoy our families. Any time we allow something into our lives that Jesus speaks against, there will be consequences. When stress is a part of our lives, we can expect anxiety and physical difficulties. We demonstrate to those around us that our Lord Jesus is unable to deal with the problems of our life. We shout that our faith is insufficient to trust in our sovereign Lord being able to manage our life.

Failing to rest in my Savior last week was a good reminder of my need for greater trust and rest. Therefore, I was determined to cast all my cares on Him this week when I had a similar opportunity. May my family have a daddy who is trusting in his Lord in a very real way and being at peace and at rest even after a difficult day. Galatians 5:22-23: "But the fruit of the Spirit is love, joy, peace, longsuffering, gentleness, goodness, faith, Meekness, temperance: against such there is no law."

# Are You a Yes Man?
## by Steve

What does it take to be a leader? How would we score if we were rated in our leading abilities? More importantly, what will the results of our leadership be in five, ten, or twenty years?

Mary, our seven-year-old daughter, wanted to know if she and Jesse could go with the other three children to their appointment this afternoon. Unfortunately, the car we were taking would not have had enough seatbelts for all five of the children. I had planned on taking the smaller vehicle and was hesitant to change plans.

It is so easy for me to lock in on my own agenda and preferences. I would like to automatically choose to put others first. It amazes me that I can struggle with that, but it is true. I have to make it a conscious decision. *"Let* nothing *be done* through strife or vainglory; but in lowliness of mind let each esteem other better than themselves"* (Philippians 2:3). Vainglory means self-conceit. We are not to do anything based on the (false) assumption of our importance. In other words, we are not to put our interests first.

That can be a difficult thing when Dad is the one who is able to make the final decision. It is easy to think that means we can make the decision that is best for us. However, the best decision is the Lord's decision.

I find I need to run each situation past the Lord and ask Him to tell me what I should do. As I took this decision to the Lord, He quickly impressed on me that my choosing the vehicle that would exclude my little ones was ridiculous. I love my time with them, and here I was willing to pass it up because I wanted to take the smaller car. It was hard to believe I was about to make such a silly decision.

We love our home, but one thing it lacks is storage for items like bicycles. With seven bicycles, that poses a real problem! Part of the solution is that I have three bicycles hanging upside down in the garage. That works out okay most of the time, but when the children want to ride those bikes, I have to pull the car out of the garage so we can get the bikes down. That probably doesn't sound like a huge problem, but selfishly, there are times when it is very inconvenient; I may be working, in the middle of a project, or on the telephone. It is pretty easy to justify not taking the time to pull out the car to get down the bicycles when I'm in the middle of something "important."

The other morning I was doing my beginning-workday routine of clearing out e-mail and doing other desk-related chores when one of the children asked me to go through his birthday list with him. I wasn't officially on the "clock" yet, but I had to deal with those other things so I could begin "work." To make matters worse, the previous evening I had told this child that I was available to go through his list with him, but he had something else going then that he wanted to complete. So now it was convenient for him but not for me. I was beginning to feel irritated about it because I was forced to make a decision: was he more important than what I was doing? I'm not saying we drop everything every time, just because our children want something, but are we willing to if the Lord directs?

This verse should ring loud and clear in our minds: "And, ye fathers, provoke not your children to wrath: but bring them up in the nurture and admonition of the Lord" (Ephesians 6:4). As we evaluate the decisions that are brought to us each day, are we thinking of our children's best interests? Are we zealous not to provoke them to wrath or cause them to be discouraged (Colossians 3:21)?

I expect we may have forgotten what it is like to have to go to someone else for a decision when we want to do something. I know it has been a few years for me. If every time I wanted to do something all I heard was "no," I would get pretty frustrated. That is the difficulty of being a real leader: knowing when to say "yes" and when to say "no."

On the other side of this discussion can be a tendency to say "yes" just because it is what the child wants. However, it might be against the direction the Lord is leading the family. Dads will justify the "yes" as only a small compromise or not a battle worth fighting. Don't fall for that trap. If the Lord has directed in an area, it is a battle that must be fought and won! There can be no compromise.

How sad when we hear dads justify wrong decisions that they knew they shouldn't have made, but the child "really wanted to." The truth is, Dad said "yes" when he should have said "no." But so often the dads are afraid of losing their children's hearts if they say "no."

We don't lose our children's hearts when we do the right thing. We lose their hearts when we do the wrong things for many years. Keeping our children's hearts means purposing to say "yes" every time I can, even if it costs me something. It may be an inconvenience or an outright difficulty for me. If it is an opportunity to show them I love them, I value them, and want their best, then I am committed to saying "YES!"

As I shared, this does not come naturally for me because I'm selfish. However, the Lord Jesus has been working on me in this area, and I'm so grateful He has. "And he said to *them* all, If any *man* will come after me, let him deny himself, and take up his cross daily, and follow me" (Luke 9:23). It is hard to even use that verse here. I know nothing of taking up my cross daily. The minor inconveniences I face cannot even be compared to taking up my cross. Yet, if that is the case, why do I struggle?

May we be committed to being "yes" men. May we purpose that we will do everything we can to say "yes" to our children, because we know that there are many "no's" that must be served if we are to be faithful and trusted fathers. There will be numerous things that our children want to do that will not be good for them. If we have proven our love through the years, they will continue to trust us with their hearts.

# Aiiiiiiiiiiiiiiiiiiiiiiiiiiiiiiiiiiiiiiiiiiiiiiiiiiiiii

## by Steve

The two men looked quite sleepy and were chatting as they waited for the train. One of them was probably six foot, four inches and had a hardened look. I struck up a conversation with them, asking where they were going. They were headed a very short distance on the train and would be hiking to the top of the cliffs that were near us. Then they would run, jump off the cliff, and free-fall. The maximum time they would wait to open their parachutes was nine seconds. They said it was the greatest thrill on earth. The tall guy had traveled a long distance to go there and plummet off the cliff. It would take them close to an hour to make the full circuit and arrive back on top for the next fall.

Another group of guys I met also were cliff-jumping and said they would jump four or five times before heading for the bars. Then they would have a few beers and brag to the girls about how brave they were. They were living out their dreams. When I told a friend with military jump experience about this, he asked how high the cliff was and, after a quick mental calculation, said those guys were crazy. They were not allowing enough time to adequately slow down before they hit the ground.

Reflecting back on my discussion with those guys, I remember how they reacted to my incredulity. It gave them great satisfaction that I thought it was a bit dangerous and not the best idea. I'm still amazed that they would spend a great deal of money and risk their lives, all for the pleasure of a nine-second thrill.

In June I spoke to a good-looking man in his mid-thirties at the homeless mission. He spoke well and had a bright smile. I could not figure out why this Christian man was living at the homeless shelter. I sat down to talk with him and soon knew why. He had a professional practice that had been doing well until he ran into a personal crisis in his life. To help him through his sadness, a "friend" encouraged him to try some crack. He was instantly hooked. He said crack was the most pleasurable experience imaginable. For the sake of pleasure, he traded problems of one sort for tribulations far worse.

The Bible talks about men like this in 2 Timothy 3:1-5. "This know also, that in the last days perilous times shall come. For men shall be lovers of their own selves, covetous, boasters, proud, blasphemers, disobedient to parents, unthankful, unholy, Without natural affection, trucebreakers, false accusers, incontinent, fierce, despisers of those that are good, Traitors, heady, highminded, lovers of pleasures more than lovers of God; Having a form of godliness, but denying the power thereof: from such turn away."

The men described in that passage won't have all of those characteristics, but we will see these in general in the society. It is not a flattering list, and clearly we see these traits now. Most Christians are wary of evil things because even a shallow understanding of life in Christ warns that we stay away from bad things. I wonder how many of us would see pleasure as something to treat with great caution?

Now, not all men at the shelter are there because of addictions or substance abuse; however, it does seem to be a common thread in most with whom we speak. Think about this. They are in bondage to something that gives them pleasure. Legal or illegal, whether they have the money for it or not, they are bound by their pleasure. Those I've spoken with about it say they want to be free, yet they are bound—pleasure can be addicting and shipwreck a man's life.

We don't have statistics, but we do have the general impression that a majority of the men we talk to at the homeless shelter come from Christian homes. It never ceases to amaze us as we hear a tragic tale of a man's life and how it began in a Christian home. Frequently, it will come up that their parents would like them to come to their church and are praying for them. We would be wise to consider how easy it is to lose our children.

Our country and, yes, maybe even so many as call themselves Christians, are in hot pursuit of pleasure. If it is fun, thrilling entertainment, we want it, but where are we told in the Bible to seek it? Scripture says, "If ye then be risen with Christ, seek those things which are above, where Christ sitteth on the right hand of God. Set your affection on things above, not on things on the earth" (Colossians 3:1-2).

Our time is the most valuable thing we have. It would be a good exercise to write down how we have spent the last two weeks. How many hours did we sleep, work, read the Bible, pray, lead our family in devotions, spend time with our children, with our wives, on hobbies, on sports, on recreation, in front of the TV, etc.? How does the time spent on pleasure compare to the time we spent with the Lord? Might we be described as being lovers of pleasure more than lovers of God? If so, may we repent before God and make different choices, as we can be sure we are heavily influencing our children.

It would be risky to believe that we can live a life seeking pleasure, and it won't affect our children. In John 8:38 Jesus said, "I speak that which I have seen with my Father: and ye do that which ye have seen with your father." He was speaking to Jews that had "believed" on Him (verse 31). Jesus is saying that our children will do what they see us doing. They are going to follow after what we pursue.

I'm grieved as I have observed many Christians pursuing pleasure with the same gusto that the world does. Christians may seek somewhat different things, but it is all for the sake of pleasure. May we not deceive ourselves and think that just because we go to church, our children will live for the Lord. May we evaluate the message we are sending our children. May we live for the Lord Jesus with all of our hearts.

"And every man that striveth for the mastery is temperate in all things. Now they *do it* to obtain a corruptible crown; but we an incorruptible" (1 Corinthians 9:25).

# I Just Don't Understand It
## *by Steve*

We were on a trip one time when Teri noticed this big mustard-colored stain on my shirt. I had been out of the van getting gas, and the stain would have been very obvious to everyone I encountered. However, I was totally unaware of it. When Teri later saw the stain, we were quite perplexed as to how I might have acquired it because I had eaten nothing that resembled mustard. Upon closer examination, we found that it was actually a bug. We remembered there had been something that had deflected off of my side mirror through the open window, but we hadn't known where it went. Now we knew that my shirt was the final resting place for a yellow-filled bug. Are there aspects of our lives that might resemble that—something of which we aren't aware but others can easily see?

Recently a dad told me that for over five years he has been having his own personal time every morning reading the Bible and praying. He said that during that time Jesus has changed him into a new man. Additionally, the Lord has used his devotional time to springboard changes in the entire family. He said the transformation has been wonderful. "For the word of God *is* quick, and powerful, and sharper than any twoedged sword, piercing even to the dividing asunder of soul and spirit, and of the joints and marrow, and *is* a discerner of the thoughts and intents of the heart" (Hebrews 4:12).

Teri tells people that she saw the most incredible difference in my life when I began reading the Bible and praying every morning. There is real, life-changing power as the Holy Spirit strengthens and convicts a man when he reads the Word and prays. I wonder if that isn't the single most significant factor that makes the difference between a man who grows in his faith and a lukewarm Christian. That is the main reason why, when someone writes us with a question, I generally respond by asking whether they are reading their Bible and praying daily.

I expect pastors are keenly aware of, by outward evidence, those dads who are daily in the Word and those who aren't. Maybe they can see the mustard-colored stain in lives void of the Word. Could it be that pastors would have far fewer problems to deal with if men were in the Word? Could it be Christian marriages would have fewer difficulties if Dad (and Mom) were feeding daily on the sweet and precious Word of God? I believe the answer is a resounding "YES"! If this is true, then why is it that fewer than one out of ten dads (based on unofficial polling) will get up at least half an hour earlier in the morning to fellowship with Jesus? I can't really answer that for other dads, but I know what hindered me in earlier years.

In truth, personal Bible reading and prayer just wasn't important enough, and I didn't see it as the lifeline that it is. That is another way of saying it was my pride. It was as if I was saying, "Jesus, I really don't love You and Your Word enough to spend time with You. I have more important things to do, one of which is sleep. If I need You, I will definitely cry out to You."

I'm convinced that if every man in a church would begin his day with Bible reading and prayer, pastors would be delighted. Their counseling times would be almost nonexistent. We would see churches on fire for Jesus Christ because Jesus would be daily fanning the flames of purifying and strengthening hearts. I believe we would also see marriages transformed and being true examples of Christ and His bride. Husbands would have hearts turned toward their wives and children. The lost would be saved in record numbers because they would finally be seeing Jesus Christ at work in lives.

Some might say, "Wait a minute, just because a man reads the Bible every day doesn't mean he will live it out." That may be true of any old book, and this Book is an old one, but it isn't true of the Bible. Just this week a brother shared how he was drawn out of a false church into fellowship with Jesus. It all began when he started reading the Word every day. It changes the soul of a person.

I have struggled to keep my weight where it should be for a long time. There is one thing that makes a difference as to how successful I am in controlling my eating. That is whether I weigh myself consistently. If I have been eating too much and gaining weight, I don't want to weigh myself. I don't want to see the reality of my decisions reflected in the scale.

That is the way it is with the Bible and the Holy Spirit. As we read God's Word every day, it speaks to our hearts. It builds us up and also convicts us of areas that don't line up with Scripture. It gives us direction. It provides an "Amen" to what the Holy Spirit is telling our hearts. Then the Holy Spirit works in us to bring about the changes He desires.

When Paul, by the Holy Spirit, commands us to ". . . put off all these; anger, wrath, malice, blasphemy, filthy communication out of your mouth" (Colossians 3:8), I don't want to be angry ever again. Then when I am, I confess, repent, and cry out to Jesus to work in my heart.

When I read, "If ye love me, keep my commandments" (John 14:15), I am struck in my heart that as a Christian, I am called to obey—period. Then I am encouraged to read, "He that hath my commandments, and keepeth them, he it is that loveth me: and he that loveth me shall be loved of my Father, and I will love him, and will manifest myself to him" (John 14:21). I see that obedience isn't simply to avoid God disciplining me, but that in obedience Jesus manifests more of Himself to me. That means that somehow He reveals more of Himself to me as my walk deepens and gets sweeter. I can testify that has been my experience and the experience of others with whom I have discussed this.

Then why is it that as brothers in Christ, we don't hold each other accountable? Here is something very simple to do, and it could dramatically change a man's life, his marriage, his family, and ultimately the church. If we love our brothers, why don't we take those with whom we have a relationship aside and discuss this issue with them? Why is it that we don't then ask them, or plead with them, that they let us hold them accountable for having a time with Jesus every morning?

I know one reason is that if a dad isn't in the Word and praying himself, it will prevent him from discussing this with someone else. It may be like the mustard-colored stain on my shirt—something of which the person wearing the shirt isn't even aware but others can observe. We may think no one would know whether we spend time with Jesus each day or not, but perhaps it really is evident. If dads would realize how critical personal time reading the Bible and praying is, they would do it. If we love Jesus, we must do it. If our love for Jesus isn't enough to motivate us to spend time with Him, may we do it because we love our families and how it will affect our ability to love and lead them. If we don't love them enough, could we do it because we love ourselves and want the best for ourselves? Whatever it takes, may we spend time with Jesus and encourage everyone we know to do the same out of our love for Jesus and our love and concern for our families.

# Who Has Time?
## *by Steve*

He lay in bed with his broken right arm strapped to his waist. It must have been broken in such a way that they couldn't cast it but had to immobilize it in this fashion. He wanted to call his brother, and with great difficulty, he reached with his left arm to grab the phone from the hospital bed holder. He had hiked up his nightshirt to dial with a finger from the restrained arm. I asked if I could help him, and with a twinkle in his eighty-year-old eye he said, "I learned a long time ago, you can do anything you really want to!"

Another dear brother in Christ has paralyzed legs. Helpers have to use a hoist to get him from his bed to his wheelchair. Not only do his legs not work, but they are quite painful. That is his life, patient suffering. He is always waiting on someone to help him with his every need. Yet, I can't ever remember him complaining. He shares Jesus first by the peace and joy everyone witnesses and then by the confession of his lips. He speaks of how Jesus saved him and that He will save you as well. Finally, he shares about how good God is.

Most families are getting close to a new homeschool year beginning again. The books have been ordered and received by now. Mom has looked over her curriculum and is doing some planning and mapping out of the year. Yet, homeschooling often provides some real challenges.

In our home there is usually a spirit of anticipation mixed with a bit of apprehension. The new year always brings about some character-training challenges. For example, a while ago, during the confession time of our evening family worship, there were no confessions at all. We try to ask forgiveness when offenses occur during the day. However, if anyone didn't ask forgiveness earlier, then the evening time is when we clear our consciences before bed. After a long, quiet pause, I asked, "Hasn't someone offended someone else in the day and not made it right?"

One of the younger ones stated innocently, "Daddy, we didn't have school today."

We can let the difficult situations of homeschooling that arise be discouraging or embrace them as occasions to prove and hone our children's (and all too frequently our own) character. This is the area where Teri seems to need my help with homeschooling the most. I am asked to help differentiate between such things as sin and youthful carelessness in the children, slothfulness and inability, and then provide direction and motivation for improvement.

I have found there is never a good time in my schedule for the difficulties that arise. However, these situations tend to expose my real priorities. If raising men and women of God is one of my highest priorities, then how can I not have time to intervene, think, pray, and restore as needed when one of these growth opportunities comes along for the children?

When I find myself thinking I am too busy and resent the need for my attention when a situation arises, I'm showing that I am not committed to Teri's success in teaching the children. It is a real wake-up call for me when I sense I'm feeling like that. I then repent of my selfish and sinful attitude and ask Jesus for wisdom in both the situation and managing my time. "Husbands, love your wives, even as Christ also loved the church, and gave himself for it" (Ephesians 5:25). When I think of the investment Teri is making in our children's lives as she teaches them, I am ashamed if I find myself resentful when she needs my time.

Those two men whom I shared about in the beginning of this Dad's Corner are powerful reminders as to how I am called to love and lead this family. My time is not my own. "For ye are bought with a price: therefore glorify God in your body, and in your spirit, which are God's" (1 Corinthians 6:20).

When situations requiring my attention cause resentment in my heart, I am showing I'm no more mature than one of the children who is struggling in doing what they must do. I am humbled as I look to those two men I wrote about in the beginning. We can do anything that Christ is leading us to do, if we put our mind to it. If we are hopelessly buried in our work, then we must depend all the more on Jesus. "And he said unto me, My grace is sufficient for thee: for my strength is made perfect in weakness. Most gladly therefore will I rather glory in my infirmities, that the power of Christ may rest upon me" (2 Corinthians 12:9).

We don't give of our time grudgingly but cheerfully. We demonstrate the fruit of the Spirit in these times. "But the fruit of the Spirit is love, joy, peace, longsuffering, gentleness, goodness, faith, Meekness, temperance: against such there is no law. And they that are Christ's have crucified the flesh with the affections and lusts. If we live in the Spirit, let us also walk in the Spirit" (Galatians 5:22-25). We live out the reality of our walk with Jesus each day with our family. May we be leaders putting our families' needs first and helping our wives to be successful no matter what it costs us. "And whatsoever ye do in word or deed, *do* all in the name of the Lord Jesus, giving thanks to God and the Father by him" (Colossians 3:17).

# Would You Go?
## *by Steve*

It was 1971, and the man was quickly convicted of murdering a U.S. military officer. He was sentenced to public execution. The town buzzed. It seemed like everyone had come to the gravel pit near the city to see the man put to death. The police set up a barricade to keep the crowd back. Soon there were refreshments and souvenirs being sold, making the execution resemble more a carnival than a solemn occasion meting out due justice. A post was driven into the ground before a wall of dirt, and then a cloth screen was placed in front of it. A target was strategically fastened to the screen in line with the post behind it.

The condemned man was led in, blindfolded, and tied to the post behind the screen. The foreign military's firing squad lined up facing the target. On command, the five men fired. It took only a second for the death sentence to be carried out. What happened next surprised those overseeing the event. The crowd surged forward past the barricades and tore down the screen to get a closer look at the result of the five bullets.

At first I believe most Christians would be amazed at how people might actually want to see such a sight. However, we must remember the lost will act like the lost, and therefore, we should not be surprised by such behavior. Jesus said about the lost in John 8:44, "Ye are of *your* father the devil, and the lusts of your father ye will do. He was a murderer from the beginning, and abode not in the truth, because there is no truth in him. When he speaketh a lie, he speaketh of his own: for he is a liar, and the father of it." Jesus said that the unsaved will imitate their father.

Many years ago, Christians were victims of activities that were beyond what I will describe here. Men, women, and children were condemned and brought into an arena for the entertainment of others. Wild beasts were also released, and in time only the wild beasts remained alive. Unwillingly, Christians were brutally killed for the pleasure of others. How could humanity ever stoop so low as to take enjoyment watching others suffer? The answer to this is that Satan is a murderer and takes joy in it. Satan takes delight in the evil and violence that is perpetuated against human beings in our world. Therefore, we can expect the lost to take enjoyment in it as well. This isn't being said in a harsh, judgmental way. It is simply the way it is for a man without Jesus Christ.

The Bible is very clear regarding the depravity of the lost soul. "And GOD saw that the wickedness of man *was* great in the earth, and *that* every imagination of the thoughts of his heart *was* only evil continually" (Genesis 6:5). "The earth also was corrupt before God, and the earth was filled with violence" (Genesis 6:11). "How much more abominable and filthy *is* man, which drinketh iniquity like water?" (Job 15:16). "The fool hath said in his heart, *There* is no God. They are corrupt, they have done abominable works, *there is* none that doeth good" (Psalms 14:1). "The heart *is* deceitful above all *things*, and desperately wicked: who can know it?" (Jeremiah 17:9). "For out of the heart proceed evil thoughts, murders, adulteries, fornications, thefts, false witness, blasphemies" (Matthew 15:19). Whew! Would you believe there is more about this in Scripture that we don't have room for here?

As we read what the Bible says about the depravity of the soul, it is easy to see how a lost person could take enjoyment and be entertained watching violence, including someone being brutalized or murdered. I must confess that I attended the execution with my military friends and the local townspeople. I was there participating in the festive spirit. I didn't rush forward afterwards, but I might as well have. I remember even in junior high school how I was part of the crowd hurrying outside to see a couple of boys fight it out.

But would I go now to that type of public execution for the sake of seeing the gore, or a legal event for entertainment where people could hurt, injure, maim, or even kill others? NO! At salvation, Jesus gave me a new heart and changed me. "A new heart also will I give you, and a new spirit will I put within you: and I will take away the stony heart out of your flesh, and I will give you an heart of flesh" (Ezekiel 36:26). My new heart no longer enjoys seeing fights, strife, brutality, and killing.

"Therefore if any man *be* in Christ, *he is* a new creature: old things are passed away; behold, all things are become new" (2 Corinthians 5:17). The key is "if any man *be* in Christ." I am a new creature in Christ: the old has passed away and all things are become new. My new heart is now indwelt by the Spirit of God. My Lord Jesus came to earth to die on a cross for mankind. He loves man so much He gave His life as a ransom so that man wouldn't suffer for all eternity in hell. "For God so loved the world, that he gave his only begotten Son, that whosoever believeth in him should not perish, but have everlasting life" (John 3:16). Think about that love. If I have even an ounce of the love of Jesus in me, just a portion of His Spirit, how then could I ever take pleasure in or be entertained watching someone being hurt? Is it possible for a believer to enjoy such a thing? How could I ever call human suffering entertainment?

Even though we should expect the unsaved to act like the unsaved and not judge them for it, Christians should not act like the lost. "For they that are after the flesh do mind the things of the flesh; but they that are after the Spirit the things of the Spirit. For to be carnally minded *is* death; but to be spiritually minded *is* life and peace. Because the carnal mind *is* enmity against God: for it is not subject to the law of God, neither indeed can be. So then they that are in the flesh cannot please God. But ye are not in the flesh, but in the Spirit, if so be that the Spirit of God dwell in you. Now if any man have not the Spirit of Christ, he is none of his" (Romans 8:5-9).

My question for each of us is: "Would we ever go to see some act of brutality if we had the chance?" If your answer is "yes," I would encourage you to evaluate your heart in light of Scripture. Maybe the "yes" came without really realizing that Jesus would not have one of His children observe such a thing. However, think about it, and ask God to try your heart, and seek to find out what is wrong.

Now for those who answered "No!" I have a few thoughts to share. Praise God that we realize that we could not be entertained in such a fashion. However, for the sake of our children, let's take this to a deeper level. Jesus said in John 8:38, "I speak that which I have seen with my Father: and ye do that which ye have seen with your father." What do our children see us doing?

If children see their fathers being entertained by violence, they will want that for themselves. Maybe a father enjoys watching TV shows or movies that are violent. Perhaps they are actually tame ones by today's standards, where people are neatly killed. Still, they involve violence against those Jesus died to save. Regardless of the fact that it is fake, it is being presented as real. If this is the example a father sets in how he spends his time, according to John 8:38, his children are likely going to find pleasure in the same.

If someone tells us about a "great" movie or TV show where this type of stuff is going on, do we want to hear all about it, or do we challenge them as to how they could consider watching such a thing? Are we salt and light not only to a lost and dying world but also to "brothers" who are being shameful in their conduct and being a stumbling block for their children? It only takes one generation to lose one's children.

Men, if you find yourselves drawn to ungodly viewing, I implore you to reconsider. May we identify with our Father in heaven and not with the father of lies. May we be good role models for our children and not be stumbling blocks. May we love the light and flee the darkness. May our children observe in us the fruit of the Spirit and not the fruit of Satan.

"And this is the condemnation, that light is come into the world, and men loved darkness rather than light, because their deeds were evil. For every one that doeth evil hateth the light, neither cometh to the light, lest his deeds should be reproved. But he that doeth truth cometh to the light, that his deeds may be made manifest, that they are wrought in God" (John 3:19-21).

"But the fruit of the Spirit is love, joy, peace, longsuffering, gentleness, goodness, faith, Meekness, temperance: against such there is no law. And they that are Christ's have crucified the flesh with the affections and lusts. If we live in the Spirit, let us also walk in the Spirit" (Galatians 5:22-25).

# Candy Bars, Checkers, and Pepper
## by Steve

"What is your favorite candy bar?" I asked the very tired-looking, aging checker at the grocery store where we shop weekly. She paused from passing the food in front of the scanner for several seconds, looked at me with a little suspicion, and replied, "Three Musketeers." I gave the nod to one of the children and off he went on his mission. Momentarily he returned and slid the named candy bar onto the conveyor belt. After it had been scanned, another child grabbed it before being bagged and looked at me. I smiled and nodded. Mary, holding the candy bar out in her hand, said to the checker, "Here, we would like you to have this."

For a second, the tired face had a puzzled look, but in a flash it was exchanged for a bright smile as she exclaimed, "That is so kind. Thank you! You just made my day."

We had driven down to load the moving truck my dad had rented. We stopped to eat before heading to a motel and bed. When the waiter came to take our order, Nathan (our oldest son) spoke to him. Nathan said that we would be asking the Lord to bless the food in a few minutes and was there anything we might pray for him concerning. The waiter was a bit taken aback, recovered, and then said that his girlfriend's father was in the hospital with serious heart difficulties, and they would appreciate prayer for him. The waiter was clearly moved and grateful that we had asked. I told Nathan how thankful I was for this idea and example because I was looking forward to asking others this same question in the future. Nathan explained that he had been with someone who had done this, and he had purposed to do it when he remembered.

When Jesus was asked about whether it was right to pay taxes, He responded with, ". . . Render therefore unto Caesar the things which are Caesar's; and unto God the things that are God's" (Matthew 22:21). What a startling thing for Jesus to say. The Romans were harsh and cruel to the Jews. It would have been reasonable for Jesus to have said, "This government is as corrupt as the Pharisees. Don't give them even a penny." But He didn't. He said give Caesar what you owe him. Israel was under the control of a wicked and ruthless government. Jesus was telling them to pay the taxes that were required. It would be certain that some of the money would be used to pay troops who would commit horrible crimes against Jews. Yet Jesus said to pay the taxes. The money Jesus was instructing them to render to Caesar ultimately would pay the soldiers who would crucify the Lord of Glory.

The Jews were seeking a political and national savior who would free them from Rome. We can understand that all too well. It was easy to be caught up in the emotion surrounding the 2004 Presidential elections. However, have you noticed, when listening to Christians discussing politics, that it sounds like they too could be looking for a political savior? It is as if a righteous leader can change the country. Now, don't get me wrong, I want a righteous leader; however, a righteous leader will not make righteous citizens. As the morals of the general population slide, we can expect it to become impossible to elect godly men.

What, then, can be done? "Be not overcome of evil, but overcome evil with good" (Romans 12:21). ". . . Come ye after me, and I will make you to become fishers of men" (Mark 1:17). "And that repentance and remission of sins should be preached in his name among all nations, beginning at Jerusalem" (Luke 24:47). "Go ye therefore, and teach all nations, baptizing them in the name of the Father, and of the Son, and of the Holy Ghost" (Matthew 28:19). The only reason believers make right choices, when they do, is because they are obeying the Lord Jesus. Then why should we be surprised when lost people make the choices that they do?

The long-term answer to the real need of our country is Jesus Christ. How will they know unless they are told? "Now then we are ambassadors for Christ . . ." (2 Corinthians 5:20) bringing the Good News of eternal life. We are to be salt to a decaying society. "Ye are the salt of the earth . . ." (Matthew 5:13). We are to be light exposing sin and leading others to the Savior. "Ye are the light of the world . . ." (Matthew 5:14).

Jesus' time on earth was spent waging war for the hearts of men, and that is what He has called us to also. "A new heart also will I give you, and a new spirit will I put within you: and I will take away the stony heart out of your flesh, and I will give you an heart of flesh" (Ezekiel 36:26). Are we any different from our fathers before us who had little impact in their society for Christ? Even worse, by our example we are infecting our children with the same lifestyle—a cozy, comfortable, complacent walk with the Lord. If that doesn't sound lukewarm, I don't know what does.

Brothers, are we willing to own our failure to reach the lost? Will we repent? I say that in general as I'm confident some of you are faithful in sharing Jesus every chance you get. From my experience, though, it may be one in a thousand or even fewer who have a passion for telling others about Jesus. Are we embarrassed to hand someone a tract or to ask them where they will spend eternity? "Whosoever therefore shall be ashamed of me and of my words in this adulterous and sinful generation; of him also shall the Son of man be ashamed, when he cometh in the glory of his Father with the holy angels" (Mark 8:38).

I read a pastor's comments after he had visited Christians in Africa. He said he was amazed at how much the African Christians had done with so little materially. He was also amazed at how little the United States Christians have done with so much materially.

Our decisions for how we use our time and money document our priorities and theology. We will spend our time and money on what is most important to us. We can tell ourselves witnessing is important, but if we aren't actively doing it, frankly, it really isn't important to us.

Sarah shared with the family something she had just read about D. L. Moody. Now there is someone who had significant impact on those around him. Mr. Moody had made a commitment to the Lord to share Christ with someone every day. One night he was lying in bed about to go to sleep when he realized that he had not shared Jesus with anyone that day. So he got up, dressed, and went out to tell another about Jesus Christ. Heavenly Father, may I be that serious about other men's souls.

For years I have sought to share my faith frequently; however, the Lord has shown us that we really haven't been passionate for the souls of men. I am ashamed to say that I don't remember the last time I wept over someone's lost condition. Our family desires revival in our hearts so we will be ". . . instruments of righteousness unto God" (Romans 6:13). Would you even now pause for a moment to pray for my heart and those in my family? Pray that our hearts would be broken for the lost. As Jesus was approaching Jerusalem during His triumphal entry, He broke down and wept over the city. "And when he was come near, he beheld the city, and wept over it" (Luke 19:41). Jesus was looking at a people who would reject their Savior and choose a convicted criminal instead of the Righteous One. May my heart be broken as well.

Our next-door neighbors have a small mixed-breed dog that is a "people magnet." Everyone in the neighborhood loves Pepper. Since Pepper's backyard runs next to the street, anyone walking by can see the dog. On spotting someone, Pepper repeatedly leaps vertically in the air almost to the top of the fence, with her tail furiously wagging. It looks as if Pepper has springs on her feet as she boings up and down showing her intense love for any morsel of time you might "cast" her way. Once she has won your heart and you reach over the fence to pet her, she presses her head against your hand, whines, and tries to lick you. It makes you feel like you are the most important thing in her life. People can't resist her because of the love that just flows from her.

It is our desire to be like that little dog. I would like others to feel our deep love for them and be drawn to us on every encounter we have with them. When I speak to them about their souls, I hope they would sense a sincere love, a love that only Jesus Christ can give. I don't believe I have ever pleaded for those receiving the Corners to pray for us like this before, but from the depth of my soul I'm asking now.

There are limitless ways to be salt and light, to show the love of Jesus and proclaim His name throughout each day. Just this morning someone had dialed a wrong number and left a message on our phone. Instead of hanging up, they left a most beautiful message proclaiming the goodness of God and inviting us to know Him if we didn't already. We have found that buying candy bars for checkers, to show them we appreciate what they do for us, and by asking people how we can pray for them, we have purpose in every outing and trip. We have found a source for tracts that are very captivating, and we are learning how to share them effectively. (If you'd like to find about more information about these tracts, please visit: www.FamiliesforJesus.com)

We have heard some former waiters say that they dreaded the Sunday lunch after-church crowd. They felt that Christians were the most ungrateful, cheap people they had to serve. How can this be? We should be the most generous, grateful people on the face of the earth. Instead of a good testimony and chance to share Christ, a bad taste for the name of Jesus is left in the waiters' mouths.

It all starts in the heart, which is why I ask you to pray for us, and we will pray for you on the Corners list. There is no other reason that I don't weep for the lost than having a cold, hard heart. Please pray that the Father would pour out His Spirit into our family and give us abundantly of Himself. I know I'm being very vulnerable in asking this, but that is okay because it is the deepest desire of my heart. That is why I feel led to ask for your help. Together may we be used of the Father to share Christ with our nation and the world.

"How then shall they call on him in whom they have not believed? and how shall they believe in him of whom they have not heard? and how shall they hear without a preacher? And how shall they preach, except they be sent? as it is written, How beautiful are the feet of them that preach the gospel of peace, and bring glad tidings of good things" (Romans 10:14-15).

# He Loved Her
### *by Steve*

She was married at the age of sixteen with her mother's consent. Her father was a cruel and harsh man, and to protect the daughter, a marriage license was quickly obtained. Soon she was married to a young man seven years older, whom she had been seeing twice a week for the last year with her father's consent.

The situation had erupted when the daughter had asked the father if she might now see the young man three times a week. This had made the father very angry, and he had whipped her mercilessly. After the dad left the house, the girl went over to her boyfriend's. When the boy's mother saw the girl, she was broken-hearted and sought a solution. Together they went to the girl's mother, who soon consented to signing the marriage license for the daughter.

Through a dear older woman, she came to know Jesus as Lord and Savior at the age of nineteen, and she is a beautiful testimony of God's faithful work in the human heart. I detected no bitterness or anger as she spoke of her father, but a sweet and tender heart. Truly, it is amazing how the love of Christ Jesus can change a person.

One would think that to have been married fifty-three years it must have been a beautiful, storybook kind of marriage. Yes, one might think that, but instead it was a dramatic testimony of God's grace. The good man of twenty-three who rescued her from a terrible home situation brought her into a new set of undesirable circumstances. Her knight in shining armor was to become an alcoholic and a gambler. He then shared with her the multitude of difficulties that go with those addictions.

She gives credit to the Lord Jesus for sustaining her through those fifty-three years of marriage. Does she harbor bitterness toward her husband? No. She says, "He loved me." Many times she repeated, "He loved me." Even with such a hard life, by God's grace, she chose to look back on her husband's love instead of the injustice that she received through the years.

As a lost man, her husband could not love her as Christ has called husbands to love their wives. "Husbands, love your wives, even as Christ also loved the church, and gave himself for it" (Ephesians 5:25). Brothers, do we love our wives? Not "do we provide for them," but do we love them? When they think of us, do they think of our love for them? Do our wives find comfort in knowing we love them? Do we love them not just in word but in deed? To love our wives as Christ loved the church is not just a nice saying, it is a command of God through the Holy Spirit.

Here is a secondary thought for us to consider. What appetites are we creating in our children? This woman's husband of fifty-three years became an alcoholic and a gambler largely due to his well-meaning mother. She felt it was special for her family to have some home-brew always available. That she did, and her son developed a real taste for alcohol as he grew up. I said "largely due" because we are all individually accountable to God for the sin in our life. Others may place a stumbling block in our path, but we are still responsible and will be judged accordingly.

The well-meaning mom also wanted her family to spend time together in the evenings, so they began playing cards together. They never played for money, not even pennies, but they used matches and toothpicks. After years of playing cards in the home, he was hooked as a youth and became a serious gambler as an adult.

A brother in Christ once shared with me how his mother taught him to play penny-pat when he was young, and that gave him a hunger for gambling. Even though his mother was well-intentioned and wanted to spend some time with her son, in reality what she did was to give him the appetite for gambling. Therefore, he was addicted to it even at middle-school age.

Brothers, what sort of appetites are we creating in our children? Whether it is a part of our lives that they observe, something we allow in their lives, the gifts that we give, or something we encourage them to do, they will readily develop appetites. "I speak that which I have seen with my Father: and ye do that which ye have seen with your father" (John 8:38). "Then said he unto the disciples, It is impossible but that offences will come: but woe *unto him*, through whom they come! It were better for him that a millstone were hanged about his neck, and he cast into the sea, than that he should offend one of these little ones" (Luke 17:1-2).

May we evaluate our lives and what we encourage in the lives of our children for the fruit it will produce in them. I'm amazed how occasionally I will see a child doing something they shouldn't, and when I correct them, they will say, "But you saw me doing this before and didn't say anything." Since they weren't corrected previously, they took that as approval to do it again, when in fact we might not have really noticed what was going on.

Men, may our hearts be turned toward our family. May we love our wives sincerely with great honor and respect. May we guard the hearts of our children and be ever so careful of what appetites we introduce in their lives. As we love Jesus Christ and obey Him in all that He calls us to, our family will be drawn to Christ as well, and He will be glorified.

# Dad's and Mom's Corners Via E-mail

If you enjoy what you read in this book, you may want to sign up for the monthly Dad's and Mom's Corners e-mail.

To be on the Dad's and Mom's Corners list (which is never given away or sold—all addresses are kept strictly confidential), stop by our website, www.Titus2.com, or call us (913) 772-0392.

# Index

# D

decisions 17, 18, 119

bad 219, 235, 239-240, 278-279

husband's 32, 35-36, 167, 220-221, 231-234, 235-237, 239, 245, 254, 278-279, 349-350

mom's 108, 112, 169, 189, 197, 279

depression 58, 131, 133, 186

devotions

children's 125, 283

dad's 241, 250, 254, 283, 311-315, 318, 335, 355, 357-360

family 59, 91, 275, 283, 285, 307, 309, 318-320, 334, 344, 355

mom's 43, 53, 58, 80, 98, 130, 154, 183-184, 186, 283

difficulties 35-36, 54, 108, 125, 133, 150-151, 154-155, 183, 197, 209, 211, 213, 223, 226, 228-229, 234, 265, 338, 346-348, 358, 362, 369, 375

discipline 41, 97, 246, 329

self- 54, 69, 78, 103, 123, 171, 186, 189

discouragement 58, 131, 137, 151, 195

# E

Easter 201-202

entertainment 367

dad's 249, 265, 291, 355

family's 283

exercise 22, 44, 48, 130, 133, 183

# F

family planning 31-33, 296

fear 36, 84, 186, 193, 221, 226-229, 298, 335, 343

friends 219, 324, 354

children's 35, 89, 93, 96-97, 283, 305, 321, 323

mom's 133, 189

# G

goals

biblical 51, 123, 306

for children 47-48, 75, 105, 120, 172, 204-206

dad's 196, 275, 300, 306, 314

family's 99-100, 305

mom's 41, 128, 135, 156

gratefulness 15, 18, 41, 55, 65, 93-94, 103, 114, 133, 136, 172, 255, 351, 369, 373

# H

# I

# L

Lord's 23, 249

mom's 21, 37, 43, 63, 91, 117-118, 125-128, 129-132, 157, 159, 173-174, 184, 186, 191, 218

projects 15, 21-22, 43, 51, 126-127, 148, 207, 305, 346

protection

children 83, 93, 96, 98, 281

Christ's 186, 253, 315

emotional 257

father's 238, 249-250, 303-305

purity 94, 98, 249

**R**

rebellion 97, 295, 301

relationships

mother-daughter 13

with children 135, 154, 174, 257, 294-296, 297

with husband 63, 166, 304

with Jesus Christ 58, 91, 104, 106, 107, 109, 130, 294, 296, 300, 338

with wife 211, 256, 304

respect 123, 196, 200

for adult children 96-97

for dad 245

for wife 377

wife's 167

responsibility

child's 93, 173, 181

dad's 197, 211, 273, 298, 303-304, 306, 318

mom's 28, 114, 141, 157-158, 162, 167

**S**

salvation 55, 70, 235, 245, 296, 331-332, 366

schedule 19, 21, 45, 46, 48, 92, 120, 139, 161-163, 181, 183, 243, 362

benefits of 43, 116, 128, 163

chore 23

summer 21-23, 125-128

shelter 51, 83-84, 93, 98, 287, 293, 297, 301

sleep 39, 41, 44-46, 115-118, 177, 183-184, 186, 222, 225, 267, 302, 312-313, 328, 335, 355, 358, 372

spirit

angry 283

critical 36-37, 259-261, 293

meek and quiet 41, 62-63, 153-156, 161-162, 167, 173, 186

sports 123, 131, 300, 305, 322, 355

stress 102, 131, 335-336, 339, 345-348

# Additional Resources
## Books (pages 386-394)
## Audios (pages 395-400)
## Websites (see below)

**www.Titus2.com**—Titus2.com provides information and resources to encourage, exhort, and equip homeschooling parents. On the site you will find articles, information about the Maxwells' books, audios, and other resources. Steve and Teri Maxwell write free monthly e-mail articles for Christian parents. The Dad's and Mom's Corners address issues that are at the heart of Christian families. You may sign up on the website.

**www.ChorePacks.com**—Ancillary to *Managers of Their Chores.* Book owners can download chore forms and make pre-reader chore cards. Also, check out ChoreWare, which greatly facilitates ChorePack development, on www.ChorePacks.com. ChoreWare is available for a small yearly subscription fee to owners of *Managers of Their Chores.*

**www.FamiliesforJesus.com**—A website dedicated to building up and challenging Christian families as they share Jesus with a lost and dying world.

**www.HomeschooleCards.com**—eCards designed to encourage homeschoolers and Christians in the Lord Jesus Christ!

**www.PreparingSons.com**—Work project center, messageboard, and more!

**www.PreparingDaughters.com**—A website especially for daughters who are striving to be women of God.

## Managers of Their Homes
## A Practical Guide to Daily Scheduling
## for Christian Homeschool Families

### by Steven and Teri Maxwell

A homeschool mother's greatest challenge may be "getting it all done." *Managers of Their Homes* offers solutions! Responses by families who have read *Managers of Their Homes* and utilized the Scheduling Kit indicate the almost unbelievable improvements they have realized.

Step-by-step instructions and a unique Scheduling Kit make the setting up of a daily schedule easily achievable for any homeschooling family. *"People have told me for years that I need a schedule, but every time I tried I couldn't get one to work. I always had problems fitting everything that needed to be done into one day. With your system, I am actually accomplishing more, and I have more time left over! The key to it is the great worksheets. They are invaluable."* Who wouldn't like to accomplish more and have time left over?

How does one schedule school time? Are you struggling with keeping up in areas such as laundry, dishes, or housekeeping? Does it seem like there is no time for you in the day? Do you feel stressed over the busyness of your days or not accomplishing all you want? It doesn't matter whether you have one child or twelve, this book will help you to plan your daily schedule.

*Managers of Their Homes: A Practical Guide to Daily Scheduling for Christian Homeschool Families* sets a firm biblical foundation for scheduling, in addition to discussing scheduling's numerous benefits. Chapter after chapter is filled with practical suggestions for efficient, workable ways to schedule a homeschooling family's days. Thirty real-life schedules in the Appendix give valuable insight into creating a personalized schedule. Also included is a special chapter by Steve for homeschool dads.

*"My schedule has given me back my sanity!! I can't believe the way my life has changed since implementing a schedule."* Tracy L.

*"I had read almost every organizational book there was, and I still couldn't get to where I wanted to be until I applied this method!"* Corrie

*"In retrospect, having used the book, I would have paid $100 for it, if I could have know beforehand the tremendous benefits I would gain: peace in my busy home, and the ability my schedule gives me to accomplish the things I feel God wants me to do in my family."* Tracy

*"Making and using a schedule has helped me, and there were people who thought I was hopeless!"* Sheri

*"Your book helped to make our second year of homeschooling much smoother than the first! My three boys (8, 6, 6) have learned to be very helpful around the house and much more independent with their assignments for school. God has used your book to help prepare us for His plans! I feel totally confident and able to handle mothering and homeschooling and the new baby that will be arriving in January."* Julie

*"The advice and easy-to-apply information in the book are a must for large and small families alike. It is flexible and anyone can do it; I love that. Even those who normally wouldn't be that structured are saying they love it, and it's so much fun. It's not just adding structure—it's advancing confidence!"* Tina

Moms who have applied these methods have gained new hope from MOTH *(Managers of Their Homes)*. They have moved from chaos, stress, and disorganization to peace, contentment, and productivity. You can as well!

For information visit: www.Titus2.com

Or call: (913) 772-0392

You may also e-mail: managers@Titus2.com

# Managers of Their Chores
## A Practical Guide to Children's Chores

### by Steven and Teri Maxwell

In the same way that *Managers of Their Homes* helped tens of thousands of moms "get it all done," *Managers of Their Chores* helps families conquer the chore battle. The book and included ChorePack system have the potential to revolutionize the way your family accomplishes chores. Whether you are chore challenged or a seasoned chore warrior, you will gain motivation and loads of practical advice on implementing a stress-free chore system.

Most would view the question of whether their children do chores or not as a simple parental-preference decision. We took a survey in the spring of 2005, and hundreds of families responded to our request for information on their experience with chores.

Response after response revealed the lifelong benefits of chores or the long-term consequences of not having chores. When we saw how the vast majority of those surveyed indicated that chores were crucial to their preparation for being a parent, a chore book took on a whole new urgency for us.

Many questions arise as families look at the issue of chores: Should children be expected to do chores? How many chores should they have? What age do we begin assigning chores? How do we encourage our children to accomplish their work? Is there a biblical basis for chores? Do chores bring benefits or burdens to our children? There are a multitude of questions that arise when we begin to discuss chores. *Managers of Their Chores* tackles these questions, giving answers and direction.

Written by parents of eight, *Managers of Their Chores* begins with the biblical foundation for chores and the many benefits chores will bring to a child—both now and in the future. It moves into key factors in parents' lives that will affect a chore system. The book gives pertinent information about what kinds of chores should reasonably be done in a home with children.

One chapter is devoted to helping moms work with their preschoolers on chores. For those moms who say they have no idea where to even begin, the book develops various pieces of a chore system and how it can be set up. Aspects of accountability, rewards, and consequences are addressed. Finally, *Managers of Their Chores* provides step-by-step directions for setting up a ChorePack chore system.

*Managers of Their Chores* comes with all the ChorePack materials typically needed for four children, including ChorePacks, chore card paper, and a ChorePack holder. In the appendix of the book, you will find a chore library with more than 180 chores listed, forms for use and future photocopying, and sample chore assignments from eight families. Help prepare your children—from preschoolers to teens—for life by teaching them to do chores.

*"I can't believe how much time we have gained in our days now that we have our ChorePack system in place." A mom*

*"Its simplicity and ease of use encouraged independence and accountability at a young age." A mom*

*"I have just implemented* Managers of Their Chores. *Wow! My children are consistently doing their chores and I am free from the daily burden of trying to do it all. Now I know it will get done at a certain time, and my children are growing in responsibility and independence and obedience. Thank you for such a wonderful resource." Heather*

For information visit: www.Titus2.com

Or call: (913) 772-0392.

You may also e-mail: managers@Titus2.com

## Keeping Our Children's Hearts
## Our Vital Priority
### by Steven and Teri Maxwell

Written for parents of young children to teenagers, this book shares the joys and outcomes of our vital priority—keeping our children's hearts. Rebellion and immorality are common among teens even within the Christian community. Does Scripture offer any path of hope for more than this for our children? What can parents do to direct their children toward godliness rather than worldliness? When does this process begin? What is the cost?

Steve and Teri Maxwell believe the key factors in raising children in the nurture and admonition of the Lord (Ephesians 6:4) are whether or not the parents have their children's hearts and what they are doing with those hearts. *Keeping Our Children's Hearts* offers direction and encouragement on this critically important topic.

Included in this book is a chapter co-authored by the three adult Maxwell children concerning their thoughts, feelings, experiences, and outcomes of growing up in a home where their parents wanted to keep their hearts. There are also questions at the end of each chapter, which are thought provoking and helpful.

*"The most complete and most balanced book I have read on how to raise children who won't rebel!" Dr. S. M. Davis*

*"This book is making me rethink what my purpose as a Christian, mother, and homeschooler should be." A mom*

*"The Scripture and its experiential application was encouraging and refreshing." A dad*

To order or for more information: www.Titus2.com

Or call: (913) 772-0392

# Homeschooling with a Meek and Quiet Spirit
## by Teri Maxwell

The desire of a homeschooling mother's heart is to have a meek and quiet spirit instead of discouragement, fear, and anger.

Because Teri Maxwell, a mother of eight, has walked the homeschooling path since 1985, she knows first-hand the struggle for a meek and quiet spirit. The memories from her early home-schooling years of often being worried and angry rather than having a meek and quiet spirit are not what she would like them to be. Her prayer is that as she shares the work the Lord has done in her heart, through homeschooling, you would be encouraged that He can do the same for you. She also desires that you could learn from the lessons He has taught her so that you would begin to have a meek and quiet spirit long before she did.

Will your journey toward a meek and quiet spirit be completed upon finding the perfect spelling curriculum or deciding which chores your child should be doing? Perhaps the answer lies on a different path.

In these pages, Teri offers practical insights into gaining a meek and quiet spirit that any mom can apply to her individual circumstances. She transparently shares the struggles God has brought her through and what He has shown her during these many home-schooling years.

In *Homeschooling with a Meek and Quiet Spirit,* you will discover the heart issues that will gently lead you to a meek and quiet spirit. Come along and join Teri as you seek the Lord to homeschool with a meek and quiet spirit!

*"This is one of the best, most helpful, encouraging, and empathetic books I've read during my 5 years of homeschooling." A mom*

To order or for more information: www.Titus2.com

Or call: (913) 772-0392

# Preparing Sons to Provide for a Single-Income Family

## by Steven Maxwell

In today's world of two-income families, preparing a son to provide for a single-income family seems an overwhelming task. Christian parents will find it helpful to have a purpose and plan as they raise sons who will one day be responsible for supporting a family.

Steve Maxwell presents the groundwork for preparing your son to be a wage-earning adult. He gives practical suggestions and direction to parents for working with their sons from preschool age all the way through to adulthood. You will be challenged to evaluate your own life and the example you are setting for your son.

As the father of eight children, four of them now wage-earning adults, Steve has gained valuable experience he openly shares with other parents. Learn these principles from a dad whose twenty-four-year-old homeschooled son purchased a home debt free a year before his marriage, and whose second son is doing the same. Steve explains how it is possible for parents, with a willing commitment, to properly prepare their sons to provide for a single-income family.

*"You are dealing with topics that no one I know of has dealt with as thoroughly and practically as you have." Dr. S. M. Davis*

"Preparing Sons *was a big blessing to my husband. All you ladies should get a copy for your husband and every church library needs one."* Shelly

*Preparing Sons* is available in paperback or unabridged audiobook.

To order or for more information: www.Titus2.com or www.PreparingSons.com

Or call: (913) 772-0392

# Just Around the Corner
## Encouragement and Challenge
## for Homeschooling Dads and Moms
## Volume 1

### by Steven and Teri Maxwell

*Just Around the Corner,* Volume 1 is a compilation of over five years' worth of Steve and Teri Maxwell's monthly Dad's and Mom's Corners. Steve's writing will challenge dads in their role as the spiritual head of the family. Teri's writing addresses many aspects of daily life that often frustrate or discourage a mom.

You will find the Mom's Corners grouped together in the front of the book and the Dad's Corners in the back. The Corners are all indexed so that you can read the ones relating to a specific topic you are interested in, if you so choose.

Because most of these articles deal with family life in general, many Christian non-homeschool families find them useful as well. Topics addressed in *Just Around the Corner* include anger, depression, child training, and husbands loving their wives.

With four of the Maxwell children now adults, Steve and Teri write from the perspective of having seen the truth of God's Word put into practice. At the same time, they are still in the trenches homeschooling four children.

*"The Maxwells are so encouraging and down to earth. I had been feeling down about some negative behavior in my children, things in my marriage, homeschooling, and the list goes on. This book has helped me to regain my focus and carry on to what God has called me to do." Michelle*

To order or for more information: www.Titus2.com

Or call: (913) 772-0392

# The Moody Family Series
## Summer with the Moodys
## Autumn with the Moodys
## Winter with the Moodys
## Spring with the Moodys

Often parents are concerned about negative examples and role models in books their children are reading. One goal in writing the Moody Series was to eliminate those kinds of examples replacing them with positive, godly ones.

In the four books, you'll find the Moodys helping a widowed neighbor, starting small businesses for the children, enjoying a family fun night, training their new puppy, homeschooling, Mom experiencing morning sickness, and much more! Woven throughout the books is the Moodys' love for the Lord and their enjoyment of time together. Children (parents too!) will enjoy Mr. and Mrs. Moody, Max, Mollie, Mitch, and Maddie—they'll come away challenged and encouraged.

*"My six-year-old son asked Jesus into his heart while we were reading* Autumn with the Moodys. *These books are wonderful, heartwarming Christian reading. The Moodys will always have a special place in our hearts!"* A mom

*"At last, a Christian book series that is engaging and encourages my children to love Jesus more and bless their family and friends."* A mom

To order or for more information: www.Titus2.com, or call: (913) 772-0392. You may also e-mail: managers@Titus2.com

# Audio Resources
## Encouragement for the Homeschool Family

### by the Maxwell Family

*Encouragement for the Homeschool Family* is an eight-session audio seminar which will encourage, exhort, and equip homeschooling families. Included in the album: *The Homeschooling Family—Building a Vision, Managers of Their Homes, Manager of His Home, Loving Your Husband, Sports—Friend or Foe, Anger—Relationship Poison, Experiencing the Joy of Young Womanhood,* and *Success or Failure* (for young men).

For information visit: www.Titus2.com

Or call: (913) 772-0392.

## Feed My Sheep
## A Practical Guide to Daily Family Devotions

### by Steve Maxwell

Tried them and failed? Never tried because you knew it would be too big of a battle? No time for them even if you wanted to? Do any of these questions describe your experience with family devotions? This two CD set is highly motivational and practical.

In the first CD, Steve Maxwell gives realistic advice for achieving success with family devotions. He reveals the secret that he guarantees will work. He also explains common problems causing many families to fail with daily family devotions and then gives solutions to these difficulties.

The second CD contains two of the Maxwells' family devotions recorded live. You'll feel like you're right at home with Steve as you listen to him lead his family in their time in the Word. You will see how easy it is to lead your family in the most important time of the day.

Join Steve, father of eight, as he shares about the Maxwells' favorite part of their day. We pray you'll come away with an excitement for the daily feeding of your family from God's Word!

For information visit: www.Titus2.com

Or call: (913) 772-0392.

# *Manager of His Home*
# *Helping Your Wife Succeed*
# *As She Manages Your Home*

### by Steve Maxwell

Do you desire to know what practical, spiritual headship actually means, and does your wife long for this? How do you lead and still allow her to manage the home?

In this two-hour audio session you will be given real-life, biblical suggestions for how you can support and facilitate your wife in her role as a homeschooling mom.

*"I would recommend this message to others because it provided plenty of practical, daily examples of how to lead the family." A dad*

For information visit: www.Titus2.com

Or call: (913) 772-0392.

# Individual Audio Titles

## The Homeschooling Family — Building a Vision

### by Steve and Teri Maxwell

Whether new or experienced home-schoolers, this motivational and practical session helps a family attain their heartfelt goals for raising and educating their children. Doubts, discouragement, and burnout can easily shipwreck the family that doesn't know "where they are going."

Together, Steve and Teri will give you concrete examples from homeschooling struggles they have experienced and how they made it through. With four adult children whom they homeschooled and four more children who are currently being homeschooled, they have the experience to know how to keep on while still being in the trenches of day to day homeschooling.

## Loving Your Husband

### By Teri Maxwell

This is an incredible message every woman should listen to. One area Titus 2:4-5 tells the older women to teach the younger women is to love their husbands. In this practical workshop, Teri discusses both the starting point and the keys to loving your husband.

Are you a helpmeet or a wife who tries to control her husband? No Christian wife wants to be the "brawling" or "contentious" woman from Proverbs. Teri shares many examples from her own life and how the Lord has used them to both convict her and teach her how to love her husband. Join Teri as she evaluates how a meek and quiet spirit can help us be godly wives, building our houses rather than tearing them down (Proverbs 14:1).

## *Sports — Friend or Foe?*

### By Steve Maxwell

Homeschooling families are heavily involved in sports. What are the parents' goals in having their children participate in organized sports? Are these goals being met? Are the children better or worse by being one of the team? Steve shares data from a large on-line survey that he conducted regarding Christian families and sports.

## *Anger — Relationship Poison*

### By Steve and Teri Maxwell

Homeschooling families have a heart's desire to raise godly children. However, it seems that anger is found in many homeschooling parents, and it can undermine all the hours invested in positive teaching. Is a little anger beneficial? Do you have difficulty controlling your anger? Is a harsh tone in your voice anger? Steve and Teri Maxwell will encourage you on this universally needed topic as they share from God's Word and personal testimonies.

# *Experiencing the Joy of Young Womanhood*

## By Sarah Maxwell

Young ladies, what are your goals in life? Are you waiting for something to happen? Sarah shares truth from Scripture and true-life testimonies about the importance of seeking God's will for your life and resting in Him. She gives practical applications concerning joyfully serving the Lord.

# *Success or Failure—Where Are You Headed?*

## By Christopher Maxwell

Homeschooled young men have incredible potential for success in their lives—both spiritually and vocationally. There are tragic pitfalls that might appear innocuous on the surface to be avoided. In addition there are basic elements crucial for success in the spiritual world and in the business world.

*To order any of the audio titles or for more information: www.Titus2.com*
*Or call: (913) 772-0392*

## *Freedom from the Spirit of Anger*
### by Dr. S. M. Davis

We feel this to be the most important audio message you could hear to help you overcome the spirit of anger. Dr. Davis will grip your heart as he shares about this life-changing issue. Even if you just have a "tone" in your voice, it is still anger. Dr. Davis gives ten key steps to find freedom from the spirit of anger. It has helped us make tremendous positive change in our family as we seek to overcome anger.

## *Changing the Heart of a Rebel*
### by Dr. S. M. Davis

This audio message is for parents only. We feel it is a very important topic and ties in with the theme of *Keeping Our Children's Hearts*. Even if your child is not rebelling, you will glean great insight from listening to this sermon. You'll discover warning signs for which to watch plus a strong resolve to keep your child from rebelling.

## *The Attitude No Lady Should Have*
### by Dr. S. M. Davis

This is an incredible message that every woman should listen to. Do you struggle with submission to your husband or wrong attitudes toward him? We believe this message holds the key to many areas of struggle Christian women face concerning their husbands. Dr. Davis contrasts the Mary versus Martha attitude, making it applicable to a husband/wife relationship.

**To order or for more information: www.Titus2.com
Or call: (913) 772-0392**